Theory Test
for Car Drivers

Theory Test
for Car Drivers

The recommended revision
questions and answers for car drivers

Save £40

on your first 10 lessons*

theaa.com/driving-school

AA Driving School

Published by AA Publishing (a trading name of AA Media Limited, whose registered office is Fanum House, Basing View, Basingstoke, Hampshire RG21 4EA; registered number 06112600).

© AA Media Limited 2022
Fifteenth edition.

ISBN: 978-0-7495-8307-1

Printed and bound in the UK by Bell & Bain Ltd.

A05826

For driving lessons, visit AA Driving School at www.theaa.com/driving-school

CONTENTS

Getting your licence

You want to pass your driving test and take advantage of the freedom and mobility that driving a car can give you. The following three things will help you to achieve your goal.

- Acquire knowledge of the rules of the road by learning *The Highway Code*.
- Take the right attitude. Be careful, courteous and considerate to all other road users.
- Learn and understand the skills of driving by taking lessons from a trained and qualified driving instructor.

This book has been designed to help you become a careful and safe driver and help you take the first steps towards achieving your goal – preparing for your theory test.

SIX ESSENTIAL STEPS TO GETTING YOUR LICENCE:

1 Get your provisional licence
You can apply online for your provisional licence at www.gov.uk/apply-first-provisional-driving-licence or apply using form D1 available from Post Offices.

The driving licence is issued as a photocard.

You must be at least 17 before you can legally begin learning to drive and you must be in possession of the correct licence documents. Take care when completing all the forms. Many licences cannot be issued for the required date because of errors or omissions on the application. You will need to provide proof of identity, such as a UK passport.

2 Learn *The Highway Code*
The Highway Code is essential reading for all drivers and not just those learning to drive. It sets out all the rules for good driving, as well as the rules for other road users such as pedestrians and motorcycle riders. When you have learned the rules you will be able to answer most of the questions in the theory test and be ready to start learning the driving skills you will need to pass your practical test.

3 Apply for and take the theory test
The driving test is in two parts, the theory test and the practical test. Once you have a valid provisional licence you may take the theory test at any time, but you must pass it before you are allowed to apply for the practical test. It is important, however, not to take your theory test too early in your course of practical lessons. This is because you need the experience of meeting real hazards while you are learning to drive, to help you pass the hazard perception element of the theory test.

You can book your theory test online or by phone. You will need your Driver and Vehicle Licensing Agency (DVLA) licence number and your debit or credit card details to hand.

Online: www.gov.uk/book-theory-test
Enquiries and booking support: 0300 200 1122
Welsh speakers: 0300 200 1133
Textphone: 0300 200 1166
Lines are open Monday to Friday, from 8am to 4pm
Post: DVSA, PO Box 381, M50 3UW

4 Learn to drive

It is recommended that you learn to drive with an Approved Driving Instructor (ADI). Only an ADI may legally charge for providing tuition. A fully qualified ADI must display a green badge on the windscreen of the car while teaching you. Some trainee driving instructors display a pink badge on the windscreen.

Choose an instructor or driving school by asking friends or relatives for recommendations. Price is important, so find out whether the school offers any discounts for blocks or lessons paid in advance; if you decide to pay in advance, make sure the driving school is reputable. If lesson prices are very low, ask yourself 'why?' Check how long the lesson will last. Ask about the car you'll be learning to drive in. Is it modern and reliable? Is it insured? Does it have dual controls?

The most efficient and cost-effective way to learn to drive is to accept that there is no short-cut approach to learning the necessary skills. Agree with your instructor on a planned course of tuition suited to your needs, take regular lessons, and don't skip weeks and expect to pick up where you left off. Ensure the full official syllabus is covered and, as your skills develop, get as much driving practice on the road as possible with a relative or friend. Ensure they are legally able to supervise you; they must be over 21 years of age and have held a full driving licence for at least three years.

5 Apply for and take the practical test

Once you have passed the theory test, and with your instructor's guidance based on your progress, you can plan ahead for a suitable test date for the practical test. You can book your practical test online or by phone.

Online: www.gov.uk/book-driving-test
Enquiries and booking support:
0300 200 1122
Welsh speakers: 0300 200 1133
Lines are open Monday to Friday, from 8am to 12pm

Make sure you have the following details to hand when booking your practical test:

- theory test pass certificate number
- driver number shown on your licence
- driving school code number (if known)
- your preferred date
- unacceptable days or periods
- if you can accept a test at short notice
- disability or any special circumstances
- your credit/debit card details (the person who books the test must be the cardholder)

If you need to, you can change your practical test appointment online.

Saturday and weekday evening tests are available at some driving test centres. The fee is higher than for a driving test during normal working hours on weekdays. Evening tests are available during the summer months only.

6 Apply for your full driving licence

If you have a photocard provisional driving licence issued after 1 March 2004, and pass your driving test, the examiner can issue your full driving licence immediately. The DVLA will send your new full licence by post within four weeks of passing your practical test.

If you don't have a photocard provisional driving licence, you need to send your Pass Certificate and your provisional licence to the DVLA in Swansea, within two years of passing your practical test.

AFTER THE PRACTICAL TEST

Drivers may wish to enhance their basic skills and widen their experience by taking further training in the form of the Pass Plus scheme.

This is a six-module syllabus that covers town and rural driving, night driving, driving in adverse weather conditions and driving on dual carriageways and motorways. It offers you the opportunity to gain more driving experience with the help of an instructor. Insurance companies may be prepared to offer discounts to new drivers who have completed the course. There is no test to take at the end of the course.

MORE INFORMATION

For more information on learning to drive, including the theory test, the practical test and Pass Plus, visit www.gov.uk/browse/driving.

ABOUT THE THEORY TEST

Revising for the theory test

The theory test is all about making you a safer driver and it is a good idea to prepare for the theory test at the same time as you develop your skills behind the wheel for the practical test. By preparing for both tests at the same time, you will reinforce your knowledge and understanding of all aspects of driving and improve your chances of passing both tests first time.

HOW TO USE THIS BOOK

This book is designed to help you prepare for the multiple-choice questions part of the theory test and contains all the recommended revision questions from the DVSA. The theory test consists of 50 unseen theory test questions based on the topics in this book (see pages 53–254). The real test questions are not published, but the questions in this book will help you revise for the test.

To help you study for the test, the questions are arranged into the theory test topics. Each topic has its own colour band to help you find your way through the book.

Start your revision by picking a topic; you don't have to study the topics in order. Study each question carefully to make sure you understand what it is asking you. Look carefully at any diagram or photograph before reading the explanatory information and deciding on your answer.

All the answers are given in the back of this book (see pages 255–260).

REMEMBER

- Learning *The Highway Code* and taking lessons with an ADI (approved driving instructor) are the best way to prepare for your theory test.
- Don't attempt too many questions at once.
- Don't try to learn the questions and answers by heart; the real test questions are not available for you to practice and are different from the revision questions given in this book.

Questions marked **NI** are **not** found in theory tests in Northern Ireland.

1 Study the question carefully and make sure you understand what it is asking you

19 Mark *one* answer
You're travelling along this road.
How should you pass the cyclist?

3 Look carefully at any photograph, symbol or diagram given within the question.

☐ **A** Sound your horn as you pass
☐ **B** Keep close to them as you pass
☐ **C** Leave them plenty of room as you pass
☐ **D** Change down one gear before you pass

2 Read through all the possible options.

Allow the cyclist plenty of room in case they wobble or swerve around a pothole or raised drain. Look well ahead before you start to overtake, because you'll need to cross the hazard line. Look for entrances where vehicles could be waiting to pull out.

4 Each question in this book is accompanied by an explanation that will help you understand the theory behind the question and what answer may be appropriate. Make sure you read through this text before answering the question. This text will not appear in your actual theory test.

What to expect in the theory test

The theory test consists of two parts: 50 multiple-choice questions and hazard perception (see page 18). You have to pass both parts in order to pass your theory test. You will receive your test scores at the end of the test. Even if you only failed on one part of the theory test, you still have to take both parts again next time.

MULTIPLE-CHOICE QUESTIONS
You will have 57 minutes to complete the question part of the test using a touch-screen and all the questions are multiple-choice. Three questions will be case studies, based on a video clip (see page 16).

The 50 questions appear on the screen one at a time and you can return to any of the questions within the 57 minutes to re-check or change your answers (an example of how they might appear is shown opposite). You have to score a minimum of 43 out of 50 to pass. The Government may change the pass mark from time to time. Your driving school or the DVSA will be able to tell you if there has been a change.

Each question has four possible options. You must select the one correct answer. Don't worry about accidentally missing marking an answer because you'll be reminded that you haven't chosen an answer before moving on to the next question.

Study each question carefully and look carefully at any diagram, drawing or photograph. Before you look at the options given, decide what you think the correct answer might be. Read through the options and then select the answer that matches the one you had decided on. If you follow this system, you will avoid being confused by answers that appear to be similar.

You can answer the questions in any order you choose by moving forwards and backwards through the questions. You can also change your answer if necessary and flag questions you're unsure about. This means that you can go back to them later in the test. In the actual test, the remaining time you have left in the test is shown clearly on the screen.

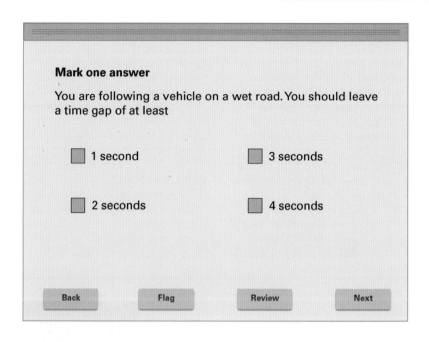

Mark one answer

You are following a vehicle on a wet road. You should leave a time gap of at least

☐ 1 second

☐ 3 seconds

☐ 2 seconds

☐ 4 seconds

Back   Flag   Review   Next

Mark one answer

You have just gone through deep water. To dry off the brakes you should

☐ accelerate and keep to a high speed for a short time

☐ avoid using the brakes at all for a few miles

☐ go slowly while gently applying the brakes

☐ stop for at least an hour to allow them time to dry

Back   Flag   Review   Next

CASE STUDY QUESTIONS

Currently, 3 of the 50 questions will take the form of a case study. The case study is based on a short, silent, video clip and you will be asked 3 multiple-choice questions about it. You can watch the video clip as many times as you like during the multiple-choice part of the theory test. For example, you could watch the video, answer a question, and then watch the video again before you answer the next question.

Case studies are designed to test that you not only know your car theory but also that you understand how to apply your knowledge when faced with a given driving situation.

The case study in your theory test could be based on any driving scenario and ask questions from a range of topics in the DVSA's database of questions.

The sample case study on the next page demonstrates how the case study questions may appear in your live test, so you'll know what to expect.

WHAT WILL I SEE?

The video clip (see below) will show you a situation from the driver's viewpoint, such as driving through a town centre or driving on a country road. You'll then be given three questions, such as:

1. Why are motorcyclists considered vulnerable road users?
2. Why should the driver, on the side road, look out for motorcyclists at junctions?
3. In this clip, who can cross the chevrons to overtake other vehicles, when it's safe to do so?

For each of the 3 questions, you'll have to choose the correct answer from 4 possible answers. The left-hand side of The screen will show the video clip much like below with controls to:

– play the video
– pause the video
– move to a specific part of the video on a progress bar
– watch the video using the full screen

The right-hand side of the screen will show the multiple-choice questions.

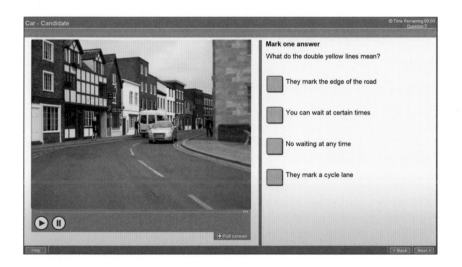

HAZARD PERCEPTION

The second part of the theory test is known as 'hazard perception' and is based on video clips. Its aim is to find out how good you are at noticing hazards developing on the road ahead. The test will also show how much you know about the risks to you as a driver, the risks to your passengers and the risks to other road users.

> Who do you think have the most accidents – new or experienced drivers? New drivers have just had lessons, so they should remember how to drive safely, but in fact statistics show that new drivers have the most accidents.

Learner drivers need training in how to spot hazards because they are often so busy thinking about the car's controls that they forget to watch the road and traffic. Losing concentration for even a second could prove fatal to you or another road user.

Proper training can help you to recognize more of the hazards that you will meet when driving and to spot those hazards earlier, so you are less likely to have an accident.

Your driving instructor has been trained to help you learn hazard perception skills and can give you plenty of practice in what to look out for when driving, how to anticipate hazards, and what action to take to deal with hazards of all kinds.

WHAT IS A HAZARD?

A hazard is anything that might cause you to change speed or direction when driving. The hazard perception element of the theory test is about spotting developing hazards. This is one of the key skills of good driving and is also called 'anticipation'. Anticipating hazards, such as car doors opening or children running into the road, means looking out for them in advance and taking the appropriate action.

As you get more driving experience you will start to learn about the times and places where you are most likely to meet hazards. An example of this is the rush hour. You know people take more risks when they are in a hurry. Maybe they have to drop their children at school before going to work. Perhaps they are late for a meeting or want to get home. So you have to be prepared for bad driving, such as another driver pulling out in front of you.

You won't be able to practise with the real clips used in the official test, of course, but training books and practice videos are widely available.

TAKING THE THEORY TEST: HAZARD PERCEPTION

After answering the multiple-choice questions, you will be given a short break before you begin the hazard perception part of the test. The hazard perception test lasts for about 20 minutes. Before you start you will be given some instructions explaining how the test works; you'll also get a chance to practise with the computer and mouse before you start. This is to make sure that you know what to expect on the test and that you are happy with what you have to do.

Next you will see 14 clips of street scenes with traffic such as cars, cyclists, pedestrians etc. The scenes are from the point of view of a driver in a car. You have to notice potential hazards that are developing on the road ahead – that is, problems that could lead to an incident. As soon as you notice a hazard developing, click the mouse. You will have plenty of time to see the hazard and the sooner you notice it, the more marks you score.

Each clip has at least one hazard in it but some clips may have more than one hazard. You have to score a minimum of 44 out of 75 to pass, but the pass mark may change so check with your instructor or the DVSA before sitting your test.

Note that the computer has checks built in to show anyone trying to cheat – for example someone who keeps clicking the mouse all the time. Be aware that, unlike the theory test questions, you will not have an opportunity to go back to an earlier clip and change your response, so you need to concentrate throughout the test.

Above: Click the mouse when you spot potential hazards – the tractor emerging from the side road (ringed in red).

About the theory test

You responded to this clip in an unacceptable manner. You will score zero for this clip.

Left: You may see a warning screen similar to this one if the computer detects a clicking pattern or you click the mouse constantly.

FURTHER INFORMATION

For more practical information on learning to drive including the theory test, practical test and Pass Plus visit www.gov.uk/browse/driving.

UNDERSTANDING THE THEORY BEHIND THE TEST

Section 1

Alertness

The first section in the theory test revision questions is headed ALERTNESS. Alertness is a short section and is a good place to start.

- Alertness means being wide awake and concentrating on what you are doing – driving – not being distracted by mobile phones or loud music
- Alertness means looking out for hazards
- Alertness means noticing all road signs and road markings, and acting on the instructions and information they give

ARE YOU FIT TO DRIVE?

'Fit' can mean:

- Did you have any alcoholic drinks before you set out?
- Are you under the influence of illegal substances (drugs)?
- Are you feeling groggy or unwell?
- Are you taking prescription medicine that could affect your ability to control the car?
- Are you too tired to drive?

It's unwise to set out on a journey if you're not well, on the basis of 'I'll see how I go – I'll probably be all right':

- Your reactions are likely to be slower
- You may be unable to judge distances properly
- Your actions may be less well co-ordinated than usual and it's not legal

If you are tired, open the window for a few moments to let in some fresh air. If you drive when you are too tired, you risk falling asleep at the wheel – an all too common cause of serious accidents. Driving for long stretches on a motorway at night can be especially dangerous. If you sense that you are losing your concentration, then take a break at a motorway service station. Plan your journey ahead, giving yourself plenty of time for rest stops – at least every couple of hours.

TACKLING THE QUESTIONS

Look at the questions in the Alertness section.
You'll see that the Alertness questions are all about these:

- anticipation
- observation
- signalling
- reversing
- using your mirrors
- concentration
- getting distracted
- feeling sleepy
- using mobile phones

DID YOU KNOW?

The main causes of distraction are:

- Loud music in the car
- Passengers (usually children)
- Events happening outside (such as accidents)
- Using a mobile phone

Now test yourself on the questions on pages 54–60

Section 2
Attitude

The government road safety
organisations believe that the ATTITUDE
of learner drivers is extremely important
for road safety.

ATTITUDE MEANS:
- Your frame of mind when you
  get in the car
- How you react when you meet
  hazards on the road
- How you behave towards
  other drivers

Attitude is a very important part of being
a good driver. Your attitude when you
are driving plays a big part in ensuring
your safety and that of other road users.

Do you aim to be a careful and safe
driver or a fast and skilful driver? If you
don't want to end up as another road
accident statistic, then carefully and
safely is the way to go.

Remember that a car is not an offensive
weapon, and often people don't realise
what a potentially lethal machine they
are in control of when they get behind
the wheel. You only have to think about
this to understand the importance of
your attitude when driving.

You'll see that questions in this section
are concerned with encouraging you to
be a careful and safe driver, and cover:
- Tailgating
- Consideration for other road users,
  including pedestrians, buses, slow-
  moving vehicles and horse riders
- Driving at the right speed for
  the conditions

- When to flash headlights
- The right place, time and way
  to overtake

And remembering a few dos and don'ts
will help you achieve the right attitude
for driving and make passing this
section of the test much easier.

GOOD DRIVERS DO:
- drive at the right speed for the road
  and traffic conditions
- observe speed limits
- overtake only when it is safe to do so
- park in correct and safe places
- wait patiently if the driver in front is a
  learner or elderly or hesitant
- look out for vulnerable road users
  such as cyclists, pedestrians
  and children
- concentrate on their driving at
  all times
- plan their journey so that they
  have plenty of time to get to
  their destination

GOOD DRIVERS DON'T:
- allow themselves to become involved
  in road rage
- break speed limits
- drive too fast, particularly in wet,
  foggy or icy weather
- accelerate or brake too harshly
- overtake and 'cut in', forcing others
  to brake sharply
- put pressure on other drivers by
  driving too close behind them (this is
  called 'tailgating'), flashing headlights
  or gesturing
- allow their attention to be distracted
  by passengers, mobile phones or
  loud music, or what is happening
  on the road, such as staring at
  an accident

TAILGATING

Driving excessively close behind another vehicle is known as tailgating – and it's dangerous! The car in front may stop suddenly (to avoid hitting a child or animal that has dashed out into the road, for example); when this happens the car following runs the risk of crashing into it.

You should always leave enough space between your vehicle and the one in front, so that you can stop safely if the driver in front suddenly slows down or stops.

Rear-end shunts account for a large percentage of all accidents on the road. In these situations, the driver of the car behind is almost always judged to be the guilty party.

So tailgating is potentially expensive as well as dangerous.

Another time when drivers are tempted to tailgate is when attempting to pass a large, slow-moving vehicle. However, keeping well back will improve your view of the road ahead, so that you're better able to judge when it's safe to overtake and the driver of the large vehicle will also be able to see you.

USEFUL TIP

If you are being followed too closely by another driver you should slow down and increase the distance between your vehicle and the one in front. If you slow down or have to stop suddenly, the driver behind may crash into you, but you will have increased your stopping distance and will not be pushed into the vehicle in front of you.

ALWAYS REMEMBER:

- Expect the unexpected, and make provision for the potential errors of other drivers – everyone makes mistakes sometimes.
- Don't create unnecessary stress for other drivers by showing your frustration in an aggressive manner.

If you are driving at the right speed for the road and weather conditions and a driver behind tries to overtake, you should pull back a bit from the vehicle in front so that if the driver behind insists on overtaking, there is less risk of an accident.

Do not try to stop the car behind from overtaking. Do not move into the middle of the road or move up close to the car in front. These actions could be very dangerous.

You should not give confusing signals such as indicating left or waving the other driver on.

Now test yourself on the questions on pages 61–70

Section 3

Safety and your vehicle

When you go through this section you will notice that the questions are a bit of a mixture. They cover a number of topics about SAFETY, including:

- Understanding the controls of your vehicle
- What the car's warning lights tell you
- Tyres – correct inflation, pressures and tread depths
- When to use hazard warning lights
- Passenger safety
- The environment
- Security and crime prevention

Many of the questions in this section are to do with 'legal requirements' and rules regarding parking your car and using lights. Look up all the sections in *The Highway Code* that deal with parking rules. Find out the rules for red routes, white lines and zigzag lines as well as yellow lines.

SEAT BELTS

If any of your passengers are young people under 14, you are responsible for making sure that they wear seat belts or are in the correct car seat. You are responsible for them by law, even if you are still a learner driver yourself.

TIPS FOR THIS SECTION

Learn *The Highway Code* and you will be able to answer most of the questions in this section. In particular make sure you know the rules regarding seat belts, tyres, and when to use your lights, including your hazard warning lights.

A CONFUSING QUESTION

One of the most confusing questions in this section asks what kind of driving results in high fuel consumption. The answer, of course, is bad driving – especially harsh braking and acceleration. This means you will use more fuel than you should and therefore cause more damage to the environment than is necessary.

BUT many people read the word 'high' as meaning 'good' – as in a level of driving skill – and so pick the wrong answer.

Don't let it be you...

Now test yourself on the questions on pages 71–89

Section 4
Safety margins

Experienced drivers are usually better than new or learner drivers at leaving good SAFETY MARGINS. Learner drivers find it harder to keep their vehicle at a safe distance from the one in front. Therefore the questions in this section cover:
• safe stopping distances
and
• safe separation distances (these are the same as safety margins)

WHAT IS A SAFETY MARGIN?

A safety margin is the space that you need to leave between your vehicle and the one in front so that you will not crash into it if it slows downs or stops suddenly. They are also called 'separation distances' and are an important part of anticipating road and traffic hazards. When you are learning to drive, you can feel pressured to speed up by drivers behind you.

Don't let other drivers make you cut down on your safety margins. Stay a safe distance behind the vehicle in front. Then you will have time to anticipate and react to hazards.

THE TWO-SECOND RULE

In traffic that's moving at normal speed, allow at least a two-second gap between you and the vehicle in front.

STOPPING DISTANCES

Many people who are taking their theory test get confused about this. You will notice that some of the questions ask for your overall stopping distance and others ask for your braking distance. These are different.

Overall stopping distance or stopping distance is not the same as braking distance. Stopping distance is made up of thinking distance + braking distance.

In other words, the time it takes to notice that there's a hazard ahead plus the time it takes to brake to deal with it.

THINKING DISTANCE

Thinking distance is sometimes called 'reaction time' or 'reaction distance'. If you are driving at 30mph, your thinking distance will be 30 feet (9 metres). That means your vehicle will travel 30 feet (9 metres) before you start braking.

THE LINK BETWEEN STOPPING DISTANCE AND SAFETY MARGINS

You should always leave enough space between your vehicle and the one in front. If the other driver has to slow down suddenly or stop without warning, you need to be able to stop safely. The space is your safety margin.

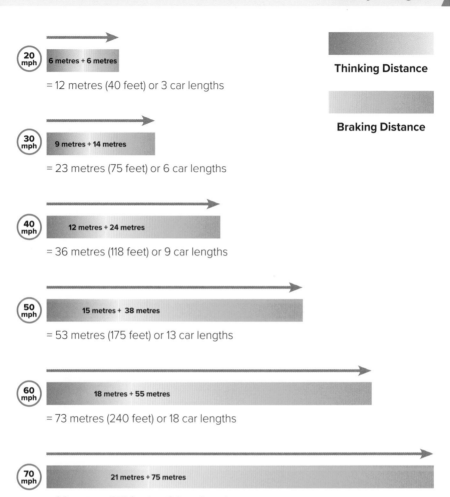

20 mph
6 metres + 6 metres
= 12 metres (40 feet) or 3 car lengths

30 mph
9 metres + 14 metres
= 23 metres (75 feet) or 6 car lengths

40 mph
12 metres + 24 metres
= 36 metres (118 feet) or 9 car lengths

50 mph
15 metres + 38 metres
= 53 metres (175 feet) or 13 car lengths

60 mph
18 metres + 55 metres
= 73 metres (240 feet) or 18 car lengths

70 mph
21 metres + 75 metres
= 96 metres (315 feet) or 24 car lengths

Thinking Distance

Braking Distance

SAFETY MARGINS FOR OTHER VEHICLES

Long vehicles and motorcycles need more room to stop – in other words, you must leave a bigger safety margin when following a long vehicle or motorbike. When driving behind a long vehicle, pull back to increase your separation distance and your safety margin so that you get a better view of the road ahead – there could be hazards developing and if you are too close he will be unable to see you in his rear view mirror. Strong winds can blow lorries and motorbikes off course. So leave a bigger safety margin.

DIFFERENT CONDITIONS AND SAFETY MARGINS

You may find that one or more questions in your theory test might be about driving in 'different conditions'. These questions aim to make sure you know what adjustments you should make to your driving when either road conditions are different from normal, for example, when parts of the road are closed off for roadworks, or weather conditions affect your driving.

Roadworks

You should always take extra care when you see a sign warning you that there are roadworks ahead. Remember, roadworks are a hazard and you have to anticipate them.

If you see the driver in front of you slowing down, take this as a sign that you should do the same – even if you can't see a hazard ahead. You still need to keep a safe distance from him. Harassing the driver in front by 'tailgating' is both wrong and dangerous and so is overtaking to fill the gap. It's especially important that you know what to do when you see a sign for roadworks ahead on a motorway.

- There may be a lower speed limit than normal – keep to it
- Use your mirrors and indicators, and get into the correct lane in plenty of time
- Don't overtake the queue and then force your way in at the last minute (this is an example of showing an inconsiderate attitude to other road users)

- Always keep a safe distance from the vehicle in front

Weather conditions

In bad weather (often called 'adverse' weather), you need to increase your safety margins.

When it's raining you need to leave at least twice as much distance between you and the vehicle in front. When there's ice on the road leave an even bigger gap because your stopping distance increases tenfold.

It's amazing how often drivers go too fast in bad weather. In adverse weather motorways have lower speed limits, but some drivers don't take any notice of them.

When it's icy you should multiply your two-second gap by ten.

QUESTIONS THAT LOOK ALIKE

There are a number of questions about anti-lock brakes in this section. Lots of questions look the same. Some are easy and some are hard. Some of them appear to be the same but they are not.

The questions test two things – your knowledge of the rules of the road and your understanding of words to do with driving.

> **Now test yourself on the questions on pages 90–98**

Section 5
Hazard awareness

How often does a motorist protest that the accident happened before they had time to realise the person they hit was there? Some accidents will inevitably happen, but part of your instructor's job while teaching you to drive is to help you learn to anticipate problems before they happen.

WHAT IS THE DIFFERENCE BETWEEN HAZARD AWARENESS AND HAZARD PERCEPTION?

Hazard awareness and hazard perception mean the same thing

- Hazard Perception is the name for the part of the theory test that uses video clips. This test is about spotting developing hazards. One of the key skills of good driving, this is called 'anticipation'
- Anticipating hazards means looking out for them in advance and taking action immediately
- Hazard awareness is about being alert whenever you are driving

That is why some of the questions in the HAZARD AWARENESS section deal with things that might make you less alert. For example feeling tired, feeling ill, taking medicines prescribed by your doctor, drinking alcohol or taking illegal drugs.

Other questions in Hazard Awareness cover noticing road and traffic signs as well as road markings, what to do at traffic lights and when to slow down for hazards ahead.

WHY ARE YOUNG MALE DRIVERS MORE AT RISK?

New drivers have a greater than average chance of being involved in accidents. Statistics show that young male drivers have the most accidents.

- Maybe it's because when they first get their licence they want to show off to other drivers
- Some people think that driving much too fast will earn them 'respect' from their friends
- Some people think that they are such good drivers that the rules of the road should not apply to them

Whatever the reason – drivers who don't watch out for hazards are at risk of being involved in an accident. The problem has a lot to do with people's attitude to driving. You'll find more about this aspect of driving in the Attitude part of the theory test.

We've already said that young drivers often don't learn to anticipate hazards until they are older and more experienced. The Hazard Perception test aims to 'fill the gap' in hazard perception for young drivers and other new drivers by making sure they have some proper training to make up for their lack of experience.

This should make them safer drivers when they start out on the road alone.

LOOKING FOR CLUES TO HAZARDS DEVELOPING ON THE ROAD

As you get more driving experience you will start to learn about the times and places where you are most likely to meet hazards. Think about some of these examples.

Rush hour

You know that people take more risks when driving in the rush hour. Maybe they have to drop their children off at school before going to work. Maybe they are late for a business meeting. So you have to be prepared for bad driving, such as other drivers pulling out in front of you.

Dustbin day

Drivers in a hurry may get frustrated if they are held up in traffic because of a hazard such as a dustcart. They may accelerate and pull out to overtake even though they cannot see clearly ahead. You should not blindly follow the lead of another driver. Check for yourself that there are no hazards ahead.

School children

Young children are often not very good at judging how far away a car is from them, and may run into the road unexpectedly. Always be on the lookout for hazards near a school entrance.

Parked cars

Imagine you are driving on a quiet one-way street with cars parked down each side of the road. You wouldn't expect to meet any vehicles coming the other way – but what about children playing? They might run out into the road after a football. It would be difficult to see them because of the parked cars, until they were in the road in front of you.

MORE EXAMPLES OF HAZARDS

So, what kinds of hazards are we talking about? And what should you do about them?

Road markings and road signs sometimes highlight likely hazards for you.

The list below gives some of the hazards you should look out for when driving along a busy street in town.

After each hazard there are some ideas about what you should be looking out for, and what to do next.

- You see a bus which has stopped in a lay-by ahead

There may be some pedestrians hidden by the bus who are trying to cross the road, or the bus may signal to pull out. Be ready to slow down and stop.

- You see a white triangle painted on the road surface ahead

This is a hazard warning sign. It tells you that there is a 'Give Way' junction just ahead. Slow down and be ready to stop.

- You see a sign for a roundabout on the road ahead

Anticipate that other drivers may need to change lane, and be ready to leave them enough room.

- You come to some road works where the traffic is controlled by temporary traffic lights

Watch out for drivers speeding to get through before the lights change.

- You look in your rear view mirror and see an emergency vehicle with flashing lights coming up behind you

An emergency vehicle wants to pass, so get ready to pull over when it's safe.

- You see a small child standing with an adult near the edge of the pavement

Check if the child is safely holding the adult's hand. Be ready to stop safely if the child suddenly steps into the road.

- You notice dustbins or rubbish bags put out on the pavement

The dustcart could be around the next corner, or the bin men could be crossing the road with bags of rubbish. Be ready to slow down and stop if necessary.

- You hear a siren

Look all around to find out where the emergency vehicle is. You may have to pull over to let it pass.

You will find out more about the different types of hazards you may encounter, including what to look for when driving on narrow country roads, or in bad (adverse) weather conditions, in the Vehicle Handling section of this book.

ALWAYS EXPECT THE UNEXPECTED

Don't forget that not all hazards can be anticipated. There are bound to be some you haven't expected.

RED FLASHING WARNING LIGHTS

Level crossings, ambulance stations, fire stations and swing bridges all have red lights that flash on and off to warn you when you must stop.

OBSERVATION

Another word for taking in information through our eyes is 'observation'. Observation is one of the three key skills needed in hazard perception. The three skills are:

- observation
- anticipation
- planning

An easy way to remember this is **O A P**

Observe
Anticipate
Plan

TALK TO YOURSELF!

It's a good idea to 'talk to yourself' when you're learning to drive – and even after you've passed your test. Talk about all the things you see that could be potential hazards. Your driving instructor might suggest this as a way of making you concentrate and notice hazards ahead.

Even if you don't talk out loud, you can do a 'running commentary' in your head on everything you see around you as you drive.

For example, you might say to yourself – 'I am following a cyclist and the traffic lights ahead are red. *When the lights change I will allow him/her plenty of time and room to move off.*'
or
'The dual carriageway ahead is starting to look very busy. There is a sign showing that the right lane is closing in 800 yards. *I must get ready to check my mirrors and, if safe to do so, drop back to allow other vehicles to move into the left-hand lane ahead of me.*'

Note: Don't forget the mirrors! This way, you will notice more hazards, and you will learn to make more sense of the information that your eyes are taking in.

SCANNING THE ROAD

Learner drivers tend to look straight ahead of their car and may not notice all the hazards that might be building up on both sides. You will spot more hazards when driving if you train yourself to scan the road.

- Practise looking up and ahead as far as possible
- Use all your mirrors to look out for hazards too
- Don't forget that you have 'blind spots' when driving – work out where they are and find safe ways of checking all round for hazards
- Ask your driving instructor to help you with all of this

LEARN YOUR ROAD SIGNS!

Notice the information at the bottom of the first page of traffic signs in *The Highway Code*. It explains that you won't find every road sign shown here.

You can buy a copy of *Know Your Road Signs* from a bookshop to see some of the extra signs that are not in *The Highway Code*.

Note: In Wales, some road signs include the Welsh spelling as well as the English, and in Scotland some signs are written using Gaelic spelling. You'll also see some 'old-style' road signs around, which are slightly different too.

How is learning to scan the road going to help me pass my theory test?

- The idea of the hazard perception element of the test is to encourage you to get some real experience of driving before you take the theory test
- If you meet real hazards on the road and learn how to anticipate them, you'll learn how to pass the hazard perception element of the test
- In the video test you may not be able to look all around you as you would when driving a car; but the clips will be as realistic as possible in giving you a wide 'view' of the road ahead

OBSERVATION QUESTIONS

Study some of the pictures in the Hazard Awareness section.

They include photographs of scenes such as:

- a cyclist at traffic lights, seen from the viewpoint of a driver in a car behind the cyclist

- what you see as a driver when you are approaching a level crossing

- what you see when coming up to a 'blind bend'

- a view of the road ahead with traffic building up where one lane is closing

Look out for situations like these when you are out driving with your instructor, and use the practice to improve your hazard awareness.

As well as photographs, there are pictures of road and traffic signs.

WHAT DO THESE SIGNS MEAN?

What actions should you take when you see these signs?

- If you are not sure, look them up in *The Highway Code*

- Think about why the square yellow sign with the two children is in the Vehicle Markings section and not with the rest of the road signs

Now test yourself on the questions on pages 99–120

Section 6
Vulnerable road users

Today's new vehicles are becoming safer all the time for the driver inside the car, but sadly this is not always the case for the pedestrian or cyclist outside. Many road users who are not driving cars have nothing to protect them if they are in an accident with a motor vehicle.

The questions in the VULNERABLE ROAD USERS section deal with the following:

- why different types of road users are vulnerable
- what you as a driver must do to keep them safe

WHO ARE VULNERABLE ROAD USERS?

You must drive with extra care when you are near the following vulnerable road users:

- pedestrians
- children
- older people
- people with disabilities
- cyclists
- motorcycle riders
- horse riders
- learner drivers, new drivers and older drivers
- animals being herded along the road

CYCLISTS

Give cyclists plenty of room. Remember to keep well back from cyclists when you are coming up to a junction or a roundabout because you cannot be sure what they are going to do. On the roundabout they may go in any direction – left, right or straight ahead. They are allowed to stay in the left lane and signal right if they are going to continue round. Leave them enough room to cross in front of you if they need to. Turn to the section headed Vulnerable Road Users in the theory test questions to see some pictures of this. You must also give way to cyclists at toucan crossings and in cycle lanes (see the rules for cyclists set out in *The Highway Code*).

Look out for cyclists!

- It can be hard to see cyclists in busy town traffic
- It can also be hard to see them coming when you are waiting to turn out at a junction. They can be hidden by other vehicles

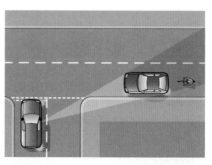

Always be on the lookout for cyclists.

Especially, check your mirror to make sure you do not trap a cyclist on your left when you are turning left into a side road. Check your blind spots for cyclists, too.

Controlling your vehicle near cyclists
When you are following a cyclist, you must be able to drive as slowly as they do, and keep your vehicle under control. Only overtake when you can allow them plenty of room, and it is safe to do so.

CYCLE LANES

Cycle lanes are reserved for cyclists and car drivers should not use them. A cycle lane is marked by a white line on the road. A solid white line means you must not drive or park in the cycle lane during the hours it is in use. A broken white line means that you should drive or park in it only if there is no alternative. You should not park there at any time when there are waiting restrictions.

When you overtake a cyclist, a motorcyclist or a horse rider, give them at least as much room as you would give a car.

Cyclists and motorcycle riders

Cyclists and motorcycle riders are more at risk than car drivers because

- they are more affected by strong winds, or by turbulence caused by other vehicles
- they are more affected by an uneven road surface, and they may have to move out suddenly to avoid a pothole
- car drivers often cannot see them

PEDESTRIANS

Pedestrians most at risk include older people and children. Older people and others who cannot move easily may be slower to cross roads – you must give them plenty of time. Children don't have a sense of danger on the road; they can't tell how close a car is, or how fast it is going. They may run out into the road without looking. Or they may step out behind you when you are reversing – you may not see them because they are small.

People who are unable to see and/or hear

A person who is blind will usually carry a white stick to alert you to their presence. If the stick has a red band, this means that the person is also deaf, so will have no warning of an approaching car either visually or from engine noise.

When to give way to pedestrians

At any pedestrian crossing, if a pedestrian has started to cross, wait until they have reached the other side. Do not harass them by revving your engine or edging forward.

At a crossing with lights (pelican, toucan or puffin crossings), pedestrians have priority once they have started to cross even if, when on a pelican crossing, the amber lights start flashing.

Once a pedestrian has stepped on to a zebra crossing, you must stop and wait for them to cross.

Note: It is courteous to stop at a zebra crossing if a pedestrian is waiting to cross.

Vulnerable road users

When you take your practical driving test, you must stop for any pedestrians who are waiting on the pavement at a zebra crossing even if they haven't stepped on to the crossing yet. However, you must not wave to them to cross.

If you want to turn left into a side road, and there are people crossing or waiting to cross, then you should give way until they finish crossing. People on foot have priority over car drivers.

> ### DID YOU KNOW?
> **If a car hits a pedestrian at 40mph, the pedestrian will probably be killed. Even at 35mph, 50% of pedestrians hit by cars will be killed.**
>
> **At 20mph, pedestrians have a better chance of surviving. This is why you will find 20mph limits and other things to slow traffic in some residential streets and near school entrances.**

OTHER TYPES OF VULNERABLE ROAD USERS
Be prepared to slow down for animals, learner drivers, and other more unusual hazards such as people walking along the road in organised groups or parades (for example, on a demonstration, or a sponsored walk). There are rules in The Highway Code that walkers must follow. But even if they break the rules, make sure you keep to them.

Animals
Drive slowly past horses or other animals. Allow them plenty of space on the road. Don't frighten them by sounding your horn or revving your engine.

If you see a flock of sheep or a herd of cattle blocking the road, you must:
- stop
- switch off your engine
- and wait until they have left the road

People riding horses on the road are often children, so you need to take extra care; when you see two riders abreast, it may well be that the one on the outside is shielding a less experienced rider.

TRAFFIC SIGNS
Look up the Traffic Signs and Vehicle Markings sections in The Highway Code and find the following signs:
- pedestrians walking in the road ahead (no pavement)
- cycle lane and pedestrian route
- advance warning of school crossing patrol ahead
- school crossing patrol
- frail or disabled people crossing
- sign on back of school bus or coach

Now test yourself on the questions on pages 121–139

Section 7
Other types of vehicle

We have already come across some of the other types of vehicle that share the road with you and your car including motorbikes and bicycles. The questions in this part of the theory test are mostly about long vehicles such as lorries. However, you also need to know what to do about:

- buses
- caravans
- trams
- tractors and other farm vehicles
- special vehicles for disabled drivers (powered invalid carriages)
- slow vehicles such as road gritters
- motorway repair vehicles

Important points to remember about these types of vehicle:

- Many of them can only move very slowly
- They cannot easily stop or change direction
- The driver's field of vision may be restricted – this means that car drivers have to allow them plenty of room

MOTORCYCLES

- Motorcycles are easily blown off course by strong winds. If you see a motorcyclist overtaking a high-sided vehicle such as a lorry, keep well back. The lorry may shield the motorcyclist from the wind as it is overtaking, but then a sudden gust could blow the motorcyclist off-course
- It can be hard to see a motorcyclist when you are waiting at a junction. Always look out for them

- If you see a motorcyclist looking over their shoulder, it could mean that they will soon give a signal to turn right. This applies to cyclists too. Keep back to give them plenty of room
- Motorcyclists and cyclists sometimes have to swerve to avoid hazards such as bumps in the road, patches of ice and drain covers. As before – give them plenty of room

LONG VEHICLES

- Like cyclists, long vehicles coming up to roundabouts may stay in the left lane even if they intend to turn right. This is because they need lots of room to manoeuvre. Keep well back so they have room to turn
- Take great care when overtaking long or high-sided vehicles. Before you pull out to overtake, make sure you have a clear view of the road ahead
- A long vehicle that needs to turn left off a major road into a minor road may prepare to do so by moving out towards the centre of the road, or by moving across to the other side

If you're following them:

- Give way, and don't try to overtake – on the right or the left
- You might need to slow down and stop while the driver of the long vehicle makes the turn

BUSES AND TRAMS

- Always give way to buses when they signal to pull out
- Always give way to trams as they cannot steer to avoid you
- Don't try to overtake a tram

Trams are **quiet** vehicles – you cannot rely on approaching engine noise to warn you that a tram is coming.

Take extra care when you see this sign, because trams are sometimes allowed to go when car drivers are not.

TRACTORS AND SLOW-MOVING VEHICLES
- Always be patient if you are following a slow vehicle

Drivers of slow vehicles will usually try to find a safe place to pull in to let the traffic go past. In the meantime you should keep well back, so that you can see the road ahead. Allow a safe distance in case they slow down or stop.

Slow vehicles are not allowed on motorways because they cannot keep up with the fast-moving traffic. Vehicles not allowed on motorways include:
- motorcycles under 50cc
- bicycles
- tractors and other farm vehicles
- powered invalid carriages

Now test yourself on the questions on pages 140–145

Section 8
Vehicle handling

The questions in this section test how much you know about controlling your vehicle on different road surfaces and in different weather.

Your control is affected by:
- the road surface – is it rough or smooth? Are there any holes or bumps? Are there any 'traffic-calming' measures, such as humps or chicanes?
- the weather conditions – you have to drive in different ways when there is fog, snow, ice or heavy rain

Other questions in this section cover driving on country roads – on narrow and one-way roads, humpback bridges, steep hills, fords. Other questions need practical knowledge, for example, on engine braking, brake fade, and coasting your vehicle – use the Glossary.

This section also has some questions on overtaking and parking.

ROAD SURFACE
The condition of the road surface can affect the way your vehicle handles. Your vehicle handles better on a smooth surface than on a surface that is damaged, bumpy or full of holes. If you have to drive on an uneven surface, keep your speed down so that you have full control of your vehicle, even if your steering wheel is jolted.

Take care also where there are tramlines on the road. The layout of the road affects the way your vehicle handles.

You may have to adjust your driving for traffic-calming measures, such as traffic humps (sometimes called 'sleeping policemen') and chicanes. These are double bends that have been put into the road layout to slow the traffic down. The sign before the chicane tells you who has priority.

Traffic calming measures are often used in residential areas or near school entrances to make it safer for pedestrians.

WEATHER CONDITIONS

Bad weather (adverse weather) such as heavy rain, ice or snow affects the way your vehicle handles. If you drive too fast in adverse weather, your tyres may lose their grip on the road when you try to brake. This means the car may skid or 'aquaplane'. Aquaplaning means sliding out of control on a wet surface.

Driving in snow

In snow, the best advice is do not drive at all unless you really have to make a journey. If you have to drive in snowy conditions, leave extra time for your journey and keep to the main roads. You can fit snow chains to your tyres to increase their grip in deep snow.

Driving in fog

In fog your field of vision can be down to a few metres. Your vehicle is fitted with fog lights to help you see and be seen in fog. But you must know how and when to use them. Look up the three rules about fog lights in *The Highway Code*. You'll see that the key points to remember are:
- Don't dazzle other road users with your fog lights

- Switch them off as soon as you can see better (as soon as the fog starts to clear)

> **REMEMBER THE TWO-SECOND RULE**
> You should double the two-second gap to four seconds when driving in rain, and increase the gap by as much as ten times when there is ice on the road.

COUNTRY DRIVING

If you have had most of your driving lessons in a town, you need to know how to drive on narrow country roads. Some are only wide enough for one vehicle ('single-track'), and some are on very steep hills.

Your control of the gears, clutch and brakes will be important if you have to follow a tractor very slowly up a hill. On a steep downward slope you have to make sure your vehicle does not 'run away'.

On country roads you might find humpback bridges and fords. The signs below warn you of these hazards.

- Find out what you must do first after you have driven through a ford

TECHNICAL KNOWLEDGE

We have already mentioned engine braking. Understanding how engine braking works is part of good vehicle handling.

Note: If you press the footbrake constantly on a long hill, you may get 'brake fade'. If you're not sure, check what that means in the Glossary near the back of this book.

Use the gears to control your vehicle on a downhill slope (or 'gradient'). If you put the vehicle in 'neutral', or drive with the clutch down (called 'coasting'), your vehicle will increase speed beyond what is safe and will not be under proper control.

This sign warns you of a steep hill downwards.

- Travelling in neutral for long distances (known as coasting) is wrong and dangerous – you should not be tempted to do it and it doesn't save fuel

Remember that if there is sudden heavy rain after a dry hot spell, the road surface can get very slippery.

Now test yourself on the questions on pages 146–157

Section 9
Motorway rules

Learner drivers are only allowed on motorways at the discretion – and under the supervision – of an Approved Driving Instructor, so you might not experience driving on them until after you've passed your test. However, you do need to know all about MOTORWAY RULES before taking your practical test, and your theory test will most likely include a question about motorways.

As soon as you pass your driving test you will be legally allowed to drive on motorways. You need to know all the motorway rules in advance, so that you are confident and ready to cope with motorway driving when you pass your test.

There are some major roads and dual carriageways that learners can drive on which are very much like motorways. You may drive on some of these fast roads during your driving test, so that your examiner can see how well you cope with hazards at higher speeds.

When driving on these fast roads you will need some of the very same skills that you will need for motorway driving – for example, using lanes properly, knowing when it is safe to overtake, and controlling your vehicle at speed.

If you don't have a lesson on motorway driving with your ADI before taking your practical test, it makes sense to arrange one after you have passed before driving on a motorway alone for the first time.

MOTORWAYS AND OTHER ROADS

- On a motorway traffic is moving at high speed all the time
- All lanes are in use
- No stopping is allowed on a motorway – traffic only slows or comes to a stop because of accidents or other types of hold-up
- Some road users are not allowed on motorways. These include:
  - pedestrians, cyclists and learner drivers not accompanied by an ADI in a car with dual controls
  - horses and other animals
  - motorcycles under 50cc
  - slow-moving vehicles, tractors and farm vehicles and invalid carriages
- You always enter and leave a motorway on the left, via a slip road
- To the left of the inside lane (left-hand lane) on a motorway is the hard shoulder. You can only drive on this in an emergency
- Special signs and signals are used on motorways. These include signs above the road on overhead gantries, signs on the central reservation, and amber and red flashing lights

CHECKS BEFORE YOUR JOURNEY

Be extra careful about doing all your regular checks before you set out on a motorway journey. You cannot stop on the motorway to fix small problems, and no one wants to break down in the middle of fast traffic.

Always check:

- oil and coolant levels, screen wash container
- tyres and tyre pressure
- fuel gauge
- that the horn works

- that all mirrors and windows are free of dirt and grease

Many of these checks are legally necessary, as well as important for your safety.

HOW TO MOVE ON TO A MOTORWAY

- Join the motorway by building up your speed on the slip road to match the speed of traffic in the left lane of the motorway
- Use MSM (Mirrors – Signal – Manoeuvre) and move into the flow of traffic when it is safe to do so

CHANGING LANES AND OVERTAKING

Driving on a motorway needs all the skills you have learned about anticipation and forward planning.

You should:

- make good use of all mirrors, and check your blind spots
- signal to move out in plenty of time
- look out for hazards ahead in the lane you want to move to
- not go ahead if it will force another vehicle to brake or swerve
- keep a safe distance from the vehicle in front

TAKE A BREAK

When you drive on motorways you will sometimes see signs that say 'Tiredness can kill – take a break!' This is very good advice. Motorways are monotonous – boring to drive, with long stretches of road that look the same for miles. A major cause of accidents is drivers falling asleep at the wheel. Plan your journey so that you have time to get out, stretch your legs and have a drink or snack.

THE RULES YOU NEED TO KNOW:

- Keep to the left-hand lane unless you are overtaking and move back to the left lane as soon as it is safe to do so. Sometimes you need to stay in the centre lane for a time – for example, when a line of lorries is travelling up a hill in the left lane. Stay in the centre lane until you have passed the hazard, then signal left and return to the left lane
- NEVER reverse, park, walk or drive in the wrong direction on a motorway
- Don't exceed the speed limit. This is normally 70mph, but lower speed limits may be signed when the road is busy, or in bad weather
- Keep to the correct separation distance (see Safety Margins)
- Don't overtake on the left. If traffic is moving slowly in all three lanes you may find that the lane on the left is moving faster than the one to its right for a short time. Or the left lane may be signed for traffic turning off at the next junction only. But these are exceptions to the rule
- If luggage falls from your vehicle, do not get out to pick it up. Stop at the next emergency phone and tell the Highways Agency or the police. Posts on the edge of the motorway show the way to the nearest emergency phone. You should use these phones rather than your mobile phone, because the emergency phone connects directly to the Highways Agency or the police and tells them exactly where you are calling from on the motorway
- Don't stop on the hard shoulder except in an emergency. The hard shoulder is an extremely dangerous place, as many as one in eight road deaths happen there.

TRAFFIC SIGNS AND ROAD MARKINGS

Light signals

In *The Highway Code* you'll find the light signals only seen on motorways. Signs above the roadway or on the central reservation are activated as needed to warn of accidents, lane closures or weather conditions. Overhead gantries display arrows or red crosses showing which lanes are open or closed to traffic and which lanes to move to when motorways merge or diverge. They may also show temporary speed limits.

Direction signs

Direction signs on motorways are blue and those on other major roads are green – other direction signs are white with black print.

Reflective studs or 'cat's eyes'

It's useful to know the colours of studs on a motorway; this can help in working out which part of the road you're on if it's dark or foggy. White studs mark lanes or the centre of the road and red studs mark the left edge of the carriageway. Amber studs are used alongside the central reservation and green studs mark the entry to a slip road.

Note: These markings are also found on some dual carriageways.

USING THE HARD SHOULDER IN AN EMERGENCY
Light signals

- Stop as far to the left as possible and, if you can, near an emergency phone

- Emergency phones are situated 1 mile apart and have blue and white marker posts every 100 metres. An arrow on the posts points the direction of the nearest phone

- If you are using a mobile phone you can identify your location from the number on the post, or from a nearby blue 'driver location sign'

- Switch on your hazard warning lights

- Use the left-hand door to get out of the vehicle, and make sure your passengers do too This is also known as a 'Dutch reach'.

- Get everyone away from the road – if possible, behind the barrier or up the bank

- Leave animals in the vehicle unless they aren't safe there

Phone the Highways Agency or the police with full details of where you are, then go back and wait in a safe place near your vehicle

Now test yourself on the questions on pages 158–174

Section 10
Rules of the road

'Rules of the Road' is a good way to describe what is in *The Highway Code*.

The questions that come under this heading in the theory test include several on road signs and road markings. There are many more road sign questions in the section on Road and Traffic Signs. Several of the topics listed in this section have already come up.

Other questions in this section cover:
- speed limits
- overtaking
- parking
- lanes and roundabouts
- clearways
- box junctions
- crossroads
- pedestrian crossings
- towing caravans and trailers

SPEED LIMITS

Driving too fast for the road, traffic or weather conditions causes accidents. Make sure that you keep below the speed limit shown on the signs for the road that you are on.

30mph in a built-up area

50mph on a long, twisty country road

or as low as 20mph in a residential area with speed humps or traffic-calming measures

The national speed limit for cars on a dual carriageway is 70mph. This is also the maximum speed for motorway driving.

National speed limit
When you leave a built-up area you will usually see this sign.

- This sign tells you that the national speed limit for this type of road applies here
- The national speed limit for cars on a normal road (single carriageway outside a built-up area) is 60mph. So on this road you must drive below 60mph even if it is straight and empty

Street lights usually mean that a 30mph limit applies, unless there are signs showing other limits.

The right speed for the conditions

If it is raining, there is snow and ice on the road, or there is a high wind, you will have to drive more slowly than the maximum speed limit. This will keep you and other road users safe.

- Remember – you have to double the time you allow for stopping and braking in wet weather. Allow even more time in snow and ice
- You need to be extra careful when driving in fog

The right speed for your vehicle

Some other vehicles have lower speed limits than cars. You can find out more about speed limits from the table in *The Highway Code*.

PARKING RULES

There are some general rules about parking that all drivers should know:

- Whenever you can, you should use off-street car parks, or parking bays. These are marked out with white lines on the road
- Never park where your vehicle could be a danger to other road users

Look for special signs that tell you that you cannot park there at certain times of the day or that only certain people may park in that place. Examples include signs showing bus lanes, cycle lanes, residents' parking zones and roads edged with red or yellow lines.

Blue badges are given to people with disabilities. Do not park in a space reserved for a driver with a disability, even if that is the only place left to park. A driver with a disability may need to park there. You will break the law if you park in that space.

Parking at night
- If you park at night on a road that has a speed limit higher than 30mph, you must switch on your parking lights. You must switch on your parking lights even if you have parked in a lay-by on this type of road
- When parking at night, always park facing in the same direction as the traffic flow
- If your vehicle has a trailer, you must switch on parking lights, even if the road has a 30mph speed limit

Where not to park
You are not permitted to park:
- on the pavement
- at a bus stop
- in front of someone's drive
- opposite a traffic island
- near a school entrance
- on a pedestrian crossing (or inside the zigzag lines either side of it)
- near a junction
- on a clearway
- on a motorway

Now test yourself on the questions on pages 175–192

Section 11
Road and traffic signs

When you look up the chapter on ROAD AND TRAFFIC SIGNS in the theory test questions you will see that it takes up a lot of pages. This is because most of the questions have a picture of a road sign or marking. You will also see that a lot of questions ask 'What does this sign mean?'

But however differently the questions are worded, it all comes down to how well you know *The Highway Code*. You can try to learn as much of *The Highway Code* as possible, but there are other ways you can get to know the road signs.

As you walk or drive around, look at the road signs you see in the street, and the different markings painted on the road surface.

ON FOOT
Look at the signs and signals that all road users must obey, whether they are in a car or walking. For example, when you use a pedestrian crossing, check what kind of crossing it is (such as a pelican, toucan or zebra crossing).

CHECK WHETHER YOU KNOW THE FOLLOWING:
- What are the rules for pedestrians and drivers coming up to the crossing?
- What kinds of crossings are controlled by traffic lights?
- What is different about a zebra crossing?

Road and traffic signs

DURING YOUR DRIVING LESSONS

If you are having a driving lesson look well ahead so that you see all the signs that tell you what to do next. Obey them in good time.

DURING YOUR TEST

When you take your test the examiner will tell you when to move off, when to make a turn and when to carry out one of the set manoeuvres. The examiner will expect you to watch out for lane markings on the road, and signs giving directions, and to decide how to react to these yourself.

SIGNS

If you see several signs all on the same post, it can be confusing. The general rule is to start at the top and read down the post. The sign at the top tells you about the first hazard you have to look out for.

If you are a passenger in a car on a motorway, look at the motorway signs, because you need to know them, even though you can't drive on a motorway yet yourself.

Check that you can answer the following:
- What colour are the signs at the side of the motorway?
- What do the light signals above the road tell you?
- What signs tell you that you are coming to an exit?

Shapes of signs

Road and traffic signs come in three main shapes. Get to know them. You must learn what the signs mean.

Circles
Signs in circles tell you to do (blue) or not do (red) something – they give orders.

Triangles
Signs in triangles tell you of a hazard ahead – they give warnings.

Rectangles
Signs in rectangles tell you about where you are or where you are going – they give information.

There is only one sign which is octagonal – that is, it has eight sides. This is the sign for STOP. The eight-sided shape makes the sign stand out.

Now test yourself on the questions on pages 193–229

Section 12
Documents

This is quite a short section in the theory test. It is also different from the other sections, because it does not deal with either your driving skills or knowledge of *The Highway Code*.

It covers all the paperwork and the laws that you need to know about when you start learning to drive.

In this section there are questions about:
• driving licences
• insurance
• MOT certificate
• Vehicle Excise Duty (road tax)
• Vehicle Registration Document (log book)

This section also covers who can supervise a learner driver and changes you must tell the licensing authority about.

DRIVING LICENCE

If you are learning to drive, you'll need a provisional licence.
• You must have a valid licence to drive legally
• The driving licence consists of a photocard (see example, above) – keep it with you at all times
• Your signature appears on the licence
• Take good care of your provisional licence. If you lose it, you can get another one but you will have to pay a fee, and wait for the new licence to come before you can drive again
• When you pass your test you can apply for a full licence

INSURANCE

You must have a valid insurance certificate that covers you at least for third party liability. If you are learning with a driving school, you are covered by their insurance while you are in the driving school car. When you are in your own or anybody else's car, you must have insurance. Third party insurance cover usually comes as 'Third Party, Fire and Theft'. It is a basic insurance policy that will pay for repairs to another person's car and allows you to claim on the other driver's insurance if you are in an accident that was not your fault. If you have comprehensive insurance, the policy will pay for repairs to your vehicle even when the accident was your fault.

MOT CERTIFICATE

Cars and motorcycles must have their first MOT test three years (four years in Northern Ireland) after they are new and first registered. After that, they must have an MOT test every year.

The MOT test checks that your vehicle:
• is roadworthy – that is, all the parts work properly and the vehicle is safe to drive
• keeps to the legal limits for exhaust emissions – that is, the level of poisons in the gas that comes from the exhaust of your vehicle

If your vehicle is more than three years old you must not drive it without a valid MOT certificate – unless you are on your way to get an MOT and you have booked it in advance.

VEHICLE EXCISE DUTY

Vehicle Excise Duty is the tax that the government charges you to drive your vehicle on the roads. It is also sometimes called 'road tax'.

To drive or keep a vehicle on the road you must pay vehicle tax. The DVLA will send you a reminder when your tax is due to expire. When you buy a vehicle, any existing tax cannot be transferred with the vehicle.

Your vehicle must have valid insurance cover before you can tax it. If required, it will also need to have a valid MOT certificate. You can tax your vehicle online, by phone or at certain post offices.

If you want to keep a vehicle off the public road you must inform the DVLA by completing a Statutory Off Road Notification (SORN). It is an offence not to do so. You then won't have to pay Vehicle Excise Duty. The SORN is valid until your vehicle is taxed, sold or scrapped.

VEHICLE REGISTRATION CERTIFICATE

The Vehicle Registration Certificate (also known as a V5C) has all the important details about you and your vehicle, such as the make and model of the vehicle. It also has your name and address as the registered keeper of the vehicle. It is a record of the vehicle's history and is sometimes called 'the log book'.

DVLA

The Driver and Vehicle Licensing Agency is known as the DVLA. You must tell the DVLA if you are going to keep your car off road and are not renewing your Vehicle Excise Duty, when you buy or sell a car and if you change your name or your address.

This is because your details go on to the Vehicle Registration Certificate and you are legally responsible for the vehicle (car tax, parking fines, etc) until you have notified the DVLA that it is off road or you have sold it.

SUPERVISING A LEARNER DRIVER

As a learner driver you cannot drive on your own. If you are not with your driving instructor, you must be supervised by a person who is at least 21 years old, has a full licence for the kind of car you drive and has had that licence for at least three years. Note that if a person has a licence to drive an automatic car only, they cannot supervise a learner in a manual car.

Now test yourself on the questions on pages 230–237

Section 13

Incidents, accidents and emergencies

Most of the questions in this section are about helping anyone who is hurt in a road accident. Some people think they might do more harm than good if they try to help. But if you have a basic knowledge of first aid you won't panic and if you are first on the scene at an accident, you could even save a life. Look up 'First Aid on the road' in *The Highway Code*.

The theory test questions in this section cover:

- what to do when warning lights come on in your vehicle
- what to do if you break down
- safety equipment to carry with you
- when to use hazard warning lights
- what to do – and what not to do – at the scene of an accident
- what to do in tunnels

BASIC FIRST AID

What to do at an accident scene:

- Check that you are not putting yourself in danger before you go to help somebody else. You may need to warn other drivers of the accident
- Check all vehicle engines are switched off
- Make sure no one is smoking
- Move people who are not injured to a safe place. If the accident has happened on a motorway, if possible get uninjured people away from the hard shoulder, behind the barrier or on to the bank
- Call the emergency services. You will need to tell them exactly where you

are, and how many vehicles are involved in the accident. On motorways, use the emergency phone which connects directly to the Highways Agency or the police and tells them exactly where you are

- Do not move injured people – unless there is a risk of fire or of an explosion
- Give essential first aid to injured people (see Annexe 7 of *The Highway Code*)
- Stay there until the emergency services arrive

Other ways to help:

- Do speak in a calm way to the injured person
- Do try to keep them warm and as comfortable as possible
- Do not give them anything to drink
- Do not give them a cigarette
- Don't let injured people wander into the road

ADVICE ON SAFETY IF YOU BREAK DOWN

If you are on a non-motorway road:

- Try to get your vehicle off the main road. At least, get it right to the side of the road or on to the verge
- If the vehicle is in a place where it might be hit by another vehicle, get any passengers out and to a safer place
- Switch on the hazard warning lights to warn other drivers
- If you have a red warning triangle, place it at least 45 metres behind your car to warn other traffic (but don't use it on a motorway)
- If you are a member of a motoring organisation, call them and tell them where you are and what has happened. Wait with your vehicle until the patrol arrives

If you are on a motorway:

- If possible, leave the motorway at the next exit. If you can't get that far, drive on to the hard shoulder. Stop far over to the left, and switch on your hazard warning lights
- Get everyone out of the vehicle, using the nearside doors (but leave pets in the vehicle). Get them to sit on the bank, well away from the traffic
- Use the nearest orange emergency phone to call the emergency services and tell them where you are and what has happened (for your safety, face the oncoming traffic while you are on the phone)
- Go back to your vehicle and wait on the bank near by until help arrives
- Do not cross the motorway on foot or try to do repairs yourself – even changing a wheel. This is too dangerous on a motorway

DID YOU KNOW?
Before driving into a tunnel you should tune into a local radio station and listen to the traffic reports in case there are any accidents or problems in the tunnel.

Now test yourself on the questions on pages 238–250

Section 14

Vehicle loading

This last section, called VEHICLE LOADING, is the shortest of all. It covers a mixture of the following:

- how to load your vehicle safely
- using a roof rack
- towing caravans and trailers
- child restraints and safety locks

When you have passed your test you can tow a trailer, if the combined weight of the vehicle and trailer is less than 3,500kg. So you need to know the rules about towing.

TOWING

When you get your first full driving licence, check it to see how much you are allowed to tow. Do not tow any trailer that comes to more than that weight. The weight of a trailer should be no more than 85% of the weight of the car that is to pull it. But it is best to stay well below that top weight, because towing a trailer will affect the way your vehicle handles. When you are towing, you need to allow more room when overtaking and more time to brake and stop.

When towing a heavy load, you might need to blow your tyres up to more than the normal pressures. Check your vehicle's handbook for advice. Remember to change back to the normal tyre pressures when you finish your journey.

When you are turning at a roundabout or junction you will need to think about where you are on the road.

ROOF RACKS

If you attach a roof rack to your car, it will make a difference to the way in which your vehicle handles. Any load that is carried on a roof rack must be tied down securely.

- The roof rack makes your vehicle taller, so more vulnerable to strong winds
- You will increase your fuel consumption
- You need to change the way you drive to allow for the extra weight

To find out more, look up the parts of *The Highway Code* that deal with 'Loads and Towing'.

LOADING A TRAILER

If the weight of the load is arranged properly, this should cut down the risk of losing control, swerving and snaking.

- Try to spread the weight evenly when you load your trailer. Do not put more weight towards the front, or the back, or to one side
- It is against the law to have a load that is sticking out in a dangerous way
- Don't forget that if you park a vehicle with a trailer overnight, it must have lights

A vehicle towing a trailer:
- must not go over a maximum speed limit of 60mph
- must not use the right (outside) lane on a motorway

If you are going to buy a trailer, make sure it fits your car's tow bar. Tow bars must keep to EU regulations, and must have electric sockets to connect to the lights on the trailer.

SNAKING

'Snaking' means moving from side to side. A caravan will snake if it is not properly attached or loaded, or if the car pulling it is going too fast.

If you are towing a caravan or trailer and it starts to snake:
- slow down – stop pressing the accelerator (do not brake suddenly)
- get back in control of the steering
- then brake gently

YOU ARE RESPONSIBLE FOR PASSENGERS IN YOUR VEHICLE

There are also questions in the Vehicle Loading section about the safety of passengers. As the driver, you are responsible for making sure your vehicle is not overloaded – and this applies to people and animals as well as to luggage. Remember that all passengers must wear a seat belt (unless they have a medical certificate saying they should not wear one) and that all children under the age of 14 must wear a seat belt or be strapped into a child seat or other 'restraint' suitable for their age. (See the section on 'Child Restraints' in *The Highway Code*).

Children

Children must not sit in the space behind the back seat of a hatchback car, and no passengers should sit in a caravan while it is being towed.

Pets

Pets should be kept under careful control. You might keep them and you safe with a special harness, or if they are kept behind a screen in a hatchback which would stop them being thrown forward in the event of an accident.

Now test yourself on the questions on pages 251–254

THEORY TEST REVISION QUESTIONS

1 Mark *one* answer
What should you do before making a U-turn?

☐ **A** Give an arm signal as well as using your indicators
☐ **B** Check road markings to see that U-turns are permitted
☐ **C** Look over your shoulder for a final check
☐ **D** Select a higher gear than normal

If you have to make a U-turn, slow down and ensure that the road is clear in both directions. Make sure that the road is wide enough for you to carry out the manoeuvre safely. Use your mirrors and look round to check it's safe before turning across the road.

2 Mark *one* answer
What should you do as you approach this bridge?

☐ **A** Move to the right
☐ **B** Slow down
☐ **C** Change gear
☐ **D** Keep to 30 mph

You should slow down and be cautious. Hump bridges are often narrow and there may not be enough room for you to pass an oncoming vehicle at this point. Also, there's no footpath, so be aware of pedestrians in the road.

3 Mark *one* answer
Where should you avoid overtaking?

☐ **A** Just after a bend
☐ **B** In a one-way street
☐ **C** On a 30 mph road
☐ **D** Approaching a dip in the road

Oncoming vehicles or other hazards can be hidden from view by dips in the road. If you can't see into the dip, wait until you have a clear view and can see that it's safe before starting to overtake.

4 Mark *one* answer
What does this curved arrow road marking mean?

☐ **A** Heavy vehicles should take the next road on the left to avoid a weight limit
☐ **B** The road ahead bends to the left
☐ **C** Overtaking traffic should move back to the left
☐ **D** The road ahead has a camber to the left

In this picture, the road marking shows that overtaking drivers or riders need to return to the left. These markings show the direction drivers must pass hatch markings or solid double white lines. They're also used to show the route that high vehicles should take under a low arched bridge.

5 Mark *one* answer
What should you do if your mobile phone rings while you're driving or riding?

- ☐ **A** Stop immediately
- ☐ **B** Answer it immediately
- ☐ **C** Leave it until you have stopped in a safe place
- ☐ **D** Pull up at the nearest kerb

It's illegal to use a hand-held mobile or similar device when driving or riding, except in a genuine emergency. The safest option is to switch off your mobile phone before you set off, and use a message service. If you've forgotten to switch your phone off and it rings, you should leave it. When you've stopped in a safe place, you can see who called and return the call if necessary.

6 Mark *one* answer
Why are these yellow lines painted across the road?

- ☐ **A** To help you choose the correct lane
- ☐ **B** To help you keep the correct separation distance
- ☐ **C** To make you aware of your speed
- ☐ **D** To tell you the distance to the roundabout

These lines are often found on the approach to a roundabout or a dangerous junction. They give you extra warning to adjust your speed. Look well ahead and do this in good time.

7 Mark *one* answer
What should you do when you're approaching traffic lights that have been green for some time?

- ☐ **A** Accelerate hard
- ☐ **B** Maintain your speed
- ☐ **C** Be ready to stop
- ☐ **D** Brake hard

The longer traffic lights have been green, the sooner they'll change. Allow for this as you approach traffic lights that you know have been green for a while. They're likely to change soon, so you should be prepared to stop.

8 Mark *one* answer
What should you do before slowing down or stopping your vehicle?

- ☐ **A** Sound the horn
- ☐ **B** Use the mirrors
- ☐ **C** Select a higher gear
- ☐ **D** Flash the headlights

Before slowing down or stopping, check the mirrors to see what's happening behind you. Also assess what's ahead and make sure you give the correct signal if it will help other road users.

9 Mark *one* answer
You're following a large vehicle. Why should you stay a safe distance behind it?

- ☐ **A** You'll be able to corner more quickly
- ☐ **B** You'll help the large vehicle to stop more easily
- ☐ **C** You'll give the driver a chance to see you in their mirrors
- ☐ **D** You'll keep out of the wind better

If you're following a large vehicle but are so close to it that you can't see its exterior mirrors, the driver won't be able to see you. Keeping well back will also allow you to see the road ahead by looking past the large vehicle.

10 Mark *one* answer
Why should you use your mirrors when you see a hazard ahead?

- ☐ **A** Because you'll need to accelerate out of danger
- ☐ **B** To assess how your actions will affect the traffic behind
- ☐ **C** Because you'll need to brake sharply and stop
- ☐ **D** To check what's happening on the road ahead

You should be constantly scanning the road for clues about what's going to happen next. Check your mirrors regularly, particularly as soon as you spot a hazard. What's happening behind may affect how you respond to hazards ahead.

11 Mark *one* answer
You're waiting to turn right at the end of a road. What should you do if your view is obstructed by parked vehicles?

- ☐ **A** Stop and then move forward slowly and carefully for a clear view
- ☐ **B** Move quickly to where you can see so you only block traffic from one direction
- ☐ **C** Wait for a pedestrian to let you know when it's safe for you to emerge
- ☐ **D** Turn your vehicle around immediately and find another junction to use

At junctions, your view is often restricted by buildings, trees or parked cars. You need to be able to see in order to judge a safe gap. Edge forward slowly and keep looking all the time. Don't cause other road users to change speed or direction as you emerge.

12 Mark *one* answer
There are objects hanging from your interior mirror. Why could this be a hazard?

- ☐ **A** Your view could be obstructed
- ☐ **B** Your sun visor might get tangled
- ☐ **C** Your radio reception might be affected
- ☐ **D** Your windscreen could mist up more easily

Ensure that you can see clearly through the windscreen of your vehicle. Stickers or hanging objects could obstruct your view or draw your attention away from the road.

13 Mark *one* answer
You're on a long motorway journey. What should you do if you start to feel sleepy?

☐ **A** Play some loud music
☐ **B** Stop on the hard shoulder for a rest
☐ **C** Drive faster to complete your journey sooner
☐ **D** Leave the motorway and stop in a safe place

If you feel sleepy, you should leave the motorway at a service area or at the next exit and stop in a safe place to rest. A supply of fresh air can help to keep you alert before you reach the exit, but it isn't a substitute for stopping and resting.

14 Mark *one* answer
Why should you switch your headlights on when it first starts to get dark?

☐ **A** To make your dials easier to see
☐ **B** So others can see you more easily
☐ **C** So that you blend in with other drivers
☐ **D** Because the street lights are lit

Your headlights and tail lights help others on the road to see you. It may be necessary to turn on your headlights during the day if visibility is reduced; for example, due to heavy rain. In these conditions, the light might fade before the street lights are timed to switch on. Be seen to be safe.

15 Mark *one* answer
What's most likely to distract you while you're driving?

☐ **A** Using a mobile phone
☐ **B** Using the windscreen wipers
☐ **C** Using the demisters
☐ **D** Using the mirrors

Except for emergencies, it's illegal to use a hand-held mobile phone while you're driving. Even using a hands-free kit can severely distract your attention.

16 Mark *one* answer
You're driving your car. When may you use a hand-held mobile phone?

☐ **A** When you're receiving a call
☐ **B** When you've parked safely
☐ **C** When you're driving at less than 30 mph
☐ **D** When your car has automatic transmission

It's illegal to use a hand-held mobile phone while you're driving, except in a genuine emergency. Even using a hands-free kit can distract your attention. Park in a safe and convenient place before receiving or making a call or using text messaging. Then you'll also be free to take notes or refer to papers.

17 Mark *one* answer

You're driving on a wet road. What should you do if you have to stop your vehicle in an emergency?

- ☐ **A** Apply the parking brake and footbrake together
- ☐ **B** Keep both hands on the steering wheel
- ☐ **C** Select reverse gear
- ☐ **D** Give an arm signal

As you drive, look well ahead and all around so that you're ready for any hazards that might develop. If you have to stop in an emergency, react as soon as you can while keeping control of the vehicle. Keep both hands on the steering wheel so you can control the vehicle's direction of travel.

18 Mark *one* answer

What should you do when you move off from behind a parked car?

- ☐ **A** Give a signal after moving off
- ☐ **B** Look around before moving off
- ☐ **C** Look around after moving off
- ☐ **D** Use the exterior mirrors only

Before moving off, you should use both the interior and exterior mirrors to check that the road is clear. Look around to check the blind spots and, if necessary, give a signal to warn other road users of your intentions. Also look well ahead as you'll have to steer out into the road to pass the parked car.

19 Mark *one* answer

You're travelling along this road. How should you pass the cyclist?

- ☐ **A** Sound your horn as you pass
- ☐ **B** Keep close to them as you pass
- ☐ **C** Leave them plenty of room as you pass
- ☐ **D** Change down one gear before you pass

Allow the cyclist plenty of room in case they wobble or swerve around a pothole or raised drain. Look well ahead before you start to overtake, because you'll need to cross the hazard line. Look for entrances where vehicles could be waiting to pull out.

20 Mark *one* answer
When do windscreen pillars cause a serious obstruction to your view?

☐ **A** When you're driving on a motorway
☐ **B** When you're driving on a dual carriageway
☐ **C** When you're approaching a one-way street
☐ **D** When you're approaching bends and junctions

Windscreen pillars can obstruct your view, particularly at bends and junctions. Look out for other road users – especially cyclists, motorcyclists and pedestrians who can easily be overlooked.

21 Mark *one* answer
What should you do if you can't see clearly behind when you're reversing?

☐ **A** Open the window to look behind
☐ **B** Open the door to look behind
☐ **C** Look in the nearside mirror
☐ **D** Ask someone to guide you

If you want to turn your car around, try to find a place where you have good all-round vision. If this isn't possible, and you're unable to see clearly, then get someone to guide you.

22 Mark *one* answer
What does the term 'blind spot' mean?

☐ **A** An area covered by your right-hand mirror
☐ **B** An area not covered by your headlights
☐ **C** An area covered by your left-hand mirror
☐ **D** An area not visible to the driver

Modern vehicles provide the driver with a good view of both the road ahead and behind using well-positioned mirrors. However, the mirrors can't see every angle of the scene behind and to the sides of the vehicle. It's essential that you know when and how to check the vehicle's blind spots, so that you're aware of any hidden hazards.

23 Mark *one* answer
What's likely to happen if you use a hands-free phone while you're driving?

☐ **A** It will improve your safety
☐ **B** It will increase your concentration
☐ **C** It will reduce your view
☐ **D** It will divert your attention

Talking to someone while you're driving can distract you and, unlike when someone is in the car with you, the person on the other end of a mobile phone is unable to see the traffic situations you're dealing with. They won't stop speaking to you even if you're approaching a hazardous situation. You need to concentrate on your driving at all times.

24 Mark *one* answer
You're turning right onto a dual carriageway. What should you do before emerging?

- ☐ **A** Stop, apply the parking brake and then select a low gear
- ☐ **B** Position your vehicle well to the left of the side road
- ☐ **C** Check that the central reservation is wide enough for your vehicle
- ☐ **D** Make sure that you leave enough room for a vehicle behind

Before emerging right onto a dual carriageway, make sure that the central reservation is deep enough to protect your vehicle. If it isn't, you should treat the dual carriageway as one road and check that it's clear in both directions before pulling out. Neglecting to do this could place part or all of your vehicle in the path of approaching traffic and cause a collision.

25 Mark *one* answer
You're waiting to emerge from a junction. The windscreen pillar is restricting your view. What should you be particularly aware of?

- ☐ **A** Lorries
- ☐ **B** Buses
- ☐ **C** Motorcyclists
- ☐ **D** Coaches

Windscreen pillars can completely block your view of pedestrians, motorcyclists and cyclists. You should make a particular effort to look for these road users; don't just rely on a quick glance.

26 Mark *one* answer
How can you make sure that a satellite navigation (satnav) system doesn't distract you when you're driving?

- ☐ **A** Turn it off while you're driving in built-up areas
- ☐ **B** Choose a voice that you find calming
- ☐ **C** Only set the destination when you're lost
- ☐ **D** Set it before starting your journey

Satnavs can be useful when driving on unfamiliar routes. However, they can also distract you and cause you to lose control if you look at or adjust them while you're driving. Set the satnav before starting your journey, or pull up in a safe place before making any changes to it.

27 Mark *one* answer
**What must you do when the amber
light is flashing at a pelican crossing?**

☐ **A** Stop and wait for the green light
☐ **B** Stop and wait for the red light
☐ **C** Give way to pedestrians waiting
    to cross
☐ **D** Give way to pedestrians already on
    the crossing

Pelican crossings are signal-controlled
crossings operated by pedestrians.
Push-button controls change the signals.
Pelican crossings have no red-and-amber
stage before green; instead, they have a
flashing amber light. This means you must
give way to pedestrians who are on the
crossing but if the crossing is clear you
can continue.

28 Mark *one* answer
**Why should you never wave people
across at pedestrian crossings?**

☐ **A** Another vehicle may be coming
☐ **B** They may not be looking
☐ **C** It's safer for you to carry on
☐ **D** They may not be ready to cross

If people are waiting to use a pedestrian
crossing, slow down and be prepared to
stop. Don't wave them across the road,
because another driver may not have seen
them, may not have seen your signal, and
may not be able to stop safely.

29 Mark *one* answer
**Why is it dangerous to drive too close
to the vehicle ahead?**

☐ **A** Your engine will overheat
☐ **B** Your mirrors will need adjusting
☐ **C** Your view of the road ahead will
    be restricted
☐ **D** Your satnav will be confused

'Tailgating' is the term used when a driver or
rider follows the vehicle in front too closely.
It's dangerous because it restricts your view
of the road ahead and leaves no safety
margin if the vehicle in front needs to slow
down or stop suddenly. Tailgating is often
the underlying cause of rear-end collisions
or multiple pile-ups.

30 Mark *one* answer
**What will happen if you follow this
vehicle too closely?**

☐ **A** Your brakes will overheat
☐ **B** Your fuel consumption will
    be increased
☐ **C** Your engine will overheat
☐ **D** Your view ahead will be reduced

Staying back will increase your view of the
road ahead. This will help you to see any
hazards that might occur and give you more
time to react.

Section 2 – **Attitude**

31 Mark *one* answer
What's the minimum time gap you should leave when following a vehicle on a wet road?

- ☐ **A** One second
- ☐ **B** Two seconds
- ☐ **C** Three seconds
- ☐ **D** Four seconds

Water will reduce your tyres' grip on the road. The safe separation gap of at least two seconds in dry conditions should be doubled, to at least four seconds, in wet weather.

32 Mark *one* answer
You're being overtaken by a long, heavily laden lorry. What should you do if it's taking a long time for it to overtake?

- ☐ **A** Speed up
- ☐ **B** Slow down
- ☐ **C** Hold your speed
- ☐ **D** Change direction

A long lorry with a heavy load will need more time to pass you than a car, especially on an uphill stretch of road. Slow down and allow the lorry to pass.

33 Mark *one* answer
Which vehicle will use a blue flashing beacon?

- ☐ **A** Motorway maintenance
- ☐ **B** Bomb disposal
- ☐ **C** Snow plough
- ☐ **D** Breakdown recovery

Emergency vehicles use blue flashing lights. If you see or hear one, move out of its way as soon as it's safe and legal to do so.

34 Mark *one* answer
What should you do if you're being followed by an ambulance showing flashing blue lights?

- ☐ **A** Pull over as soon as it's safe to do so
- ☐ **B** Accelerate hard to get away from it
- ☐ **C** Maintain your speed and course
- ☐ **D** Brake harshly and stop well out into the road

Pull over in a place where the ambulance can pass safely. Check that there are no bollards or obstructions in the road that will prevent it from passing.

35 Mark *one* answer
What type of emergency vehicle is fitted with a green flashing beacon?

☐ **A** Fire engine
☐ **B** Road gritter
☐ **C** Ambulance
☐ **D** Doctor's car

A green flashing beacon on a vehicle means the driver or passenger is a doctor on an emergency call. Give way to them if it's safe to do so. Be aware that the vehicle may be travelling quickly or may stop in a hurry.

36 Mark *one* answer
Who should obey diamond-shaped traffic signs?

☐ **A** Tram drivers
☐ **B** Bus drivers
☐ **C** Lorry drivers
☐ **D** Taxi drivers

These signs apply only to tram drivers, but you should know their meaning so that you're aware of the priorities and are able to anticipate the actions of the driver.

37 Mark *one* answer
On a road where trams operate, which vehicles will be most at risk from the tram rails?

☐ **A** Cars
☐ **B** Cycles
☐ **C** Buses
☐ **D** Lorries

The narrow wheels of a bicycle can become stuck in the tram rails, causing the cyclist to stop suddenly, wobble or even lose balance altogether. The tramlines are also slippery, which could cause a cyclist to slide or fall off.

38 Mark *one* answer
When should you use your vehicle's horn?

☐ **A** To alert others to your presence
☐ **B** To allow you right of way
☐ **C** To greet other road users
☐ **D** To signal your annoyance

You mustn't use your vehicle's horn between 11.30 pm and 7 am in a built-up area or when you're stationary, unless a moving vehicle poses a danger. Its function is to alert other road users to your presence.

39 Mark *one* answer

You're in a one-way street and want to turn right. Where should you position your vehicle when there are two lanes?

☐ **A** In the right-hand lane
☐ **B** In the left-hand lane
☐ **C** In either lane, depending on the traffic
☐ **D** Just left of the centre line

When you're in a one-way street and want to turn right, you should take up a position in the right-hand lane. This will allow other road users, not wishing to turn, to pass on the left. Indicate your intention and take up the correct position in good time.

40 Mark *one* answer

You wish to turn right ahead. Why should you take up the correct position in good time?

☐ **A** To allow other drivers to pull out in front of you
☐ **B** To give you a better view into the road that you're joining
☐ **C** To help other road users know what you intend to do
☐ **D** To allow drivers to pass you on the right

If you wish to turn right into a side road, take up your position in good time. Move to the centre of the road when it's safe to do so. This will allow vehicles to pass you on the left. Early planning will show other traffic what you intend to do.

41 Mark *one* answer

Which type of crossing allows cyclists to ride across while pedestrians are also crossing?

☐ **A** Toucan
☐ **B** Puffin
☐ **C** Pelican
☐ **D** Zebra

A toucan crossing is designed to allow pedestrians and cyclists to cross at the same time. Look out for cyclists approaching the crossing at speed.

42 Mark *one* answer

You're travelling at the legal speed limit. What should you do if the vehicle behind approaches quickly, flashing its headlights?

☐ **A** Accelerate to make a gap behind you
☐ **B** Touch the brakes sharply to show your brake lights
☐ **C** Maintain your speed to prevent the vehicle from overtaking
☐ **D** Allow the vehicle to overtake

Don't enforce the speed limit by blocking another vehicle's progress. This will only cause frustration. Allow the other vehicle to pass when you can do so safely.

43 Mark *one* answer
When should you flash your headlights at other road users?

☐ **A** When showing that you're giving way
☐ **B** When showing that you're about to turn
☐ **C** When telling them that you have right of way
☐ **D** When letting them know that you're there

You should only flash your headlights to warn others of your presence. Don't use them to greet others, show impatience or give priority to other road users, because they could misunderstand your signal.

44 Mark *one* answer
You're approaching an unmarked crossroads. How should you deal with the junction?

☐ **A** Accelerate and keep to the middle
☐ **B** Slow down and keep to the right
☐ **C** Accelerate and look to the left
☐ **D** Slow down and look both ways

Be cautious, especially when your view is restricted by hedges, bushes, walls, large vehicles, etc. In the summer months, these junctions can become more difficult to deal with, because growing foliage may further obscure your view.

45 Mark *one* answer
The conditions are good and dry. When should you use the 'two-second rule'?

☐ **A** Before restarting the engine after it has stalled
☐ **B** When checking your gap from the vehicle in front
☐ **C** Before using the 'Mirrors – Signal – Manoeuvre' routine
☐ **D** When traffic lights change to green

In good conditions, the 'two-second rule' can be used to check the distance between your vehicle and the one in front. This technique works on roads carrying faster traffic. Choose a fixed object, such as a bridge, sign or tree. When the vehicle ahead passes this object, say to yourself 'Only a fool breaks the two-second rule.' If you reach the object before you finish saying this, you're too close.

46 Mark *one* answer
Which colour follows the green signal at a puffin crossing?

☐ **A** Steady red
☐ **B** Flashing amber
☐ **C** Steady amber
☐ **D** Flashing green

Puffin crossings have infra-red sensors that detect when pedestrians are crossing and hold the red traffic signal until the crossing is clear. The use of a sensor means there's no flashing amber phase as there is with a pelican crossing.

47 Mark *one* answer
You're in a line of traffic. What action should you take if the driver behind is following very closely?

- [ ] **A** Ignore the driver behind and continue to travel within the speed limit
- [ ] **B** Slow down, gradually increasing the gap between you and the vehicle in front
- [ ] **C** Signal left and wave the driver behind to come past
- [ ] **D** Move over to a position just left of the centre line of the road

If the driver behind is following too closely, there's a danger they'll collide with the back of your vehicle if you stop suddenly. You can reduce this risk by slowing down and increasing the safety margin in front of you. This reduces the chance that you'll have to stop suddenly and allows you to spread your braking over a greater distance. This is an example of defensive driving.

48 Mark *one* answer
You're driving on a clear night. Which lights should you use if the national speed limit applies and there's a steady stream of oncoming traffic?

- [ ] **A** Full-beam headlights
- [ ] **B** Sidelights
- [ ] **C** Dipped headlights
- [ ] **D** Fog lights

Use the full-beam headlights only when you can be sure that you won't dazzle other road users.

49 Mark *one* answer
You're driving behind a large goods vehicle. What should you do if it signals left but steers to the right?

- [ ] **A** Slow down and let the vehicle turn
- [ ] **B** Drive on, keeping to the left
- [ ] **C** Overtake on the right of it
- [ ] **D** Hold your speed and sound your horn

Large, long vehicles need extra room when making turns at junctions. They may move out to the right in order to make a left turn. Keep well back and don't attempt to pass them on their left.

50 Mark *one* answer
You're driving along this road. What should you do if the red car cuts in close in front of you?

- [ ] **A** Accelerate to get closer to the red car
- [ ] **B** Give a long blast on the horn
- [ ] **C** Drop back to leave the correct separation distance
- [ ] **D** Flash your headlights several times

There are times when other drivers make incorrect or ill-judged decisions. Be tolerant and try not to retaliate or react aggressively. Always consider the safety of other road users, your passengers and yourself.

51 Mark *one* answer
You're waiting in a traffic queue at night. How can you avoid dazzling drivers behind you?

- ☐ **A** Use the parking brake and release the footbrake
- ☐ **B** Keep your foot on the footbrake
- ☐ **C** Balance the clutch with the accelerator
- ☐ **D** Use the parking brake and footbrake together

In queuing traffic, your brake lights can dazzle drivers behind you. If you apply your parking brake, you can take your foot off the footbrake. This will turn off the brake lights so that they can't dazzle the driver behind you.

52 Mark *one* answer
You're driving in traffic at the speed limit for the road. What should you do if the driver behind is trying to overtake?

- ☐ **A** Move closer to the car ahead, so the driver behind has no room to overtake
- ☐ **B** Wave the driver behind to overtake when it's safe
- ☐ **C** Keep a steady course and allow the driver behind to overtake
- ☐ **D** Accelerate to get away from the driver behind

Keep a steady course to give the driver behind an opportunity to overtake safely. If necessary, slow down. Reacting incorrectly to another driver's impatience can lead to danger.

53 Mark *one* answer
What does it mean if the signs at a bus lane show no times of operation?

- ☐ **A** The lane isn't in operation
- ☐ **B** The lane is only in operation at peak times
- ☐ **C** The lane is in operation 24 hours a day
- ☐ **D** The lane is only in operation in daylight hours

Bus-lane signs show the vehicles allowed to use the lane and its times of operation. Where no times are shown, the bus lane is in operation 24 hours a day.

54 Mark *one* answer
What should you do when a person herding sheep asks you to stop?

- ☐ **A** Ignore them as they have no authority
- ☐ **B** Stop and switch off your engine
- ☐ **C** Continue on but drive slowly
- ☐ **D** Try to get past quickly

If someone in charge of animals asks you to stop, you should do so and switch off your engine. Animals are unpredictable and startle easily; they could turn and run into your path or into the path of another moving vehicle.

55 Mark *one* answer
What should you do when you're overtaking a horse and rider?

- ☐ **A** Sound your horn as a warning
- ☐ **B** Go past as quickly as possible
- ☐ **C** Flash your headlights as a warning
- ☐ **D** Go past slowly and carefully

Horses can be startled by the sound of a car engine or the rush of air caused by a vehicle passing too closely. Keep well back and only pass when it's safe. Leave them plenty of room; you may have to use the other side of the road to go past safely.

56 Mark *one* answer
You're approaching a zebra crossing. What should you do if pedestrians are waiting to cross?

- ☐ **A** Give way to older and infirm people only
- ☐ **B** Slow down and prepare to stop
- ☐ **C** Use your headlights to indicate they can cross
- ☐ **D** Wave at them to cross the road

As you approach a zebra crossing, look for pedestrians waiting to cross. Where you can see them, slow down and prepare to stop. Be especially careful of children and older people, who may have difficulty judging when it's safe to cross.

57 Mark *one* answer
What should you do if a vehicle pulls out in front of you at a junction?

- ☐ **A** Swerve past it and sound your horn
- ☐ **B** Flash your headlights and drive up close behind
- ☐ **C** Slow down and be ready to stop
- ☐ **D** Accelerate past it immediately

Try to anticipate what other drivers might do. Look and plan ahead so that you're ready to respond safely if a hazard develops. Be tolerant of road users who make mistakes.

58 Mark *one* answer
You're approaching a red light at a puffin crossing. Pedestrians are on the crossing. When will the red light change?

- ☐ **A** When you start to edge forward onto the crossing
- ☐ **B** When the pedestrians have cleared the crossing
- ☐ **C** When the pedestrians push the button on the far side of the crossing
- ☐ **D** When a driver from the opposite direction reaches the crossing

A sensor will automatically detect that the pedestrians have reached a safe position. Don't drive on until the green light shows and it's safe for you to do so.

59 Mark *one* answer
Which instrument-panel warning light would show that headlights are on main beam?

You should be aware of all the warning lights and visual aids on the vehicle you're driving. If you're driving a vehicle for the first time, you should familiarise yourself with all the controls, warning lights and visual aids before you set off.

60 Mark *one* answer
When should you leave a two-second gap between your vehicle and the one in front?

☐ **A** When it's raining
☐ **B** When it's dry
☐ **C** When it's icy
☐ **D** When it's foggy

In good, dry conditions, a driver needs to keep a distance of at least two seconds from the car in front. This should allow enough space for you to stop if the driver in front has to stop suddenly.

61 Mark *one* answer
You're driving at night on an unlit road. What should you do if you're following another vehicle?

☐ **A** Flash your headlights
☐ **B** Use dipped headlights
☐ **C** Switch off your headlights
☐ **D** Use full-beam headlights

If you follow another vehicle with your headlights on full beam, they could dazzle the driver. Leave a safe distance and make sure that the light from your dipped beam falls short of the vehicle in front.

62 Mark *one* answer
What should you do if you're driving a slow-moving vehicle on a narrow winding road?

☐ **A** Keep well out to stop vehicles overtaking dangerously
☐ **B** Wave the vehicles behind to come past you if you think they can overtake quickly
☐ **C** Pull in when you can, to let the vehicles behind overtake
☐ **D** Give a left signal when it's safe for vehicles to overtake you

If you're driving a slow-moving vehicle along a narrow road, try not to hold up faster traffic. If you see vehicles following behind, pull over in a safe place and let the traffic pass before continuing. Don't wave other traffic past – this could be dangerous if you or they haven't noticed a hazard ahead.

63 Mark *one* answer

You're driving a car that has a diesel engine. What can a loose filler cap on your fuel tank cause?

- ☐ **A** It can make the engine difficult to start
- ☐ **B** It can make the roads slippery for other road users
- ☐ **C** It can improve your vehicle's fuel consumption
- ☐ **D** It can increase the level of exhaust emissions

Diesel fuel can spill out if your filler cap isn't secured properly. This is most likely to occur on bends, junctions and roundabouts, where it will make the road slippery, especially if it's wet. At the end of a spell of dry weather, road surfaces may be especially slippery where diesel has been spilled but it hasn't been washed away by rain.

64 Mark *one* answer

What should you do to avoid fuel spillage?

- ☐ **A** Check that your tank is only three-quarters full
- ☐ **B** Check that you've used a locking filler cap
- ☐ **C** Check that your fuel gauge is working
- ☐ **D** Check that your filler cap is securely fastened

When learning to drive, it's a good idea to practise filling your car with fuel. Ask your instructor if you can use a petrol station and fill the fuel tank yourself. You need to know where the filler cap is on the car you're driving, so you know which side of the pump to park at. Take care not to overfill the tank and make sure you secure the filler cap correctly, so that no fuel leaks onto the road while you're driving.

65 Mark *one* answer

What style of driving causes increased risk to everyone?

- ☐ **A** Considerate
- ☐ **B** Defensive
- ☐ **C** Competitive
- ☐ **D** Responsible

Competitive driving increases the risks to everyone and is the opposite of responsible, considerate and defensive driving. Defensive driving is about questioning the actions of other road users and being prepared for the unexpected. Don't be taken by surprise.

66 Mark *one* answer
How would under-inflated tyres affect your vehicle?

- [ ] **A** The vehicle's stopping distance would increase
- [ ] **B** The flash rate of the vehicle's indicators would increase
- [ ] **C** The vehicle's gear change mechanism would become stiff
- [ ] **D** The vehicle's headlights would aim high

Your tyres are your only contact with the road. To prevent problems with braking and steering, keep your tyres free from defects; they must have sufficient tread depth and be correctly inflated. Correct tyre pressures help reduce the risk of skidding and provide a safer and more comfortable drive or ride.

67 Mark *one* answer
When are you not allowed to sound your vehicle's horn?

- [ ] **A** Between 10.00 pm and 6.00 am in a built-up area
- [ ] **B** At any time in a built-up area
- [ ] **C** Between 11.30 pm and 7.00 am in a built-up area
- [ ] **D** Between 11.30 pm and 6.00 am on any road

Every effort must be made to prevent excessive noise, especially in built-up areas at night. Don't rev your engine or sound the horn unnecessarily. It's illegal to sound your horn in a built-up area between 11.30 pm and 7.00 am, except when another road user poses a danger.

68 Mark *one* answer
What makes the vehicle in the picture 'environmentally friendly'?

- [ ] **A** It's powered by gravity
- [ ] **B** It's powered by diesel
- [ ] **C** It's powered by electricity
- [ ] **D** It's powered by unleaded petrol

Trams are powered by electricity and therefore don't emit exhaust fumes. They ease traffic congestion by offering drivers an alternative to using their car, particularly in busy cities and towns.

69 Mark *one* answer
Why have 'red routes' been introduced in major cities?

- [ ] **A** To raise the speed limits
- [ ] **B** To help the traffic flow
- [ ] **C** To provide better parking
- [ ] **D** To allow lorries to load more freely

Inconsiderate parking can obstruct the flow of traffic and so make traffic congestion worse. Red routes are designed to prevent this by enforcing strict parking restrictions. Driving slowly in traffic increases fuel consumption and causes a build-up of exhaust fumes.

70 Mark *one* answer
What's the purpose of road humps, chicanes and narrowings?

☐ **A** To separate lanes of traffic
☐ **B** To increase traffic speed
☐ **C** To allow pedestrians to cross
☐ **D** To reduce traffic speed

Traffic-calming measures help to keep vehicle speeds low in congested areas where there are pedestrians and children. A pedestrian is much more likely to survive a collision with a vehicle travelling at 20 mph than they are with a vehicle travelling at 40 mph.

71 Mark *one* answer
What's the purpose of a catalytic converter?

☐ **A** To reduce fuel consumption
☐ **B** To reduce the risk of fire
☐ **C** To reduce harmful exhaust gases
☐ **D** To reduce engine wear

Catalytic converters reduce a large percentage of harmful exhaust emissions. They work more efficiently when the engine has reached its normal working temperature.

72 Mark *one* answer
When should tyre pressures be checked?

☐ **A** After any lengthy journey
☐ **B** After travelling at high speed
☐ **C** When tyres are hot
☐ **D** When tyres are cold

Check the tyre pressures when the tyres are cold. This will give you a more accurate reading. The heat generated on a long journey will raise the pressure inside the tyre.

73 Mark *one* answer
When will your vehicle use more fuel?

☐ **A** When its tyres are under-inflated
☐ **B** When its tyres are of different makes
☐ **C** When its tyres are over-inflated
☐ **D** When its tyres are new

Check your tyre pressures frequently – normally once a week. If they're lower than those recommended by the manufacturer, there will be more 'rolling resistance'. The engine will have to work harder to overcome this, leading to increased fuel consumption.

74 Mark *one* answer
How should you dispose of a used vehicle battery?

☐ **A** Bury it in your garden
☐ **B** Put it in the dustbin
☐ **C** Take it to a local-authority disposal site
☐ **D** Leave it on waste land

Batteries contain acid, which is hazardous, and they must be disposed of safely. This means taking them to an appropriate disposal site.

---

75 Mark *one* answer
What's most likely to increase fuel consumption?

☐ **A** Poor steering control
☐ **B** Accelerating around bends
☐ **C** Staying in high gears
☐ **D** Harsh braking and accelerating

Accelerating and braking gently and smoothly will help to save fuel and reduce wear on your vehicle. This makes it better for the environment too.

---

76 Mark *one* answer
The fluid level in your battery is low. What fluid should you use to top it up?

☐ **A** Battery acid
☐ **B** Distilled water
☐ **C** Engine oil
☐ **D** Engine coolant

Some modern batteries are maintenance free. Check your vehicle handbook and, if necessary, make sure that the plates in each battery cell are covered with fluid.

77 Mark *one* answer
You're parked on the road at night. When must you use parking lights?

☐ **A** When there are continuous white lines in the middle of the road
☐ **B** When the speed limit exceeds 30 mph
☐ **C** When you're facing oncoming traffic
☐ **D** When you're near a bus stop

When parking at night, park in the direction of the traffic. This will enable other road users to see the reflectors on the rear of your vehicle. Use your parking lights if the speed limit is over 30 mph.

---

78 Mark *one* answer
How can you reduce the environmental harm caused by your motor vehicle?

☐ **A** Only use it for short journeys
☐ **B** Don't service it
☐ **C** Drive faster than normal
☐ **D** Keep engine revs low

Engines that burn fossil fuels produce exhaust emissions that are harmful to health. The harder you make the engine work, the more emissions it will produce. Engines also use more fuel and produce higher levels of emissions when they're cold. Anything you can do to reduce your use of fossil fuels will help the environment.

79 Mark *one* answer

What can cause excessive or uneven tyre wear?

☐ **A** A faulty gearbox
☐ **B** A faulty braking system
☐ **C** A faulty electrical system
☐ **D** A faulty exhaust system

If you see that parts of the tread on your tyres are wearing before others, it may indicate a brake, suspension or wheel-alignment fault. Regular servicing will help to detect faults at an early stage and this will avoid the risk of minor faults becoming serious or even dangerous.

80 Mark *one* answer

You need to top up your battery with distilled water. What level should you fill it to?

☐ **A** The top of the battery
☐ **B** Halfway up the battery
☐ **C** Just below the cell plates
☐ **D** Just above the cell plates

Top up the battery with distilled water and make sure each cell plate is covered.

81 Mark *one* answer

How can you plan your route before starting a long journey?

☐ **A** Check your vehicle handbook
☐ **B** Ask your local garage
☐ **C** Use a route planner on the internet
☐ **D** Consult a travel agent

Various route planners are available on the internet. Most of them give you several options, allowing you to choose between the most direct route and quieter roads. They may also identify rest and fuel stops. Print off the directions and take them with you.

82 Mark *one* answer

Why is it a good idea to plan your journey to avoid busy times?

☐ **A** You'll have an easier journey
☐ **B** You'll have a more stressful journey
☐ **C** Your journey time will be longer
☐ **D** It will cause more traffic congestion

No-one likes to spend time in traffic queues. Try to avoid busy times related to school or work travel.

83 Mark *one* answer

How will your journey be affected by travelling outside the busy times of day?

☐ **A** Your journey will use more fuel
☐ **B** Your journey will take longer
☐ **C** Your journey will be more hazardous
☐ **D** Your journey will have fewer delays

If possible, avoid the early morning, late afternoon and early evening 'rush hour'. Doing this should allow you to have a better journey, with fewer delays. This should help you to arrive at your destination feeling less stressed.

84 Mark *one* answer

You plan your route before starting a journey. Why should you also plan an alternative route?

☐ **A** Your original route may be blocked
☐ **B** Your maps may have different scales
☐ **C** You may find you have to pay a congestion charge
☐ **D** You may get held up by a tractor

It can be frustrating and worrying to find your planned route is blocked by roadworks or diversions. If you've planned an alternative, you'll feel less stressed and more able to concentrate fully on your driving or riding. If your original route is mostly on motorways, it's a good idea to plan an alternative using non-motorway roads. Always carry a map with you just in case you need to refer to it.

85 Mark *one* answer

You have to arrive on time for an appointment. How should you plan for the journey?

☐ **A** Allow plenty of time for the trip
☐ **B** Plan to travel at busy times
☐ **C** Avoid roads with the national speed limit
☐ **D** Prevent other drivers from overtaking

Always allow plenty of time for your journey in case of unforeseen problems. Anything can happen; for example, punctures, breakdowns, road closures, diversions and delays. You'll feel less stressed and less inclined to take risks if you aren't 'pushed for time'.

86 Mark *one* answer

What can you expect if you drive using rapid acceleration and heavy braking?

☐ **A** Reduced pollution
☐ **B** Increased fuel consumption
☐ **C** Reduced exhaust emissions
☐ **D** Increased road safety

Using the controls smoothly can reduce fuel consumption by about 15%, as well as reducing wear and tear on your vehicle. Plan ahead and anticipate changes of speed well in advance. This will reduce the need to accelerate rapidly or brake sharply.

87 Mark *one* answer
What could cause you to crash if the level is allowed to get too low?

- ☐ **A** Anti-freeze level
- ☐ **B** Brake-fluid level
- ☐ **C** Battery-water level
- ☐ **D** Radiator-coolant level

You should carry out frequent checks on all fluid levels but particularly brake fluid. As the brake pads or shoes wear down, the brake-fluid level will drop. If it drops below the minimum mark on the fluid reservoir, air could enter the hydraulic system and lead to a loss of braking efficiency or even complete brake failure.

88 Mark *one* answer
What should you do if your anti-lock brakes (ABS) warning light stays on?

- ☐ **A** Check the brake-fluid level
- ☐ **B** Check the footbrake free play
- ☐ **C** Check that the parking brake is released
- ☐ **D** Have the brakes checked immediately

Consult the vehicle handbook or a garage before driving the vehicle any further. Only drive to a garage if it's safe to do so. If you aren't sure, get expert help.

89 Mark *one* answer
What does it mean if this light comes on while you're driving?

- ☐ **A** A fault in the braking system
- ☐ **B** The engine oil is low
- ☐ **C** A rear light has failed
- ☐ **D** Your seat belt isn't fastened

If this light comes on, you should have the brake system checked immediately. A faulty braking system could have dangerous consequences.

90 Mark *one* answer
Why is it important to wear suitable shoes when you're driving?

- ☐ **A** To prevent wear on the pedals
- ☐ **B** To maintain control of the pedals
- ☐ **C** To enable you to adjust your seat
- ☐ **D** To enable you to walk for assistance if you break down

When you're going to drive, make sure that you're wearing suitable clothing. Comfortable shoes will ensure that you have proper control of the foot pedals.

91 Mark *one* answer
If you're involved in a collision, what will reduce the risk of neck injury?

☐ **A** An air-sprung seat
☐ **B** Anti-lock brakes
☐ **C** A collapsible steering wheel
☐ **D** A properly adjusted head restraint

If you're involved in a collision, head restraints will reduce the risk of neck injury. They must be properly adjusted. Make sure they aren't positioned too low: in a crash, this could cause damage to the neck.

92 Mark *one* answer
What does it mean if your vehicle keeps bouncing after you sharply press down and release on the bodywork over a wheel?

☐ **A** The tyres are worn
☐ **B** The tyres are under inflated
☐ **C** The vehicle is on soft ground
☐ **D** The shock absorbers are worn

If you find that your vehicle bounces as you drive around a corner or bend in the road, the shock absorbers might be worn. To test your shock absorbers, sharply press down and release above each wheel. If the vehicle continues to bounce, take it to be checked by a qualified mechanic.

93 Mark *one* answer
How will a roof rack affect your car?

☐ **A** There will be less wind noise
☐ **B** The engine will use more oil
☐ **C** The car will accelerate faster
☐ **D** Fuel consumption will increase

A roof rack increases your car's wind resistance. This will cause an increase in fuel consumption, so you should remove it when it isn't being used. An aerodynamically designed roof rack or box will help reduce wind resistance to a minimum, but the rack or box should still be removed when it isn't in use.

94 Mark *one* answer
What makes your tyres illegal?

☐ **A** If they were bought second-hand
☐ **B** If they have any large, deep cuts in the side wall
☐ **C** If they're of different makes
☐ **D** If they have different tread patterns

Your tyres may be of different treads and makes. They can even be second-hand, as long as they're in good condition. They must, however, be intact, without cuts or tears. When checking the side walls for cuts and bulges, don't forget to check the side of the tyre that's hidden from view, under the car.

95 Mark *one* answer
What's the legal minimum depth of tread for car tyres?

☐ **A** 1 mm
☐ **B** 1.6 mm
☐ **C** 2.5 mm
☐ **D** 4 mm

Car tyres must have sufficient depth of tread to give them a good grip on the road surface. The legal minimum for cars is 1.6 mm. This depth should be across the central three-quarters of the breadth of the tyre and around the entire circumference.

96 Mark *one* answer
You're carrying two 13-year-old children and their parents in your car. Who's responsible for seeing that the children wear seat belts?

☐ **A** The children's parents
☐ **B** You, the driver
☐ **C** The front-seat passenger
☐ **D** The children

Seat belts save lives and reduce the risk of injury. If you're carrying passengers under 14 years old, it's your responsibility as the driver to ensure that their seat belts are fastened or they're seated in an approved child restraint.

97 Mark *one* answer
How can drivers help the environment?

☐ **A** By accelerating harshly
☐ **B** By accelerating gently
☐ **C** By using leaded fuel
☐ **D** By driving faster

Rapid acceleration and heavy braking lead to increased
- fuel consumption
- wear on your vehicle.

Having your vehicle serviced regularly will maintain its efficiency, produce cleaner emissions and reduce the risk of a breakdown.

98 Mark *one* answer
How can you avoid wasting fuel?

☐ **A** By having your vehicle serviced regularly
☐ **B** By revving the engine in the lower gears
☐ **C** By keeping an empty roof rack on your vehicle
☐ **D** By driving at higher speeds where possible

If you don't have your vehicle serviced regularly, the engine will gradually become less efficient. This will cause increased fuel consumption and, in turn, an increase in the amount of harmful emissions it produces.

99 Mark *one* answer
What could you do to reduce the volume of traffic on the roads?

- ☐ **A** Drive in a bus lane
- ☐ **B** Use a car with a smaller engine
- ☐ **C** Walk or cycle on short journeys
- ☐ **D** Travel by car at all times

Try not to use your car as a matter of routine. For shorter journeys, consider walking or cycling instead - this is much better for both you and the environment.

100 Mark *one* answer
What's most likely to waste fuel?

- ☐ **A** Reducing your speed
- ☐ **B** Driving on motorways
- ☐ **C** Using different brands of fuel
- ☐ **D** Under-inflated tyres

Wasting fuel costs you money and also causes unnecessary pollution. Ensuring your tyres are correctly inflated, avoiding carrying unnecessary weight and removing a roof rack that's not in use will all help to reduce your fuel consumption.

101 Mark *one* answer
What part of the car does the law require you to keep in good condition?

- ☐ **A** The gearbox
- ☐ **B** The transmission
- ☐ **C** The door locks
- ☐ **D** The seat belts

Unless exempt, you and your passengers must wear a seat belt (or suitable child restraint). The seat belts in your car must be in good condition and working properly; they'll be checked during its MOT test.

102 Mark *one* answer
How much more fuel will you use by driving at 70 mph, compared with driving at 50 mph?

- ☐ **A** About 5%
- ☐ **B** About 15%
- ☐ **C** About 75%
- ☐ **D** About 100%

Your vehicle will use less fuel if you avoid heavy acceleration. The higher the engine revs, the more fuel you'll use. Using the same gear, and covering the same distance, a vehicle travelling at 70 mph will use about 15% more fuel than it would at 50 mph. However, don't travel so slowly that you inconvenience or endanger other road users.

103 Mark *one* answer
What should you do if your vehicle pulls to one side when you use the brakes?

☐ **A** Increase the pressure in your tyres
☐ **B** Have the brakes checked as soon as possible
☐ **C** Change gear and pump the brake pedal
☐ **D** Use your parking brake at the same time

The brakes on your vehicle must be effective and properly adjusted. If your vehicle pulls to one side when braking, take it to be checked by a qualified mechanic as soon as you can.

104 Mark *one* answer
What will happen if your car's wheels are unbalanced?

☐ **A** The steering will pull to one side
☐ **B** The steering will vibrate
☐ **C** The brakes will fail
☐ **D** The tyres will deflate

If your wheels are out of balance, it will cause the steering to vibrate at certain speeds. This isn't a fault that will put itself right, so take your vehicle to a garage or tyre fitter to have the wheels rebalanced.

105 Mark *one* answer
What can be damaged if you turn the steering wheel when the car isn't moving?

☐ **A** The gearbox
☐ **B** The engine
☐ **C** The brakes
☐ **D** The tyres

Turning the steering wheel when the car isn't moving is known as dry steering. It can cause unnecessary wear to the tyres and steering mechanism.

106 Mark *one* answer
What's the safest thing to do if you have to leave valuables in your car?

☐ **A** Put them in a carrier bag
☐ **B** Park near a school entrance
☐ **C** Lock them out of sight
☐ **D** Park near a bus stop

If you have to leave valuables in your car, lock them out of sight. This is the best way to deter an opportunist thief.

107 Mark *one* answer
What may help to deter a thief from stealing your car?

☐ **A** Always keeping the headlights on
☐ **B** Fitting reflective glass windows
☐ **C** Always keeping the interior light on
☐ **D** Etching the registration number on the windows

Having your car registration number etched on all your windows is a cheap and effective way to deter professional car thieves.

108 Mark *one* answer
What should you remove from your car before leaving it unattended?

☐ **A** The car dealer's details
☐ **B** The owner's manual
☐ **C** The service record
☐ **D** The vehicle registration document

Never leave the vehicle registration document inside your car. This document would help a thief to dispose of your car more easily.

109 Mark *one* answer
What should you do when leaving your vehicle parked and unattended?

☐ **A** Park near a busy junction
☐ **B** Park in a housing estate
☐ **C** Lock it and remove the key
☐ **D** Leave the left indicator on

An unlocked car is an open invitation to thieves. Leaving the keys in the ignition not only makes your car easy to steal but could also invalidate your insurance.

110 Mark *one* answer
What will reduce fuel consumption?

☐ **A** Driving more slowly
☐ **B** Accelerating rapidly
☐ **C** Late and heavy braking
☐ **D** Staying in lower gears

Harsh braking, frequent gear changes and harsh acceleration increase fuel consumption. A car uses less fuel when travelling at a constant low speed in an appropriate high gear. You need to look well ahead so you're able to anticipate hazards early. Easing off the accelerator and timing your approach at junctions, for example, can reduce the fuel consumption of your vehicle.

111 Mark *one* answer
You service your own vehicle. How should you dispose of the old engine oil?

- ☐ **A** Take it to a local-authority site
- ☐ **B** Pour it down a drain
- ☐ **C** Tip it into a hole in the ground
- ☐ **D** Put it in your dustbin

It's illegal to pour engine oil down any drain. Oil is a pollutant and harmful to wildlife. Dispose of it safely at an authorised site.

112 Mark *one* answer
Why do MOT tests include an exhaust emission test?

- ☐ **A** To recover the cost of expensive garage equipment
- ☐ **B** To help protect the environment against pollution
- ☐ **C** To discover which fuel supplier is used the most
- ☐ **D** To make sure diesel and petrol engines emit the same fumes

Emission tests are carried out to make sure your vehicle's engine is operating efficiently. This ensures the pollution produced by the engine is kept to a minimum. If your vehicle isn't serviced regularly, it may fail the MOT emissions test.

113 Mark *one* answer
How can you reduce the damage your vehicle causes to the environment?

- ☐ **A** Use narrow side streets
- ☐ **B** Brake heavily
- ☐ **C** Use busy routes
- ☐ **D** Anticipate well ahead

By looking well ahead and recognising hazards in good time, you can avoid late and heavy braking. Watch the traffic flow and look well ahead for potential hazards so you can control your speed in good time. Avoid over-revving the engine and accelerating harshly, as this increases wear to the engine and uses more fuel.

114 Mark *one* answer
How will you benefit from following the manufacturer's service schedule for your vehicle?

- ☐ **A** Your vehicle will be cheaper to insure
- ☐ **B** Your vehicle tax will be lower
- ☐ **C** Your vehicle will remain reliable
- ☐ **D** Your journey times will be reduced

All vehicles need to be serviced to keep working efficiently. An efficient engine uses less fuel and produces fewer harmful emissions than an engine that's running inefficiently. Keeping the vehicle serviced to the manufacturer's schedule should also keep it reliable and reduce the chance of it breaking down.

115 Mark *one* answer
How should you drive when you're driving along a road that has road humps?

- ☐ **A** Maintain a reduced speed throughout
- ☐ **B** Accelerate quickly between the humps
- ☐ **C** Always keep to the maximum legal speed
- ☐ **D** Drive slowly at school times only

Road humps are there for a reason – to protect vulnerable road users by reducing the speed of traffic. Don't accelerate harshly between the humps. Put the safety of others first and maintain a reduced speed throughout the zone.

116 Mark *one* answer
When should you check the engine oil level?

- ☐ **A** Before a long journey
- ☐ **B** When the engine is hot
- ☐ **C** Early in the morning
- ☐ **D** Every time you drive the car

An engine can use more oil during long journeys than on shorter trips. Insufficient engine oil is potentially dangerous: it can lead to excessive wear, mechanical breakdown and expensive repairs. Most cars have a dipstick to allow the oil level to be checked. If not, you should refer to the vehicle handbook.

117 Mark *one* answer
You're having difficulty finding a parking space in a busy town. Can you park on the zigzag lines of a zebra crossing?

- ☐ **A** No, not unless you stay with your car
- ☐ **B** Yes, in order to drop off a passenger
- ☐ **C** Yes, if you don't block people from crossing
- ☐ **D** No, not under any circumstances

It's an offence to park on the zigzag lines of a zebra crossing. You'll be causing an obstruction by obscuring the view of both pedestrians and drivers.

118 Mark *one* answer
What should you do when you leave your car unattended for a few minutes?

- ☐ **A** Leave the engine running
- ☐ **B** Switch the engine off but leave the key in
- ☐ **C** Lock it and remove the key
- ☐ **D** Park near a traffic warden

Always switch off the engine, remove the key and lock your car, even if you're only leaving it for a few minutes.

119 Mark *one* answer
Why should you try and park in a secure car park?

- ☐ **A** It makes it easy to find your car
- ☐ **B** It helps deter thieves
- ☐ **C** It stops the car being exposed to bad weather
- ☐ **D** It doesn't cost anything to park here

Whenever possible, leave your car in a secure car park. This will help deter thieves.

120 Mark *one* answer
Where would parking your vehicle cause an obstruction?

- ☐ **A** Alongside a parking meter
- ☐ **B** In front of a property entrance
- ☐ **C** On your driveway
- ☐ **D** In a marked parking space

Don't park your vehicle where it may obstruct access to a business or property. Think carefully before you slow down and stop. Look at road markings and signs to ensure that you aren't parking illegally.

121 Mark *one* answer
What's the most important reason for having a properly adjusted head restraint?

- ☐ **A** To make you more comfortable
- ☐ **B** To help you avoid neck injury
- ☐ **C** To help you relax
- ☐ **D** To help you maintain your driving position

In a collision, rapid deceleration will violently throw vehicle occupants forward and then backwards as the vehicle stops. Seat belts and airbags protect occupants against the forward movement. Head restraints should be adjusted so they give maximum protection to the head and neck during the backward movement.

122 Mark *one* answer
What can you do to reduce environmental damage caused by your vehicle?

- ☐ **A** Avoid using the cruise control
- ☐ **B** Use the air conditioning whenever you drive
- ☐ **C** Use the gears to slow the vehicle
- ☐ **D** Avoid making a lot of short journeys

Avoid using your car for short journeys. On a short journey, the engine is unlikely to warm up fully and will therefore be running less efficiently. This will result in the car using more fuel and emitting higher levels of harmful emissions.

123 Mark *one* answer

What can people who live or work in towns and cities do to help reduce urban pollution levels?

- ☐ **A** Drive more quickly
- ☐ **B** Over-rev in a low gear
- ☐ **C** Walk or cycle
- ☐ **D** Drive short journeys

Using a vehicle for short journeys means the engine doesn't have time to reach its normal operating temperature. When an engine is running below its normal operating temperature, it produces increased amounts of pollution. Walking and cycling don't create pollution and have health benefits as well.

124 Mark *one* answer

How can you reduce the chances of your car being broken into when leaving it unattended?

- ☐ **A** Take all valuables with you
- ☐ **B** Park near a taxi rank
- ☐ **C** Place any valuables on the floor
- ☐ **D** Park near a fire station

When leaving your car, take all valuables with you if you can. Otherwise, lock them out of sight.

125 Mark *one* answer

How can you help to prevent your car radio being stolen?

- ☐ **A** Park in an unlit area
- ☐ **B** Leave the radio turned on
- ☐ **C** Park near a busy junction
- ☐ **D** Install a security-coded radio

A security-coded radio can deter thieves, as it's likely to be of little use when removed from the vehicle.

126 Mark *one* answer

How can you reduce the risk of your vehicle being broken into at night?

- ☐ **A** Leave it in a well-lit area
- ☐ **B** Park in a quiet side road
- ☐ **C** Don't engage the steering lock
- ☐ **D** Park in a poorly lit area

Having your vehicle broken into or stolen can be very distressing and inconvenient. Avoid leaving your vehicle unattended in poorly lit areas.

127 Mark *one* answer
What will help you to keep your car secure?

- ☐ **A** Being a member of a vehicle breakdown organisation
- ☐ **B** Registering with a Vehicle Watch scheme
- ☐ **C** Passing an advanced driving test
- ☐ **D** Taking car maintenance classes

The Vehicle Watch scheme helps to reduce the risk of your car being stolen. By displaying high-visibility Vehicle Watch stickers in your car, you're inviting the police to stop your vehicle if it's seen in use between midnight and 5 am.

128 Mark *one* answer
On a vehicle, where would you find a catalytic converter?

- ☐ **A** In the fuel tank
- ☐ **B** In the air filter
- ☐ **C** On the cooling system
- ☐ **D** On the exhaust system

Although carbon dioxide is still produced, a catalytic converter fitted to the exhaust system reduces the toxic and polluting gases by up to 90%.

129 Mark *one* answer
What can you achieve if you drive smoothly?

- ☐ **A** Reduction in journey times by about 15%
- ☐ **B** Increase in fuel consumption by about 15%
- ☐ **C** Reduction in fuel consumption by about 15%
- ☐ **D** Increase in journey times by about 15%

By driving smoothly, you'll not only save about 15% of your fuel but will also reduce the amount of wear and tear on your vehicle and the level of pollution it produces. You're also likely to feel more relaxed and have a more pleasant journey.

130 Mark *one* answer
Which driving technique can help you save fuel?

- ☐ **A** Using lower gears as often as possible
- ☐ **B** Accelerating sharply in each gear
- ☐ **C** Using each gear in turn
- ☐ **D** Missing out some gears

Missing out intermediate gears, when appropriate, helps to reduce the amount of time spent accelerating and decelerating - the times when your vehicle uses the most fuel.

131 Mark *one* answer
How can driving in a fuel-efficient manner help protect the environment?

- ☐ **A** Through the legal enforcement of speed regulations
- ☐ **B** By increasing the number of cars on the road
- ☐ **C** Through increased fuel bills
- ☐ **D** By reducing exhaust emissions

Fuel-efficient driving is all about looking and planning further ahead. This helps raise your hazard awareness and reduces the need for late and heavy braking. This will make your journeys more comfortable, as well as considerably reducing your fuel bills and reducing emissions that can damage the environment.

132 Mark *one* answer
What does fuel-efficient driving achieve?

- ☐ **A** Increased fuel consumption
- ☐ **B** Improved road safety
- ☐ **C** Damage to the environment
- ☐ **D** Increased exhaust emissions

The emphasis is on hazard awareness and planning ahead. By looking well ahead, you'll have plenty of time to deal with hazards safely and won't need to brake sharply. This will also reduce damage to the environment.

133 Mark *one* answer
What's the legal minimum tread depth for tyres on your trailer or caravan?

- ☐ **A** 1 mm
- ☐ **B** 1.6 mm
- ☐ **C** 2 mm
- ☐ **D** 2.6 mm

Trailers and caravans may be left in storage over the winter months, and tyres can deteriorate. It's important to check their tread depth and also their pressures and general condition. The legal tread depth of 1.6 mm applies to the central three-quarters of a tyre's breadth, over its entire circumference.

134 Mark *one* answer
When is fuel consumption at its highest?

- ☐ **A** When you're braking
- ☐ **B** When you're coasting
- ☐ **C** When you're accelerating
- ☐ **D** When you're turning sharply

Accelerating uses a lot of fuel, so always try to use the accelerator smoothly. Taking your foot off the accelerator allows the momentum of the car to take you forward, especially when going downhill. This can save a considerable amount of fuel without any loss of control over the vehicle.

135 Mark *one* answer
When may a passenger travel in a car without wearing a seat belt?

- ☐ **A** When they're under 14 years old
- ☐ **B** When they're under 1.5 metres (5 feet) in height
- ☐ **C** When they're sitting in the rear seat
- ☐ **D** When they're exempt for medical reasons

If you have adult passengers, it's their responsibility to wear a seat belt, but you should still remind them to use one as they get in the car. It's your responsibility to make sure that all children in your car are secured with an appropriate restraint. Exemptions are allowed for those with a medical exemption certificate.

136 Mark *one* answer
You're driving a friend's children home from school. They're both under 14 years old. Who's responsible for making sure they wear a seat belt or approved child restraint where required?

- ☐ **A** An adult passenger
- ☐ **B** The children
- ☐ **C** You, the driver
- ☐ **D** Your friend

Passengers should always be secured and safe. Children should be encouraged to fasten their seat belts or approved restraints themselves from an early age, so that it becomes a matter of routine. As the driver, you must check that they're fastened securely. It's your responsibility.

137 Mark *one* answer
What's likely to happen if you put too much oil in your engine?

- ☐ **A** The clutch pedal will lock
- ☐ **B** The air intake will become blocked
- ☐ **C** The timing belt will slip
- ☐ **D** The oil seals will leak

Too much oil will lead to increased pressure in the engine. This could damage oil seals and lead to oil leaks. Any excess oil should be drained off.

138 Mark *one* answer
You have to make an unexpected journey. You're carrying a five-year-old child on the back seat of your car. They're under 1.35 metres (4 feet 5 inches) tall. How should you seat them if a correct child restraint isn't available?

- ☐ **A** Behind the passenger seat
- ☐ **B** Using an adult seat belt
- ☐ **C** Sharing a belt with an adult
- ☐ **D** Between two other children

In journeys of unexpected necessity, and when a correct child restraint isn't available, the child must sit on the rear seat and use an adult seat belt. In a collision, unrestrained objects and people can cause serious injury or even death.

139 Mark *one* answer

You're carrying an 11-year-old child on the front seat of your car. They're under 1.35 metres (4 feet 5 inches) tall. What seat belt security must be in place?

- ☐ **A** They must use an adult seat belt
- ☐ **B** They must be able to fasten their own seat belt
- ☐ **C** They must use a suitable child restraint
- ☐ **D** They must be able to see clearly out of the front window

As the driver, it's your responsibility to make sure that children are secure and safe in your vehicle. Make yourself familiar with the rules. When children are carried on the back seat, there are a few very exceptional cases when an adult seat belt can be used instead of a correct child restraint.

140 Mark *one* answer

You're stopped at the side of the road. What must you do if you'll be waiting there for some time?

- ☐ **A** Switch off the engine
- ☐ **B** Apply the steering lock
- ☐ **C** Switch off the radio
- ☐ **D** Use your headlights

If your vehicle is stationary and is likely to remain so for some time, you must switch off the engine unless you're stationary in traffic or diagnosing a fault.

141 Mark *one* answer

You want to put a rear-facing baby seat on the front passenger seat. What must you do if the passenger seat is protected by a frontal airbag?

- ☐ **A** Deactivate the airbag
- ☐ **B** Turn the seat to face sideways
- ☐ **C** Ask a passenger to hold the baby
- ☐ **D** Put the child in an adult seat belt

It's illegal to fit a rear-facing baby seat into a passenger seat protected by an active frontal airbag. If the airbag activates, it could cause serious injury or even death to the child. You must secure it in a different seat or deactivate the relevant airbag. Follow the manufacturer's advice when fitting a baby seat.

142 Mark *one* answer

You're leaving your vehicle parked on a road and unattended. When may you leave the engine running?

- ☐ **A** If you'll be parking for less than five minutes
- ☐ **B** If the battery keeps going flat
- ☐ **C** When parked in a 20 mph zone
- ☐ **D** Never if you're away from the vehicle

When you leave your vehicle parked on a road, switch off the engine and secure the vehicle. Make sure no valuables are visible, shut all the windows, lock the vehicle, and set the alarm if the vehicle has one.

143 Mark *one* answer
How much can stopping distances increase in icy conditions?

- ☐ **A** Two times
- ☐ **B** Three times
- ☐ **C** Five times
- ☐ **D** Ten times

Tyre grip is greatly reduced in icy conditions. For this reason, you need to allow up to ten times the stopping distance you would allow on dry roads.

---

144 Mark *one* answer
What requires extra care when you're driving or riding in windy conditions?

- ☐ **A** Using the brakes
- ☐ **B** Moving off on a hill
- ☐ **C** Turning into a narrow road
- ☐ **D** Passing pedal cyclists

Always give cyclists plenty of room when overtaking them. You need to give them even more room when it's windy. A sudden gust could easily blow them off course and into your path.

145 Mark *one* answer
Why should you keep well to the left as you approach a right-hand bend?

- ☐ **A** To improve your view of the road
- ☐ **B** To overcome the effect of the road's slope
- ☐ **C** To let faster traffic from behind overtake
- ☐ **D** To be positioned safely if you skid

Keeping to the left as you approach right-hand bends will give you an earlier view around the bend and enable you to see any hazards sooner. It also reduces the risk of collision with any oncoming vehicle that may have drifted over the centre line while taking the bend.

146 Mark *one* answer
You've just gone through flood water. What should you do to make sure your brakes are working properly?

- ☐ **A** Accelerate and keep to a high speed for a short time
- ☐ **B** Go slowly while gently applying the brakes
- ☐ **C** Avoid using the brakes at all for a few miles
- ☐ **D** Stop for at least an hour to allow them time to dry

Water on the brakes will act as a lubricant, causing them to work less efficiently. Using the brakes lightly as you go along will quickly dry them out.

147 Mark *one* answer
What will be affected if the road surface becomes soft in very hot weather?

- ☐ **A** The suspension
- ☐ **B** The exhaust emissions
- ☐ **C** The fuel consumption
- ☐ **D** The tyre grip

If the road surface becomes very hot, it can soften. Tyres are unable to grip a soft surface as well as they can a firm dry one. Take care when cornering and braking.

148 Mark *one* answer
Where is your vehicle most likely to be affected by side winds?

- ☐ **A** On a narrow country lane
- ☐ **B** On an open stretch of road
- ☐ **C** On a busy stretch of road
- ☐ **D** On a long, straight road

In windy conditions, care must be taken on exposed roads. A strong gust of wind can blow you off course. Watch out for other road users who are particularly likely to be affected, such as cyclists, motorcyclists, high-sided lorries and vehicles towing trailers.

149 Mark *one* answer
You're following a vehicle on a wet road. You stay a safe distance behind it. What should you do if a driver overtakes you and pulls into the gap you've left?

- ☐ **A** Flash your headlights as a warning
- ☐ **B** Try to overtake safely as soon as you can
- ☐ **C** Drop back to regain a safe distance
- ☐ **D** Stay close to the other vehicle until it moves on

Wet weather will affect the time it takes for you to stop and can affect your control. Your speed should allow you to stop safely and in good time. If another vehicle pulls into the gap you've allowed, ease back until you've regained your stopping distance.

150 Mark *one* answer
You're travelling on the motorway. How can you lower the risk of a collision when the vehicle behind is following too closely?

☐ **A** Increase your distance from the vehicle in front
☐ **B** Brake sharply
☐ **C** Switch on your hazard warning lights
☐ **D** Move onto the hard shoulder and stop

On busy roads, traffic may still travel at high speeds. Don't follow the vehicle in front too closely. If a driver behind seems to be 'pushing' you, gradually increase your distance from the vehicle in front by slowing down gently. This will give you more space in front if you have to brake, and will reduce the risk of a collision involving several vehicles.

151 Mark *one* answer
You're following other vehicles in fog. You have your headlights on dipped beam. What else can you do to reduce the chances of being in a collision?

☐ **A** Keep close to the vehicle in front
☐ **B** Use main beam instead of dipped headlights
☐ **C** Keep up with the faster vehicles
☐ **D** Keep a safe distance from the vehicle in front

When it's foggy, use your headlights on dipped beam. This will help you see and be seen by other road users. If visibility is seriously reduced, consider using front and rear fog lights if you have them. Keep to a sensible speed and don't follow the vehicle in front too closely. If the road is wet and slippery, you'll need to allow twice the normal stopping distance.

152 Mark *one* answer
What should you do when you're using a contraflow system?

☐ **A** Choose an appropriate lane in good time
☐ **B** Switch lanes to make better progress
☐ **C** Increase speed to get through the contraflow more quickly
☐ **D** Follow other motorists closely to avoid long queues

In a contraflow system, you'll be travelling close to oncoming traffic and sometimes in narrow lanes. You should get into the correct lane in good time, obey any temporary speed-limit signs and keep a safe separation distance from the vehicle ahead.

153 Mark *one* answer
How can you avoid wheelspin when you're driving on an icy road?

☐ **A** Drive at a slow speed in the highest gear possible
☐ **B** Use the parking brake if the wheels start to slip
☐ **C** Brake gently and repeatedly
☐ **D** Drive in a low gear at all times

If you're travelling on an icy road, extra caution will be required to avoid loss of control. Keeping your speed down and using the highest gear possible will reduce the risk of the tyres losing their grip on this slippery surface.

154 Mark *one* answer
What's the main cause of skidding?

☐ **A** The weather
☐ **B** The driver
☐ **C** The vehicle
☐ **D** The road

Skidding is usually caused by driver error. You should always adjust your driving to take account of the road and weather conditions.

155 Mark *one* answer
You're driving in freezing conditions. What should you do as you approach a sharp bend?

☐ **A** Coast into the bend
☐ **B** Apply your parking brake
☐ **C** Firmly use your footbrake
☐ **D** Slow down gently

Harsh use of the accelerator, brakes or steering is likely to lead to skidding, especially on slippery surfaces. Avoid steering and braking at the same time. In icy conditions, it's very important that you constantly assess what's ahead so that you can take appropriate action in plenty of time.

156 Mark *one* answer
You're about to start a journey in freezing weather. What part of your vehicle should you clear of ice and snow?

☐ **A** The aerial
☐ **B** The windows
☐ **C** The bumper
☐ **D** The boot

Driving in bad weather increases your risk of having a collision. If you absolutely have to travel, clear your lights, mirrors, number plates and windows of any snow or ice, so that you can see and be seen.

157 Mark *one* answer
What will help you to move off on a snowy surface?

☐ **A** Using the car's lowest gear
☐ **B** Using a higher gear than normal
☐ **C** Using a high engine speed
☐ **D** Using the parking brake and footbrake together

If you attempt to move off in a low gear, there'll be more torque (turning force) at the driven wheels than if you use a higher gear. More torque makes it easier for the tyres to lose grip and so spin the wheels.

158 Mark *one* answer
What should you do when you're driving in snowy conditions?

☐ **A** Brake firmly and quickly
☐ **B** Be ready to steer sharply
☐ **C** Use sidelights only
☐ **D** Brake gently in plenty of time

In snowy conditions, be careful with the steering, accelerator and brakes. Braking sharply while you're driving on snow is likely to make your car skid.

159 Mark *one* answer
What's the main benefit of driving a four-wheel-drive vehicle?

☐ **A** Improved grip on the road
☐ **B** Lower fuel consumption
☐ **C** Shorter stopping distances
☐ **D** Improved passenger comfort

By driving all four wheels, the vehicle has maximum grip on the road. This grip is especially helpful when travelling on slippery or uneven surfaces. However, having four-wheel drive doesn't replace the skills you need to drive safely.

160 Mark *one* answer
You're about to go down a steep hill. What should you do to control the speed of your vehicle?

☐ **A** Select a high gear and use the brakes carefully
☐ **B** Select a high gear and use the brakes firmly
☐ **C** Select a low gear and use the brakes carefully
☐ **D** Select a low gear and avoid using the brakes

When driving down a steep hill, gravity will cause your vehicle to speed up. This will make it more difficult for you to stop. To help keep your vehicle's speed under control, select a lower gear to give you more engine braking and make careful use of the brakes.

161 Mark *one* answer
What should you do when you park a car facing downhill?

☐ **A** Turn the steering wheel towards the kerb
☐ **B** Park close to the bumper of another car
☐ **C** Park with two wheels on the kerb
☐ **D** Turn the steering wheel away from the kerb

Turning the wheels towards the kerb will allow them to act as a chock, preventing any forward movement of the vehicle. It will also help to leave your car in gear, or select 'Park' if you have an automatic.

162 Mark *one* answer
You're driving in a built-up area that has traffic-calming measures. What should you do when you approach a road hump?

- ☐ **A** Move across to the left-hand side of the road
- ☐ **B** Wait for any pedestrians to cross
- ☐ **C** Check your mirror and slow down
- ☐ **D** Stop and check both pavements

Many towns have road humps as part of traffic-calming measures, designed to slow down traffic. Reduce your speed when driving over them. If you go too fast, you could lose control or damage your car. Look out for pedestrians or cyclists while you're driving in these areas.

163 Mark *one* answer
On what type of road surface may anti-lock brakes be ineffective?

- ☐ **A** Dry
- ☐ **B** Loose
- ☐ **C** Firm
- ☐ **D** Smooth

Poor contact with the road surface could cause one or more of the tyres to lose grip on the road. This is more likely to happen when braking in poor weather conditions and when the road has a loose, slippery or uneven surface.

164 Mark *one* answer
You're driving a vehicle that has anti-lock brakes. How should you apply the footbrake when you need to stop in an emergency?

- ☐ **A** Slowly and gently
- ☐ **B** Slowly but firmly
- ☐ **C** Rapidly and gently
- ☐ **D** Rapidly and firmly

You may have to stop in an emergency due to a misjudgement by another driver or a hazard arising suddenly, such as a child running out into the road. If your vehicle has anti-lock brakes, you should apply the brakes immediately and keep them firmly applied until you stop.

165 Mark *one* answer
You're driving along a country road. You see this sign. What should you do after dealing safely with the hazard?

- ☐ **A** Check your tyre pressures
- ☐ **B** Switch on your hazard warning lights
- ☐ **C** Accelerate briskly
- ☐ **D** Test your brakes

If your brakes have been thoroughly soaked, you should check that they're working properly before you build up speed again. Before you do this, remember to check your mirrors and consider what's behind you.

166 Mark *one* answer
What would suggest you're driving on an icy road?

☐ **A** There's less wind noise
☐ **B** There's less tyre noise
☐ **C** There's less transmission noise
☐ **D** There's less engine noise

Drive extremely carefully when the roads are icy. When travelling on ice, tyres make virtually no noise and the steering feels light and unresponsive. In icy conditions, be very gentle when braking, accelerating and steering.

167 Mark *one* answer
You're driving along a wet road. How can you tell if your vehicle's tyres are losing their grip on the surface?

☐ **A** The engine will stall
☐ **B** The steering will feel very heavy
☐ **C** The engine noise will increase
☐ **D** The steering will feel very light

If you drive at speed in very wet conditions, your steering may suddenly feel lighter than usual. This means that the tyres have lifted off the surface of the road and are floating on the surface of the water. This is known as aquaplaning. Reduce speed but don't brake until your steering returns to normal.

168 Mark *one* answer
In which conditions will your overall stopping distance increase?

☐ **A** In the rain
☐ **B** In fog
☐ **C** At night
☐ **D** In strong winds

Extra care should be taken in wet weather. On wet roads, your stopping distance could be double that in dry conditions.

169 Mark *one* answer
You're driving on an open road in dry weather. What distance should you keep from the vehicle in front?

☐ **A** A two-second time gap
☐ **B** One car length
☐ **C** Two metres (6 feet 6 inches)
☐ **D** Two car lengths

One way of checking there's a safe distance between you and the vehicle in front is to use the two-second rule. To check for a two-second time gap, choose a stationary object ahead, such as a bridge or road sign. When the car in front passes the object, say 'Only a fool breaks the two-second rule'. If you reach the object before you finish saying the phrase, you're too close and need to increase the gap.

170 Mark *one* answer
How can you use your vehicle's engine as a brake?

- ☐ **A** By changing to a lower gear
- ☐ **B** By selecting reverse gear
- ☐ **C** By changing to a higher gear
- ☐ **D** By selecting neutral gear

When driving on downhill stretches of road, selecting a lower gear gives increased engine braking. This will prevent excessive use of the brakes, which become less effective if they overheat.

171 Mark *one* answer
How should you use anti-lock brakes when you need to stop in an emergency?

- ☐ **A** Keep pumping the footbrake to prevent skidding
- ☐ **B** Brake normally but grip the steering wheel tightly
- ☐ **C** Brake promptly and firmly until you've stopped
- ☐ **D** Apply the parking brake to reduce the stopping distance

If you have ABS and need to stop in an emergency, keep your foot firmly on the brake pedal until the vehicle has stopped. When the ABS operates, you may hear a grating sound and feel vibration through the brake pedal. This is normal and you should maintain pressure on the brake pedal until the vehicle stops.

172 Mark *one* answer
What lights should you use when you're driving on a wet motorway and vehicles are throwing up surface spray?

- ☐ **A** Hazard warning lights
- ☐ **B** Dipped headlights
- ☐ **C** Rear fog lights
- ☐ **D** Sidelights

When surface spray reduces visibility, switch on your headlights on dipped beam. This will help other road users to see you.

173 Mark *one* answer
What can result when you travel for long distances in neutral (known as coasting)?

- ☐ **A** Improvement in control
- ☐ **B** Easier steering
- ☐ **C** Reduction in control
- ☐ **D** Increased fuel consumption

Coasting is the term used when the clutch is held down, or the gear lever is in neutral, and the vehicle is allowed to freewheel. This reduces the driver's control of the vehicle. When you coast, the engine can't drive the wheels to stabilise you through a corner, or give the assistance of engine braking to help slow the car.

174 Mark *one* answer
What should you do before starting a journey in foggy weather?

- ☐ **A** Wear a hi-visibility jacket
- ☐ **B** Have a caffeinated drink
- ☐ **C** Allow more time
- ☐ **D** Reduce your tyre pressures

Don't venture out if your journey isn't necessary. If you have to travel and someone is expecting you at the other end, let them know that you'll be taking longer than usual for your journey. This will stop them worrying if you don't turn up on time and will also take the pressure off you, so you don't feel you have to rush.

175 Mark *one* answer
What should you do when you're overtaking a motorcyclist on a windy day?

- ☐ **A** Pass closely
- ☐ **B** Pass very slowly
- ☐ **C** Pass widely
- ☐ **D** Pass immediately

In strong winds, riders of two-wheeled vehicles are particularly vulnerable. When you overtake them, allow plenty of room. Check to the left as you pass to make sure they're safe.

176 Mark *one* answer
What does it mean if the Electronic Stability Control (ESC) indicator lamp lights up while you're driving?

- ☐ **A** The ESC system has activated
- ☐ **B** The ESC system has a fault
- ☐ **C** The ESC system is running a routine test
- ☐ **D** The ESC system is switched off

ESC is a computer controlled technology that detects reduced traction and automatically makes corrective adjustments to prevent loss of control. The ESC lamp comes on to alert the driver that the system has activated and the car is approaching its handling limits. It's a powerful driver aid but it cannot save a car once its traction limits have been exceeded.

177 Mark *one* answer
Where would you expect to see these markers?

- ☐ **A** On a motorway sign
- ☐ **B** On a railway bridge
- ☐ **C** On a large goods vehicle
- ☐ **D** On a diversion sign

These markers must be fitted to vehicles over 13 metres long, large goods vehicles, and rubbish skips placed in the road. They're reflective to make them easier to see in the dark.

178 Mark *one* answer
What's the main hazard shown in this picture?

- ☐ **A** Vehicles turning right
- ☐ **B** Vehicles doing U-turns
- ☐ **C** The cyclist crossing the road
- ☐ **D** Parked cars around the corner

Look at the picture carefully and try to imagine you're there. The cyclist in this picture appears to be trying to cross the road. You must be able to deal with the unexpected, especially when you're approaching a hazardous junction. Look well ahead to give yourself time to deal with any hazards.

179 Mark *one* answer
Which road user has caused a hazard?

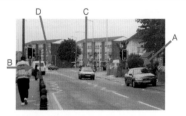

- ☐ **A** The parked car (arrowed A)
- ☐ **B** The pedestrian waiting to cross (arrowed B)
- ☐ **C** The moving car (arrowed C)
- ☐ **D** The car turning (arrowed D)

The car arrowed A is parked within the area marked by zigzag lines at the pedestrian crossing. Parking here is illegal. It also
- blocks the view for pedestrians wishing to cross the road
- restricts the view of the crossing for approaching traffic.

180 Mark *one* answer
What should the driver of the car approaching the crossing do?

- ☐ **A** Continue at the same speed
- ☐ **B** Sound the horn
- ☐ **C** Drive through quickly
- ☐ **D** Slow down and get ready to stop

Look well ahead to see whether any hazards are developing. This will give you more time to deal with them in the correct way. The man in the picture is clearly intending to cross the road. You should be travelling at a speed that allows you to check your mirror, slow down and stop in good time. You shouldn't have to brake harshly.

181 Mark *one* answer
What should the driver of the dark grey car be especially aware of?

- ☐ **A** The uneven road surface
- ☐ **B** Traffic following behind
- ☐ **C** Doors opening on parked cars
- ☐ **D** Empty parking spaces

When passing parked cars, there's a risk that a driver or passenger may not check before opening the door into the road. A defensive driver will drive slowly and be looking for people who may be about to get out of their car.

182 Mark *one* answer
What should you expect if you see this sign ahead?

- ☐ **A** The road will go steeply uphill
- ☐ **B** The road will go steeply downhill
- ☐ **C** The road will bend sharply to the left
- ☐ **D** The road will bend sharply to the right

This sign indicates that the road will bend sharply to the left. Slow down in plenty of time and select the correct gear before you start to turn. Braking hard and late, while also sharply changing direction, is likely to cause a skid.

183 Mark *one* answer
What should you do as you approach this cyclist?

- ☐ **A** Try to overtake before the cyclist gets to the junction
- ☐ **B** Flash your headlights at the cyclist
- ☐ **C** Slow down and allow the cyclist to turn
- ☐ **D** Rev your engine so the cyclist knows you're following behind

Keep well back and give the cyclist time and room to turn safely. Don't intimidate them by getting too close or trying to squeeze past.

184 Mark *one* answer
Why must you take great care when emerging from this junction?

- ☐ **A** The road surface is poor
- ☐ **B** The footpath is narrow
- ☐ **C** The kerbs are high
- ☐ **D** The view is restricted

You may have to pull forward slowly until you can see up and down the road. Be aware that the traffic approaching the junction can't see you either. If you don't know that it's clear, don't go.

185 Mark *one* answer
Which type of vehicle should you be ready to give way to as you approach this bridge?

- ☐ **A** Bicycles
- ☐ **B** Buses
- ☐ **C** Motorcycles
- ☐ **D** Cars

A bus or high-sided lorry will have to take a position in the centre of the road to clear the bridge. There's normally a sign to show this. Look well ahead, past the bridge and be ready to stop and give way to large oncoming vehicles.

186 Mark *one* answer
What type of vehicle could you expect to meet in the middle of the road?

- ☐ **A** Lorry
- ☐ **B** Bicycle
- ☐ **C** Car
- ☐ **D** Motorcycle

The highest point of the bridge is in the centre, so a large vehicle might have to move to the centre of the road to have enough room to pass safely under the bridge.

187 Mark *one* answer
What must you do at this junction?

- ☐ **A** Stop behind the line, then edge forward to see clearly
- ☐ **B** Stop beyond the line, at a point where you can see clearly
- ☐ **C** Stop only if there's traffic on the main road
- ☐ **D** Stop only if you're turning right

The 'stop' sign has been put here because the view into the main road is poor. sYou must stop because it won't be possible to take proper observation while you're moving.

188 Mark *one* answer
What should you do if a driver pulls out of a side road in front of you, causing you to brake hard?

- ☐ **A** Ignore the error and stay calm
- ☐ **B** Flash your lights to show your annoyance
- ☐ **C** Sound your horn to show your annoyance
- ☐ **D** Overtake as soon as possible

Be tolerant if a vehicle emerges and you have to brake quickly. Anyone can make a mistake, so don't react aggressively. Be alert where there are side roads and be especially careful where there are parked vehicles, because these can make it difficult for emerging drivers to see you.

189 Mark *one* answer
How would age affect an older person's driving ability?

- ☐ **A** They won't be able to obtain car insurance
- ☐ **B** They'll need glasses to read road signs
- ☐ **C** They'll take longer to react to hazards
- ☐ **D** They won't signal at junctions

As people age, their reaction time gets slower. The rate of decline varies from person to person but you can expect them to take longer to react to a hazard and they may be hesitant in some situations – for example, at a junction.

190 Mark *one* answer
Do you need to plan rest stops when you're planning a long journey?

- ☐ **A** Yes, you should plan to stop every half an hour
- ☐ **B** Yes, regular stops help concentration
- ☐ **C** No, you'll be less tired if you get there as soon as possible
- ☐ **D** No, only fuel stops will be needed

Try to plan your journey so that you can take rest stops. It's recommended that you take a break of at least 15 minutes after every two hours of driving or riding. This should help to maintain your concentration.

191 Mark *one* answer
What should you do if the red lights start flashing as you approach a level crossing?

- ☐ **A** Go over it quickly
- ☐ **B** Go over it carefully
- ☐ **C** Stop before the barrier
- ☐ **D** Switch on your hazard warning lights

At level crossings, the red lights flash before and while the barrier is down. At most crossings, an amber light will precede the red lights. You must stop behind the white line unless you've already crossed it when the amber light comes on. Don't be tempted to zigzag around half-barriers.

192 Mark *one* answer
You're approaching a crossroads. What should you do if the traffic lights have failed?

- ☐ **A** Brake and stop only for large vehicles
- ☐ **B** Brake sharply to a stop before looking
- ☐ **C** Be prepared to brake sharply to a stop
- ☐ **D** Be prepared to stop for any traffic

When approaching a junction where the traffic lights have failed, you should proceed with caution. Treat the situation as an unmarked junction and be prepared to stop.

193 Mark *one* answer

What should the driver of the red car (arrowed) do?

☐ **A** Wave towards the pedestrians who are waiting to cross

☐ **B** Wait for the pedestrian in the road to cross

☐ **C** Quickly drive behind the pedestrian in the road

☐ **D** Tell the pedestrian in the road she shouldn't have crossed

Some people might take a long time to cross the road. They may be older or have a disability. Be patient and don't hurry them by showing your impatience. If pedestrians are standing at the side of the road, don't signal or wave them to cross. Other road users might not have seen your signal and this could lead the pedestrians into a hazardous situation.

194 Mark *one* answer

You're following a slower-moving vehicle. What should you do if there's a junction just ahead on the right?

☐ **A** Overtake after checking your mirrors and signalling

☐ **B** Only consider overtaking when you're past the junction

☐ **C** Accelerate quickly to overtake before reaching the junction

☐ **D** Slow down and prepare to overtake on the left

You should never overtake as you approach a junction. If a vehicle emerged from the junction while you were overtaking, a dangerous situation could develop very quickly.

195 Mark *one* answer
What should you do as you approach this overhead bridge?

- ☐ **A** Move out to the centre of the road before going through
- ☐ **B** Find another route; this one is only for high vehicles
- ☐ **C** Be prepared to give way to large vehicles in the middle of the road
- ☐ **D** Move across to the right-hand side before going through

Oncoming large vehicles may need to move to the middle of the road to pass safely under the bridge. There won't be enough room for you to continue, so you should be ready to stop and wait.

196 Mark *one* answer
Why are vehicle mirrors often slightly curved (convex)?

- ☐ **A** They give a wider field of vision
- ☐ **B** They totally cover blind spots
- ☐ **C** They make it easier to judge the speed of the traffic behind
- ☐ **D** They make the traffic behind look bigger

Although a convex mirror gives a wide view of the scene behind, you should be aware that it won't show you everything behind or to the side of your vehicle. Before you move off, you'll need to look over your shoulder to check for anything not visible in the mirrors.

197 Mark *one* answer
You're on a three-lane motorway. How should you overtake a slow-moving lorry in the middle lane if it's showing this sign?

- ☐ **A** Cautiously approach the lorry, then overtake on either side
- ☐ **B** Follow the lorry until you can leave the motorway
- ☐ **C** Use the right-hand lane and overtake the lorry normally
- ☐ **D** Approach with care and overtake on the left of the lorry

This sign is found on slow-moving or stationary works vehicles. If you wish to overtake it, do so on the left, as indicated. Be aware that there might be workmen in the area.

198 Mark *one* answer
What should you do if you think the driver of the vehicle in front has forgotten to cancel their right indicator?

- ☐ **A** Flash your lights to alert the driver
- ☐ **B** Sound your horn before overtaking
- ☐ **C** Overtake on the left if there's room
- ☐ **D** Stay behind and don't overtake

Be cautious and don't attempt to overtake. The driver may be unsure of the location of a junction and may turn suddenly.

199 Mark *one* answer
What's the main hazard the driver of the red car (arrowed) should be aware of?

- ☐ **A** Glare from the sun may affect the driver's vision
- ☐ **B** The black car may stop suddenly
- ☐ **C** The bus may move out into the road
- ☐ **D** Oncoming vehicles will assume the driver is turning right

If you can do so safely, give way to buses signalling to move off at bus stops. Try to anticipate the actions of other road users around you. The driver of the red car should be prepared for the bus pulling out. As you approach a bus stop, look to see how many passengers are waiting to board. If the last one has just got on, the bus is likely to move off.

200 Mark *one* answer
What type of vehicle displays this yellow sign?

- ☐ **A** A broken-down vehicle
- ☐ **B** A school bus
- ☐ **C** An ice-cream van
- ☐ **D** A private ambulance

Buses which carry children to and from school may stop at places other than scheduled bus stops. Be aware that they might pull over at any time to allow children to get on or off. This will normally be when traffic is heavy during rush hour.

201 Mark *one* answer
What hazard should you be aware of when travelling along this street?

- ☐ **A** Glare from the sun
- ☐ **B** Lack of road markings
- ☐ **C** Children running out between vehicles
- ☐ **D** Large goods vehicles

On roads where there are many parked vehicles, you might not be able to see children between parked cars and they may run out into the road without looking.

202 Mark *one* answer
What's the main hazard you should be aware of when following this cyclist?

☐ **A** The cyclist may move to the left and dismount
☐ **B** The cyclist may swerve into the road
☐ **C** The cyclist may get off and push their bicycle
☐ **D** The cyclist may wish to turn right at the end of the road

When following a cyclist, be aware that they have to deal with the hazards around them. They may wobble or swerve to avoid a pothole in the road or see a potential hazard and change direction suddenly. Don't follow them too closely or rev your engine impatiently.

203 Mark *one* answer
A driver's behaviour has upset you. How can you get over this incident safely?

☐ **A** Stop and take a break
☐ **B** Shout abusive language
☐ **C** Gesture to them with your hand
☐ **D** Follow them, flashing your headlights

If you feel yourself becoming tense or upset, stop in a safe place and take a break. Tiredness can make things worse and may cause a different reaction to upsetting situations.

204 Mark *one* answer
How should you drive in areas with traffic-calming measures?

☐ **A** At a reduced speed
☐ **B** At the speed limit
☐ **C** In the centre of the road
☐ **D** With headlights on dipped beam

Traffic-calming measures such as road humps, chicanes and narrowings are intended to slow drivers down to protect vulnerable road users. Don't speed up until you reach the end of the traffic-calmed zone.

205 Mark *one* answer
Why should you slow down as you approach this hazard?

☐ **A** Because of the level crossing
☐ **B** Because it's hard to see to the right
☐ **C** Because of approaching traffic
☐ **D** Because of animals crossing

You should be slowing down and selecting the correct gear in case you have to stop at the level crossing. Look for the signals and be prepared to stop if necessary.

206 Mark *one* answer

Why are place names painted on the road surface?

☐ **A** To restrict the flow of traffic
☐ **B** To warn of oncoming traffic
☐ **C** To help you select the correct lane in good time
☐ **D** To prevent you from changing lanes

The names of towns and cities may be painted on the road at busy junctions and complex road systems. They guide you into the correct lane in good time, allowing traffic to flow more freely.

---

207 Mark *one* answer

Some two-way roads are divided into three lanes. Why are they particularly dangerous?

☐ **A** Traffic in both directions can use the middle lane to overtake
☐ **B** Traffic can travel faster in poor weather conditions
☐ **C** Traffic can overtake on the left
☐ **D** Traffic uses the middle lane for emergencies only

If you intend to overtake, you must consider that approaching traffic could be planning the same manoeuvre. When you've considered the situation and decided it's safe, indicate your intentions early. This will show the approaching traffic that you intend to pull out.

208 Mark *one* answer

What type of vehicle uses an amber flashing beacon on a dual carriageway?

☐ **A** An ambulance
☐ **B** A fire engine
☐ **C** A doctor on call
☐ **D** A tractor

An amber flashing beacon on a vehicle indicates that it's moving slowly or stopped and a possible hazard. Look well ahead on a dual carriageway and you should be able to see and respond to these vehicles in good time.

---

209 Mark *one* answer

What does this signal from a police officer mean to oncoming traffic?

☐ **A** Go ahead
☐ **B** Stop
☐ **C** Turn left
☐ **D** Turn right

Police officers may need to direct traffic; for example, at a junction where the traffic lights have broken down. Check your copy of *The Highway Code* for the signals that they use.

210 Mark *one* answer
Why should you be cautious when going past this bus waiting at a bus stop?

- ☐ **A** There's a zebra crossing ahead
- ☐ **B** There are driveways on the left
- ☐ **C** People may cross the road in front of it
- ☐ **D** The road surface will be slippery

A bus at a bus stop can hide pedestrians who might try to cross the road just in front of it. Drive at a speed that will enable you to respond safely if you have to.

211 Mark *one* answer
Where would it be unsafe to overtake?

- ☐ **A** On a single carriageway
- ☐ **B** On a one-way street
- ☐ **C** Approaching a junction
- ☐ **D** Travelling up a long hill

You should overtake only when it's really necessary and you can see it's clear ahead. Look out for road signs and markings that show it's illegal or would be unsafe to overtake; for example, approaching junctions or bends. In many cases, overtaking is unlikely to significantly improve your journey time.

212 Mark *one* answer
How can drinking alcohol affect your ability to drive?

- ☐ **A** Your ability to judge speed will be reduced
- ☐ **B** Your confidence will be reduced
- ☐ **C** Your reactions will be faster
- ☐ **D** Your awareness of danger will be improved

Alcohol will severely reduce your ability to drive or ride safely and there are serious consequences if you're caught over the drink-drive limit. It's known that alcohol can
- affect your judgement
- cause overconfidence
- reduce coordination and control.

213 Mark *one* answer
What does the solid white line at the side of the road indicate?

- ☐ **A** Traffic lights ahead
- ☐ **B** Edge of the carriageway
- ☐ **C** Footpath on the left
- ☐ **D** Cycle path

The continuous white line shows the edge of the carriageway. It can be especially useful when visibility is restricted, such as at night or in bad weather. It's discontinued in some places; for example, at junctions, lay-bys, entrances or other openings.

214 Mark *one* answer
You're driving towards this level crossing. What would be the first warning of an approaching train?

- ☐ **A** Both half-barriers down
- ☐ **B** A steady amber light
- ☐ **C** One half-barrier down
- ☐ **D** Twin flashing red lights

The steady amber light will be followed by twin flashing red lights that mean you must stop. An alarm will also sound to alert you to the fact that a train is approaching.

215 Mark *one* answer
You're behind this cyclist. When the traffic lights change, what should you do?

- ☐ **A** Try to move off before the cyclist
- ☐ **B** Allow the cyclist time and room
- ☐ **C** Turn right but give the cyclist room
- ☐ **D** Tap your horn and drive through first

Hold back and allow the cyclist to move off. Some junctions have special areas marked across the front of the traffic lane. These allow cyclists to wait for the lights to change and move off ahead of other traffic.

216 Mark *one* answer
You intend to turn left at the traffic lights. What should you do just before turning?

- ☐ **A** Check your right mirror
- ☐ **B** Move up closer to the car ahead
- ☐ **C** Move out to the right
- ☐ **D** Check for bicycles on your left

If you've been in a queue of traffic and are about to turn left, check your nearside for cyclists as they often filter past on the nearside of slow-moving or stationary vehicles.

217 Mark *one* answer
Why should you reduce your speed here?

- ☐ **A** A staggered junction is ahead
- ☐ **B** A low bridge is ahead
- ☐ **C** The road surface changes ahead
- ☐ **D** The road narrows ahead

Traffic could be turning off or pulling out ahead of you, to the left or right. Vehicles turning left will be slowing down before the junction, and any vehicles turning right may have to stop to allow oncoming traffic to clear. Be prepared for this, as you might have to slow down or stop behind them.

218 Mark *one* answer
What might you expect to happen in this situation?

- ☐ **A** Traffic will move into the right-hand lane
- ☐ **B** Traffic speed will increase
- ☐ **C** Traffic will move into the left-hand lane
- ☐ **D** Traffic won't need to change position

Be courteous and allow the traffic to merge into the left-hand lane.

219 Mark *one* answer
You're driving on a road with several lanes. What do these signs above the lanes mean?

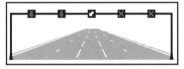

- ☐ **A** The two right lanes are open
- ☐ **B** The two left lanes are open
- ☐ **C** Traffic in the left lanes should stop
- ☐ **D** Traffic in the right lanes should stop

On some busy roads, lane control signals are used to vary the number of lanes available to give priority to the main traffic flow. A green arrow indicates that the lane is available to traffic facing the signal. A white diagonal arrow means that the lane is closed ahead and traffic should move to the next lane on the left. A red cross means that the lane is closed to traffic facing the signal.

220 Mark *one* answer
You're invited to a pub lunch. What should you do if you know that you'll have to drive in the evening?

- ☐ **A** Avoid mixing your alcoholic drinks
- ☐ **B** Don't drink any alcohol at all
- ☐ **C** Have some milk before drinking alcohol
- ☐ **D** Eat a hot meal with your alcoholic drinks

Alcohol will stay in your body for several hours and may make you unfit to drive later in the day. Drinking during the day will also affect your performance at work or study.

221 Mark *one* answer

What will become more expensive after you've been convicted of driving while unfit through drink or drugs?

☐ **A** Road fund licence
☐ **B** Insurance premiums
☐ **C** Vehicle test certificate
☐ **D** Driving licence

You've shown that you're a risk to yourself and others on the road. For this reason, insurance companies may charge you a higher premium.

222 Mark *one* answer

What advice should you give to a driver who has had a few alcoholic drinks at a party?

☐ **A** Have a strong cup of coffee and then drive home
☐ **B** Drive home carefully and slowly
☐ **C** Go home by public transport
☐ **D** Wait a short while and then drive home

Drinking black coffee or waiting a few hours won't make any difference. Alcohol takes time to leave the body. A driver who has been drinking should go home by public transport or taxi. They might even be unfit to drive the following morning.

223 Mark *one* answer

What should you do about driving if you've been taking medicine that causes drowsiness?

☐ **A** Only drive if your journey is necessary
☐ **B** Drive on quiet roads
☐ **C** Ask someone to come with you
☐ **D** Avoid driving and check with your doctor

You aren't fit to drive if you're taking medicine that makes you drowsy. Check with your doctor if you're unsure. You mustn't put other road users, your passengers or yourself at risk.

224 Mark *one* answer

What should you do if a doctor prescribes drugs that are likely to affect your driving?

☐ **A** Only drive if someone is with you
☐ **B** Avoid driving on motorways
☐ **C** Get someone else to drive
☐ **D** Never drive at more than 30 mph

You shouldn't drive if you're taking medicine that could cause you to feel drowsy at the wheel. Ask someone else to drive or, if that isn't possible, find another way to get home.

225 Mark *one* answer
What must you do if your ability to drive is impaired during a period of illness?

- ☐ **A** See your doctor each time before you drive
- ☐ **B** Take smaller doses of any medicines
- ☐ **C** Stop driving until you're fit to drive again
- ☐ **D** Take all your medicines with you when you drive

Only drive if you're fit to do so. Driving when you're ill or taking some medicines can affect your concentration and judgement. It may also cause you to become drowsy or even fall asleep.

226 Mark *one* answer
What should you do if you begin to feel drowsy while you're driving?

- ☐ **A** Stop and rest as soon as possible
- ☐ **B** Turn the heater up to keep you warm and comfortable
- ☐ **C** Close the car windows to help you concentrate
- ☐ **D** Continue with your journey but drive more slowly

You'll be putting other road users at risk if you continue to drive when you're drowsy. Pull over and stop in a safe place for a rest. If you're driving a long distance, think about finding some accommodation so you can rest for longer before continuing your journey.

227 Mark *one* answer
What should you do if you become tired while you're driving on a motorway?

- ☐ **A** Pull up on the hard shoulder and change drivers
- ☐ **B** Leave the motorway at the next exit and rest
- ☐ **C** Increase your speed and turn up the radio volume
- ☐ **D** Close all your windows and set the heating to warm

If you feel yourself becoming tired or sleepy, you should leave the motorway at the next exit or services and stop for a rest. If you have to drive a long way, leave earlier and plan your journey to include rest stops. That way, you're less likely to become tired while driving and you'll still arrive in good time.

228 Mark *one* answer
You're about to drive home. What should you do if you feel very tired and have a severe headache?

- ☐ **A** Wait until you're fit and well before driving
- ☐ **B** Drive home, but take a tablet for headaches
- ☐ **C** Drive home if you can stay awake for the journey
- ☐ **D** Wait for a short time, then drive home slowly

All of your concentration should be on your driving. Any pain you feel will distract you, and you should avoid driving when drowsy. The safest course of action is to wait until you've rested and are feeling better before starting your journey.

229 Mark *one* answer

What can you do to help prevent tiredness on a long journey?

☐ **A** Eat a large meal before driving
☐ **B** Take regular refreshment breaks
☐ **C** Play loud music in the car
☐ **D** Complete the journey without stopping

Long-distance driving can be boring. This, coupled with a stuffy, warm vehicle, can make you feel tired and sleepy. Make sure you take rest breaks to help you stay awake and alert. Stop in a safe place before you get to the stage of fighting sleep.

---

230 Mark *one* answer

You take some cough medicine given to you by a friend. What should you do before driving your car?

☐ **A** Ask your friend if taking the medicine affected their driving
☐ **B** Drink some strong coffee one hour before driving
☐ **C** Check the label to see if the medicine will affect your driving
☐ **D** Drive a short distance to see if the medicine is affecting your driving

If you've taken medicine, never drive without first checking what the side effects might be; they might affect your judgement and perception, and therefore endanger lives.

231 Mark *one* answer

You're driving on a one-way street. What should you do if you realise you've taken the wrong route?

☐ **A** Reverse out of the road
☐ **B** Turn around in a side road
☐ **C** Continue and find another route
☐ **D** Reverse into a driveway

Never reverse or turn your vehicle around in a one-way street. It's illegal and could even cause a collision. If you've taken a wrong turn, carry on along the one-way street and find another route, checking the direction signs as you drive. Stop in a safe place if you need to check a map.

---

232 Mark *one* answer

What will be a serious distraction while you're driving?

☐ **A** Looking at road maps
☐ **B** Switching on your demister
☐ **C** Using your windscreen washers
☐ **D** Looking in your door mirror

Looking at road maps while driving is very dangerous. If you aren't sure of your route, stop in a safe place and check the map. You must not allow anything to take your attention away from the road while you're driving.

233 Mark *one* answer
What should you do if the vehicle starts reversing off the driveway?

- ☐ **A** Move to the opposite side of the road
- ☐ **B** Drive through as you have priority
- ☐ **C** Sound your horn and be prepared to stop
- ☐ **D** Speed up and drive through quickly

White lights at the rear of a car show that the driver has selected reverse gear. The driver is hidden from view so can't see you approaching. Sound your horn to warn of your presence, and be ready to stop if the car reverses into your path.

234 Mark *one* answer
You've been involved in an argument that's made you feel angry. What should you do before starting your journey?

- ☐ **A** Open a window
- ☐ **B** Turn on your radio
- ☐ **C** Have an alcoholic drink
- ☐ **D** Calm down

If you're feeling upset or angry, you'll find it much more difficult to concentrate on your driving. You should wait until you've calmed down before starting a journey.

235 Mark *one* answer
You're driving on this dual carriageway. Why may you need to slow down?

- ☐ **A** There's a broken white line in the centre
- ☐ **B** There are solid white lines on either side
- ☐ **C** There are roadworks ahead of you
- ☐ **D** There are no footpaths

Look well ahead and read any road signs as you drive. They're there to inform you of what's ahead. In this case, you may need to slow down and change direction. Check your mirrors so you know what's happening around you before you change speed or direction.

236 Mark *one* answer
You've just been overtaken by this motorcyclist. What should you do if the rider cuts in sharply?

- ☐ **A** Sound the horn
- ☐ **B** Brake firmly
- ☐ **C** Keep a safe gap
- ☐ **D** Flash your lights

If another vehicle cuts in sharply, ease off the accelerator and drop back to allow a safe separation distance. Try not to overreact by braking sharply or swerving, as you could lose control. If vehicles behind you are too close or unprepared, it could lead to a crash.

237 Mark *one* answer
You're about to drive your car. What should you do if you can't find the glasses you need to wear?

- ☐ **A** Drive home slowly, keeping to quiet roads
- ☐ **B** Borrow a friend's glasses and use those
- ☐ **C** Drive home at night, so that the lights will help you
- ☐ **D** Find a way of getting home without driving

If you need to wear glasses for driving, it's illegal to drive without them. You must be able to see clearly when you're driving.

238 Mark *one* answer
How does drinking alcohol affect your driving behaviour?

- ☐ **A** It improves judgement skills
- ☐ **B** It increases confidence
- ☐ **C** It leads to faster reactions
- ☐ **D** It increases concentration

Alcohol can increase confidence to a point where your driving behaviour might become 'out of character'. Sensible behaviour might change to risk-taking behaviour. Never let yourself or your friends get into this situation.

239 Mark *one* answer
Why should you check the information leaflet before taking any medicine?

- ☐ **A** Drug companies want customer feedback on their products
- ☐ **B** You may have to let your insurance company know about the medicine
- ☐ **C** Some types of medicine can affect your ability to drive safely
- ☐ **D** The medicine you take may affect your hearing

Always check the label or information leaflet for any medication you take. The medicine might affect your driving. If you aren't sure, ask your doctor or pharmacist.

240 Mark *one* answer
You need glasses to read a vehicle number plate at the required distance. When must you wear them?

- ☐ **A** Only in bad weather conditions
- ☐ **B** Whenever you're driving
- ☐ **C** When you think it's necessary
- ☐ **D** Only at night time

Have your eyesight tested before you start your practical training. Then, throughout your driving life, have checks periodically, as your vision may change.

241 Mark *one* answer
Which type of glasses would make driving at night more difficult?

- ☐ **A** Half-moon
- ☐ **B** Round
- ☐ **C** Bifocal
- ☐ **D** Tinted

If you're driving at night or in poor visibility, tinted lenses will reduce the efficiency of your vision by reducing the amount of light reaching your eyes.

242 Mark *one* answer
What can seriously reduce your ability to concentrate?

- ☐ **A** Drugs
- ☐ **B** Busy roads
- ☐ **C** Tinted windows
- ☐ **D** Weather conditions

Both recreational drugs and prescribed medicine can affect your concentration. It's also an offence to drive with certain drugs in your body and a positive test could lead to a conviction.

243 Mark *one* answer
What must you do if your eyesight has become very poor and you're no longer able to meet the driver's eyesight requirements?

- ☐ **A** Tell the driver licensing authority
- ☐ **B** Tell your doctor
- ☐ **C** Tell the police
- ☐ **D** Tell your optician

Having very poor eyesight will have a serious effect on your ability to drive safely. If you can't meet the driver's eyesight requirements, you must tell DVLA (or DVA in Northern Ireland).

244 Mark *one* answer
When should you use hazard warning lights?

- ☐ **A** When you're double-parked on a two-way road
- ☐ **B** When your direction indicators aren't working
- ☐ **C** When warning oncoming traffic that you intend to stop
- ☐ **D** When your vehicle has broken down and is causing an obstruction

Hazard warning lights are an important safety feature and should be used if you've broken down and are causing an obstruction. Don't use them as an excuse to park illegally. You may also use them on motorways to warn traffic behind you of danger ahead.

245 Mark *one* answer

You want to turn left at this junction. What should you do if your view of the main road is restricted?

- ☐ **A** Stay well back and wait to see if anything comes
- ☐ **B** Build up your speed so that you can emerge quickly
- ☐ **C** Stop and apply the parking brake even if the road is clear
- ☐ **D** Approach slowly and edge out until you can see more clearly

You should slow right down, and stop if necessary, at any junction where your view is restricted. Edge forward until you can see properly. Only then can you decide whether it's safe to go.

246 Mark *one* answer

You're driving a car fitted with automatic transmission. When would you use 'kick down'?

- ☐ **A** To engage cruise control
- ☐ **B** To accelerate quickly
- ☐ **C** To brake progressively
- ☐ **D** To improve fuel economy

'Kick down' selects a lower gear, enabling the vehicle to accelerate faster.

247 Mark *one* answer

What should you do if it's raining and you're following this lorry on a motorway?

- ☐ **A** Allow a two-second separation gap
- ☐ **B** Switch your headlights onto main beam
- ☐ **C** Move into a lane that has less spray
- ☐ **D** Be aware of spray reducing your vision

The usual two-second time gap increases to four seconds when the roads are wet. If you stay well back, you'll
- be able to see past the vehicle
- be out of the spray thrown up by the lorry's tyres
- give yourself more time to stop if the need arises
- increase your chances of being seen by the lorry driver.

248 Mark *one* answer

You're driving towards this left-hand bend. What danger should you be anticipating?

- ☐ **A** A vehicle overtaking you
- ☐ **B** Mud on the road
- ☐ **C** The road getting narrower
- ☐ **D** Pedestrians walking towards you

Pedestrians walking on a road with no pavement should walk against the direction of the traffic. You can't see around this bend and if pedestrians are in the road you need to be able to deal with the situation safely. Always keep this in mind and give yourself time to react if a hazard does appear.

249 Mark *one* answer

What should you do if the traffic in the left-hand lane is slowing?

- ☐ **A** Slow down, keeping a safe separation distance
- ☐ **B** Accelerate past the vehicles in the left-hand lane
- ☐ **C** Pull up on the left-hand verge
- ☐ **D** Move across and continue in the right-hand lane

Allow the traffic to merge into the left-hand lane. Leave enough room so that you can maintain a safe separation distance, even if vehicles pull in ahead of you.

250 Mark *one* answer

When may you use hazard warning lights?

- ☐ **A** When driving on a motorway to warn traffic behind of a hazard ahead
- ☐ **B** When you're double-parked on a two-way road
- ☐ **C** When your direction indicators aren't working
- ☐ **D** When warning oncoming traffic that you intend to stop

Hazard warning lights are an important safety feature. Use them when driving on a motorway to warn traffic behind you of danger ahead. You should also use them if your vehicle has broken down and is causing an obstruction.

251 Mark *one* answer
You're waiting to emerge at a junction. Your view is restricted by parked vehicles. What can help you to see traffic on the road you're joining?

☐ **A** Looking for traffic behind you
☐ **B** Reflections of traffic in windows
☐ **C** Making eye contact with other road users
☐ **D** Checking for traffic in your interior mirror

You must be completely sure it's safe to emerge. Try to look for traffic through the windows of the parked cars or in the reflections in windows. Keep looking in all directions as you slowly edge forwards until you can see it's safe.

252 Mark *one* answer
What must you do if poor health affects your driving?

☐ **A** Inform your local police
☐ **B** Avoid using motorways
☐ **C** Always drive accompanied
☐ **D** Inform the licensing authority

You must tell DVLA (or DVA in Northern Ireland) if your health is likely to affect your ability to drive. The licensing authority will investigate your situation and then make a decision on whether you're fit enough to drive safely.

253 Mark *one* answer
Why should the junction on the left be kept clear?

☐ **A** To allow vehicles to enter and emerge
☐ **B** To allow the bus to reverse
☐ **C** To allow vehicles to make a U-turn
☐ **D** To allow vehicles to park

You should always try to keep junctions clear. If you're in queuing traffic, make sure that when you stop you leave enough space for traffic to flow in and out of the junction.

254 Mark *one* answer
What should you do if you start to feel drowsy while you're driving on a motorway?

☐ **A** Stop on the hard shoulder for a sleep
☐ **B** Open a window and stop as soon as it's safe and legal
☐ **C** Speed up to arrive at your destination sooner
☐ **D** Slow down and let other drivers overtake

Never stop on the hard shoulder to rest. If there's no service area for several miles, leave the motorway at the next exit and find somewhere safe and legal to pull over.

255 Mark *one* answer
Which sign means that there may be people walking along the road?

☐ A

☐ B

☐ C

☐ D

Always check the road signs. Triangular signs are warning signs: they inform you about hazards ahead and help you to anticipate any problems. There are a number of different signs showing pedestrians. Learn the meaning of each one.

256 Mark *one* answer
What should you do if you want to turn left at a junction where pedestrians have started to cross?

☐ **A** Go around them, leaving plenty of room
☐ **B** Stop and wave at them to cross
☐ **C** Sound your horn and proceed
☐ **D** Give way to them

When you're turning into a side road, pedestrians who are crossing have priority. You should wait to allow them to finish crossing safely. Be patient if they're slow or unsteady. Don't try to rush them by sounding your horn, flashing your lights, revving your engine or giving any other inappropriate signal.

257 Mark *one* answer
What hazard should you be especially aware of if you're turning left into a side road?

☐ **A** One-way street
☐ **B** Pedestrians
☐ **C** Traffic congestion
☐ **D** Parked vehicles

Make sure that you've reduced your speed and are in the correct gear for the turn. Look into the road before you turn and always give way to any pedestrians who are crossing.

258 Mark *one* answer
Why should you check for motorcyclists just before turning right into a side road?

☐ **A** They may be overtaking on your left
☐ **B** They may be following you closely
☐ **C** They may be emerging from the side road
☐ **D** They may be overtaking on your right

Never attempt to change direction to the right without first checking your right-hand mirror and blind spot. A motorcyclist might not have seen your signal and could be hidden by other traffic. This observation should become a matter of routine.

259 Mark *one* answer
Why is a toucan crossing different from other crossings?

☐ **A** Moped riders can use it
☐ **B** It's controlled by a traffic warden
☐ **C** It's controlled by two flashing lights
☐ **D** Cyclists can use it

Toucan crossings are shared by pedestrians and cyclists, who are permitted to cycle across. They're shown the green light together. The signals are push-button-operated and there's no flashing amber phase.

260 Mark *one* answer
How will a school crossing patrol signal you to stop?

☐ **A** By pointing to children waiting to cross
☐ **B** By displaying a red light
☐ **C** By displaying a 'stop' sign
☐ **D** By giving you an arm signal

If a school crossing patrol steps out into the road with a 'stop' sign, you must stop. Don't wave anyone across the road and don't get impatient or rev your engine.

261 Mark *one* answer
Where would you see this sign?

☐ **A** In the window of a car taking children to school
☐ **B** At the side of the road
☐ **C** At playground areas
☐ **D** On the rear of a school bus or coach

Vehicles that are used to carry children to and from school will be travelling at busy times of the day. If you're following a vehicle with this sign, be prepared for it to make frequent stops. It might pick up or set down passengers in places other than normal bus stops.

262 Mark *one* answer
What does this sign mean?

- ☐ **A** No route for pedestrians and cyclists
- ☐ **B** A route for pedestrians only
- ☐ **C** A route for cyclists only
- ☐ **D** A route for pedestrians and cyclists

This sign shows a shared route for pedestrians and cyclists: when it ends, the cyclists will be rejoining the main road.

263 Mark *one* answer
You see a pedestrian carrying a white stick that also has a red band. What does this mean?

- ☐ **A** They have limited mobility
- ☐ **B** They're deaf
- ☐ **C** They're blind
- ☐ **D** They're deaf and blind

When someone is deaf as well as blind, they may carry a white stick with a red reflective band or bands. They may not be aware that you're approaching and they may not be able to hear anything; so, for example, your horn would be ineffective as a warning to them.

264 Mark *one* answer
What would you do if you see older people crossing the road ahead?

- ☐ **A** Wave them across so they know that you've seen them
- ☐ **B** Be patient and allow them to cross in their own time
- ☐ **C** Rev the engine to let them know that you're waiting
- ☐ **D** Tap the horn in case they're hard of hearing

Be aware that older people might take a long time to cross the road. They might also be hard of hearing and not hear you approaching. Don't hurry older people across the road by getting too close to them or revving your engine.

265 Mark *one* answer
What should you do when you see an older person about to cross the road ahead?

- ☐ **A** Expect them to wait for you to pass
- ☐ **B** Speed up to get past them quickly
- ☐ **C** Stop and wave them across the road
- ☐ **D** Be careful; they may misjudge your speed

Older people may have impaired hearing, vision, concentration and judgement. They may also walk slowly and so could take a long time to cross the road.

266 Mark *one* answer
You're approaching a roundabout. What should you do if a cyclist ahead is signalling to turn right?

☐ **A** Overtake on the right
☐ **B** Give a warning with your horn
☐ **C** Signal the cyclist to move across
☐ **D** Give the cyclist plenty of room

If you're following a cyclist who's signalling to turn right at a roundabout, leave plenty of room. Give them space and time to get into the correct lane.

267 Mark *one* answer
Which vehicle should you allow extra room as you overtake them?

☐ **A** Lorry
☐ **B** Tractor
☐ **C** Bicycle
☐ **D** Road-sweeper

Don't pass cyclists too closely, as they may

- need to veer around a pothole, drain or other hazard
- be buffeted by side windbe made unsteady by your vehicle.

Always leave as much room as you would for a car, and don't cut in front of them.

268 Mark *one* answer
Why should you look carefully for motorcyclists and cyclists at junctions?

☐ **A** They may want to turn into the side road
☐ **B** They may slow down to let you turn
☐ **C** They're harder to see
☐ **D** They might not see you turn

Cyclists and motorcyclists are smaller than other vehicles and so are more difficult to see. They can easily be hidden from your view by cars parked near a junction.

269 Mark *one* answer
You're waiting to come out of a side road. Why should you look carefully for motorcycles?

☐ **A** Motorcycles are usually faster than cars
☐ **B** Police patrols often use motorcycles
☐ **C** Motorcycles can easily be hidden behind obstructions
☐ **D** Motorcycles have right of way

If you're waiting to emerge from a side road, look carefully for motorcycles: they can be difficult to see. Be especially careful if there are parked vehicles or other obstructions restricting your view.

270 Mark *one* answer
Why do motorcyclists use dipped headlights in daylight?

☐ **A** So that the rider can be seen more easily
☐ **B** To stop the battery overcharging
☐ **C** To improve the rider's vision
☐ **D** The rider is inviting you to proceed

A motorcycle can be lost from sight behind another vehicle. The use of headlights helps to make it more conspicuous and therefore more easily seen.

271 Mark *one* answer
Why do motorcyclists wear bright clothing?

☐ **A** They must do so by law
☐ **B** It helps keep them cool in summer
☐ **C** The colours are popular
☐ **D** To make them more visible

Motorcycles and scooters are generally smaller than other vehicles and can be difficult to see. Wearing bright clothing makes it easier for other road users to see a motorcyclist approaching, especially at junctions.

272 Mark *one* answer
Why do motorcyclists often look round over their right shoulder just before turning right?

☐ **A** To listen for traffic behind them
☐ **B** Motorcycles don't have mirrors
☐ **C** It helps them balance as they turn
☐ **D** To check for traffic in their blind area

When you see a motorcyclist take a glance over their shoulder, they're probably about to change direction. Recognising a clue like this helps you to anticipate their next action. This can improve road safety for you and others.

273 Mark *one* answer
Which is the most vulnerable road user?

☐ **A** Car driver
☐ **B** Tractor driver
☐ **C** Lorry driver
☐ **D** Motorcyclist

Pedestrians and riders on two wheels can be harder to see than other road users. Make sure you look for them, especially at junctions. Effective observation, coupled with appropriate action, can save lives.

274 Mark *one* answer
You're approaching a roundabout. What should you do if there are horses being ridden in front of you?

☐ **A** Sound your horn as a warning
☐ **B** Treat them like any other vehicle
☐ **C** Give them plenty of room
☐ **D** Accelerate past as quickly as possible

Horse riders often keep to the outside of the roundabout even if they're turning right. Give them plenty of room and remember that they may have to cross lanes of traffic.

---

275 Mark *one* answer
As you approach a pelican crossing, the lights change to green. What should you do if older people are still crossing?

☐ **A** Wave them to cross as quickly as they can
☐ **B** Rev your engine to make them hurry
☐ **C** Flash your lights in case they haven't noticed you
☐ **D** Wait patiently while they cross

If the lights turn to green, wait for any pedestrians to clear the crossing. Allow them to finish crossing the road in their own time, and don't try to hurry them by revving your engine.

276 Mark *one* answer
What action should you take when you see flashing amber lights under a school warning sign?

☐ **A** Reduce speed until you're clear of the area
☐ **B** Keep up your speed and sound the horn
☐ **C** Increase your speed to clear the area quickly
☐ **D** Wait at the lights until they stop flashing

The flashing amber lights are switched on to warn you that children may be crossing near a school. Slow down and take extra care, as you may have to stop.

277 Mark *one* answer
Why should these road markings be kept clear?

- ☐ **A** To allow children to be dropped off at school
- ☐ **B** To allow teachers to park
- ☐ **C** To allow children to be picked up after school
- ☐ **D** To allow children to see and be seen when they're crossing the road

The markings are there to show that the area should be kept clear. This is to allow an unrestricted view for
- approaching drivers and riders
- children wanting to cross the road.

278 Mark *one* answer
Where would you see this sign?

- ☐ **A** Near a school crossing
- ☐ **B** At a playground entrance
- ☐ **C** On a school bus
- ☐ **D** At a 'pedestrians only' area

School buses can stop to pick up or drop off schoolchildren at places that aren't designated bus stops. Watch out for children crossing the road to catch the bus or from the far side of the bus if they've just been dropped off.

279 Mark *one* answer
You're following two cyclists as they approach a roundabout in the left-hand lane. Where would you expect the cyclists to go?

- ☐ **A** Left
- ☐ **B** Right
- ☐ **C** Any direction
- ☐ **D** Straight ahead

Cyclists approaching a roundabout in the left-hand lane may be turning right but may not have been able to get into the correct lane due to heavy traffic. They may also feel safer keeping to the left all the way around the roundabout. Be aware of them and give them plenty of room.

280 Mark *one* answer
You're travelling behind a moped. What should you do if you want to turn left a short distance ahead?

☐ **A** Overtake the moped before the junction
☐ **B** Pull alongside the moped and stay level until just before the junction
☐ **C** Sound your horn as a warning and pull in front of the moped
☐ **D** Stay behind until the moped has passed the junction

Passing the moped and turning into the junction could mean that you cut across the front of the rider. This might force them to slow down, stop or even lose control. Stay behind the moped until it has passed the junction and then you can turn without affecting the rider.

281 Mark *one* answer
You see a horse rider as you approach a roundabout. What should you do if they're signalling right but keeping well to the left?

☐ **A** Proceed as normal
☐ **B** Keep close to them
☐ **C** Cut in front of them
☐ **D** Stay well back

Allow the horse rider to enter and exit the roundabout in their own time. They may feel safer keeping to the left all the way around the roundabout. Don't get up close behind or alongside them, because that would probably upset the horse and create a dangerous situation.

282 Mark *one* answer
How should you react to inexperienced drivers?

☐ **A** Sound your horn to warn them of your presence
☐ **B** Be patient and prepare for them to react more slowly
☐ **C** Flash your headlights to indicate that it's safe for them to proceed
☐ **D** Overtake them as soon as possible

Learners might not have confidence when they first start to drive. Allow them plenty of room and don't react adversely to their hesitation. We all learn from experience, but new drivers will have had less practice in dealing with all the situations that might occur.

283 Mark *one* answer
What should you do when you're following a learner driver who stalls at a junction?

☐ **A** Be patient, as you expect them to make mistakes
☐ **B** Stay very close behind and flash your headlights
☐ **C** Start to rev your engine if they take too long to restart
☐ **D** Immediately steer around them and drive on

Learning to drive is a process of practice and experience. Try to understand this and tolerate those who make mistakes while they're learning.

284 Mark *one* answer

You're on a country road. What should you expect to see coming towards you on your side of the road?

- ☐ **A** Motorcycles
- ☐ **B** Bicycles
- ☐ **C** Pedestrians
- ☐ **D** Horse riders

On a quiet country road, always be aware that there may be a hazard just around the next bend, such as a slow-moving vehicle or pedestrians. Pedestrians are advised to walk on the right-hand side of the road if there's no pavement, so they may be walking towards you on your side of the road.

285 Mark *one* answer

You're following a cyclist. What should you do when you wish to turn left a short distance ahead?

- ☐ **A** Overtake the cyclist before you reach the junction
- ☐ **B** Pull alongside the cyclist and stay level until after the junction
- ☐ **C** Hold back until the cyclist has passed the junction
- ☐ **D** Go around the cyclist on the junction

Make allowances for cyclists, and give them plenty of room. Don't overtake and then immediately turn left. Be patient and turn behind them when they've passed the junction.

286 Mark *one* answer

A horse rider is in the left-hand lane approaching a roundabout. Where should you expect the rider to go?

- ☐ **A** In any direction
- ☐ **B** To the right
- ☐ **C** To the left
- ☐ **D** Straight ahead

Horses and their riders move more slowly than other road users. They might not have time to cut across heavy traffic to take up a position in the right-hand lane. For this reason, a horse and rider may approach a roundabout in the left-hand lane even though they're turning right.

287 Mark *one* answer

Powered vehicles used by disabled people are small and can be hard to see. What must they display if they're travelling on a dual carriageway?

- ☐ **A** Flashing red beacon
- ☐ **B** Flashing green beacon
- ☐ **C** Flashing blue beacon
- ☐ **D** Flashing amber beacon

Powered vehicles used by disabled people are small and low making them hard to see on the road. They also travel very slowly. On an unrestricted dual carriageway, they must display a flashing amber beacon to warn other road users of their presence.

288 Mark *one* answer
What does it mean when a moving vehicle is showing a flashing amber beacon?

- ☐ **A** The vehicle is slow moving
- ☐ **B** The vehicle has broken down
- ☐ **C** The vehicle is a doctor's car
- ☐ **D** The vehicle belongs to a school crossing patrol

Different coloured beacons warn of different types of vehicle needing special attention. Blue beacons are used on emergency vehicles that need priority. Green beacons are found on doctors' cars. Amber beacons generally denote slower moving vehicles, which are often large. These vehicles are usually involved in road maintenance or local amenities and make frequent stops.

289 Mark *one* answer
What does this sign mean?

- ☐ **A** Contraflow cycle lane
- ☐ **B** With-flow cycle lane
- ☐ **C** Cycles and buses only
- ☐ **D** No cycles or buses

Usually, a picture of a cycle will also be painted on the road, and sometimes the lane will have a different coloured surface. Leave these areas clear for cyclists and don't pass too closely when you overtake.

290 Mark *one* answer
What should you do when you see these horse riders in front?

- ☐ **A** Pull out to the middle of the road
- ☐ **B** Slow down and be ready to stop
- ☐ **C** Switch on your hazard warning lights
- ☐ **D** Give a right-turn signal

Be particularly careful when approaching horse riders – slow down and be prepared to stop. Always pass wide and slowly, and look out for signals given by the riders. Horses are unpredictable: always treat them as potential hazards and take great care when passing them.

291 Mark *one* answer
What's the purpose of these road markings?

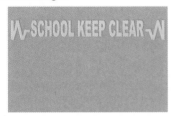

☐ **A** To ensure children can see and be seen when they're crossing the road
☐ **B** To enable teachers to have clear access to the school
☐ **C** To ensure delivery vehicles have easy access to the school
☐ **D** To enable parents to pick up or drop off children safely

These markings are found on the road outside schools. Don't stop or park on them, even to set down or pick up children. The markings are there to ensure that drivers, riders, children and other pedestrians have a clear view of the road in all directions.

292 Mark *one* answer
What should you do if the left-hand pavement is closed due to street repairs?

☐ **A** Watch out for pedestrians walking in the road
☐ **B** Use your right-hand mirror more often
☐ **C** Speed up to get past the roadworks more quickly
☐ **D** Position close to the left-hand kerb

Where street repairs have closed off pavements, proceed carefully and slowly, as pedestrians might have to walk in the road.

293 Mark *one* answer
What should you do when you're following a motorcyclist along a road that has a poor surface?

☐ **A** Follow closely so they can see you in their mirrors
☐ **B** Overtake immediately to avoid delays
☐ **C** Allow extra room in case they swerve to avoid potholes
☐ **D** Allow the same room as normal to avoid wasting road space

To avoid being unbalanced, a motorcyclist might swerve to avoid potholes and bumps in the road. Be prepared for this and allow them extra space.

294 Mark *one* answer
What does this sign mean?

☐ **A** No cycling
☐ **B** Cycle route ahead
☐ **C** Cycle parking only
☐ **D** End of cycle route

More people are cycling today and cycle routes are being extended in our towns and cities to provide safe cycling routes. Respect the presence of cyclists on the road and give them plenty of room if you need to pass.

295 Mark *one* answer
You're approaching this roundabout. What should you do when a cyclist is keeping to the left while signalling to turn right?

- ☐ **A** Sound your horn
- ☐ **B** Overtake them
- ☐ **C** Assume they're turning left
- ☐ **D** Allow them space to turn

Cycling in today's heavy traffic can be hazardous. Some cyclists may not feel safe crossing the path of traffic to take up a position in an outside lane. Be aware of this and understand that, although they're in the left-hand lane, the cyclist might be turning right.

296 Mark *one* answer
What should you do when you're approaching this crossing?

- ☐ **A** Prepare to slow down and stop
- ☐ **B** Stop and wave the pedestrians across
- ☐ **C** Speed up and pass by quickly
- ☐ **D** Continue unless the pedestrians step out

Be courteous and prepare to stop. Don't wave people across, because this could be dangerous if another vehicle is approaching the crossing.

297 Mark *one* answer
What does it mean if you see a pedestrian with a dog that has a yellow or burgundy coat?

- ☐ **A** The pedestrian is an older person
- ☐ **B** The pedestrian is a dog trainer
- ☐ **C** The pedestrian is colour-blind
- ☐ **D** The pedestrian is deaf

Dogs trained to help deaf people have a yellow or burgundy coat. If you see one, you should take extra care, as the pedestrian may not be aware of vehicles approaching.

298 Mark *one* answer
Who may use toucan crossings?

☐ **A** Motorcyclists and cyclists
☐ **B** Motorcyclists and pedestrians
☐ **C** Only cyclists
☐ **D** Cyclists and pedestrians

There are some crossings where cycle routes lead cyclists to cross at the same place as pedestrians. These are called toucan crossings. Always look out for cyclists, as they're likely to be approaching faster than pedestrians.

299 Mark *one* answer
This junction, controlled by traffic lights, has a marked area between two stop lines. What's this for?

☐ **A** To allow taxis to position in front of other traffic
☐ **B** To allow people with disabilities to cross the road
☐ **C** To allow cyclists and pedestrians to cross the road together
☐ **D** To allow cyclists to position in front of other traffic

These are known as advanced stop lines. When the lights are red (or about to become red), you should stop at the first white line. However, if you've crossed that line as the lights change, you must stop at the second line even if it means you're in the area reserved for cyclists.

300 Mark *one* answer
You're about to overtake a cyclist. Why should you leave them as much room as you would give to a car?

☐ **A** The cyclist might speed up
☐ **B** The cyclist might get off their bicycle
☐ **C** The cyclist might be unsettled if you pass too near them
☐ **D** The cyclist might have to make a left turn

Before overtaking, assess the situation. Look well ahead to see whether the cyclist will need to change direction. Be especially aware of a cyclist approaching parked vehicles, as they'll need to alter course. Don't pass too closely or cut in sharply as this could unsettle the rider.

301 Mark *one* answer
What should you do when you're passing loose sheep on the road?

☐ **A** Briefly sound your horn
☐ **B** Go very slowly
☐ **C** Pass quickly but quietly
☐ **D** Herd them to the side of the road

Slow down and be ready to stop if you see animals in the road ahead. Animals are easily frightened by noise and vehicles passing too close to them. Stop if you're signalled to do so by the person in charge.

302 Mark *one* answer

At night, what does it mean if you see a pedestrian wearing reflective clothing and carrying a bright red light?

- ☐ **A** You're approaching roadworks
- ☐ **B** You're approaching an organised walk
- ☐ **C** You're approaching a slow-moving vehicle
- ☐ **D** You're approaching a traffic danger spot

The people on the walk should be keeping to the left, but don't assume this. Pass carefully, making sure you have time to do so safely. Be aware that the pedestrians have their backs to you and may not know that you're there.

303 Mark *one* answer

You've just passed your driving test. How can you reduce your risk of being involved in a collision?

- ☐ **A** By always staying close to the vehicle in front
- ☐ **B** By never going over 40 mph
- ☐ **C** By staying in the left-hand lane on all roads
- ☐ **D** By taking further training

New drivers and riders are often involved in a collision or incident early in their driving career. Due to a lack of experience, they may not react to hazards appropriately. Approved training courses are offered by driver and rider training schools for people who have passed their test but want extra training.

304 Mark *one* answer

You're turning right from a main road into a side road. There's no oncoming traffic. What should you do if pedestrians are standing on the pavement waiting to cross the side road?

- ☐ **A** Turn in because the pedestrians are safe on the pavement
- ☐ **B** Wave at the pedestrians, inviting them to cross the road
- ☐ **C** Wait and give way to the pedestrians
- ☐ **D** Sound your horn to alert the pedestrians to your presence

You should give way to pedestrians crossing or waiting to cross the road into which or from which you're turning. Be patient if they're cautious and take their time checking that it's safe before they step into the road.

305 Mark *one* answer

You're travelling on a narrow section of road. What should you do if a horse rider ahead is riding in the centre of the lane?

- ☐ **A** Sound your horn to alert them to your presence
- ☐ **B** Stay behind and allow them to ride in this position
- ☐ **C** Move across to the right and try to ease past them
- ☐ **D** Get up close behind to encourage them to move aside

On narrow sections of road, horse riders may ride in the centre of the lane. This is for their own safety as it makes them more visible. You should be patient and only pass when it's safe to do so.

306 Mark *one* answer
You're about to overtake a cyclist on a road that has a 30 mph speed limit. How much room should you leave them as you overtake?

☐ **A** At least as much room as you would if you were overtaking a car
☐ **B** At least a car's width
☐ **C** At least a car's length
☐ **D** At least 2 car widths

You should leave cyclists at least as much room as you would if you were overtaking a car. Leave them more room if you're overtaking at speeds over 30 mph.

307 Mark *one* answer
You're turning left from a main road into a side road. What should you do if there's a pedestrian on the pavement waiting to cross the side road?

☐ **A** Flash your lights to encourage the pedestrian to cross
☐ **B** Carry on turning into the side road
☐ **C** Sound your horn to let the pedestrian know you're there
☐ **D** Wait and give way to the pedestrian

You should give way to pedestrians crossing or waiting to cross the road into which or from which you're turning. Be patient if they're cautious, and let them check that it's safe from all directions before they step into the road. Do not signal or wave them to cross.

308 Mark *one* answer
You want to reverse into a side road. What should you do if you aren't sure that the area behind your car is clear?

☐ **A** Look through the rear window only
☐ **B** Get out and check
☐ **C** Check the mirrors only
☐ **D** Carry on, assuming it's clear

If you can't tell whether there's anything behind you, it's always safest to check before reversing. There may be a small child or a low obstruction close behind your car.

309 Mark *one* answer
You're about to reverse into a side road. What should you do if a pedestrian is waiting to cross behind your car?

☐ **A** Wave to the pedestrian to stop
☐ **B** Give way to the pedestrian
☐ **C** Sound your horn to warn the pedestrian
☐ **D** Reverse before the pedestrian starts to cross

If you need to reverse into a side road, try to find a place that's free from traffic and pedestrians. Look all around before and during the manoeuvre. Stop and give way to any pedestrians who want to cross behind you. Avoid waving them across, sounding the horn, flashing your lights or giving any signals that could mislead them and create a dangerous situation.

Section 6 – **Vulnerable road users**

310 Mark *one* answer
Which road users are most difficult to see when you're reversing your car?

☐ **A** Motorcyclists
☐ **B** Car drivers
☐ **C** Cyclists
☐ **D** Children

It may not be possible to see a small child through the rear windscreen of your vehicle. Be aware of this before you reverse. If there are children about, get out and check that it's clear before reversing.

311 Mark *one* answer
You want to turn right from a junction. What should you do if your view is restricted by parked vehicles?

☐ **A** Move out quickly, but be prepared to stop
☐ **B** Sound your horn and pull out if there's no reply
☐ **C** Stop, then move forward slowly until you have a clear view
☐ **D** Stop, get out and look along the main road to check

If you want to turn right from a junction and your view is restricted, stop. Ease forward until you can see – something might be approaching. If you don't know, don't go.

312 Mark *one* answer
You're at the front of a queue of traffic waiting to turn right into a side road. Why is it important to check your right mirror just before turning?

☐ **A** To look for pedestrians about to cross
☐ **B** To check for overtaking vehicles
☐ **C** To make sure the side road is clear
☐ **D** To check for emerging traffic

A motorcyclist could be riding along the outside of the queue. Always check your mirror before turning, as situations behind you can change while you've been waiting to turn.

313 Mark *one* answer
You've driven up to a pelican crossing. What must you do while the amber light is flashing?

☐ **A** Signal the pedestrian to cross
☐ **B** Always wait for the green light before proceeding
☐ **C** Give way to any pedestrians on the crossing
☐ **D** Wait for the red-and-amber light before proceeding

The flashing amber light allows pedestrians already on the crossing to get to the other side before a green light shows to the traffic. Be aware that some pedestrians, such as older people and young children, need longer to cross. Let them do this at their own pace.

314 Mark *one* answer
You've stopped at a pelican crossing. What should you do if a disabled person is crossing slowly in front of you and the lights change to green?

- ☐ **A** Wait for them to finish crossing
- ☐ **B** Drive in front of them
- ☐ **C** Edge forward slowly
- ☐ **D** Sound your horn

At a pelican crossing, the green light means you may proceed as long as the crossing is clear. If someone hasn't finished crossing, be patient and wait for them, whether they're disabled or not.

315 Mark *one* answer
You're driving past a line of parked cars. What should you do if a ball bounces out into the road ahead?

- ☐ **A** Continue driving at the same speed and sound your horn
- ☐ **B** Continue driving at the same speed and flash your headlights
- ☐ **C** Slow down and be prepared to stop for children
- ☐ **D** Stop and wave the children across to fetch their ball

Beware of children playing in the street and running out into the road. If a ball bounces out from the pavement, slow down and be prepared to stop. Don't encourage anyone to retrieve it. Other road users may not see your signal and you might lead a child into a dangerous situation.

316 Mark *one* answer
You want to turn right from a main road into a side road. What should you do just before turning?

- ☐ **A** Cancel your right-turn signal
- ☐ **B** Select first gear
- ☐ **C** Check for traffic overtaking on your right
- ☐ **D** Stop and set the parking brake

In some circumstances, your indicators may be difficult to see and another road user may not realise you're about to turn. A final check in your mirror and blind spot can help you to see an overtaking vehicle, so that you can avoid turning across their path.

317 Mark *one* answer
You're driving in a slow-moving queue of traffic. What should you do just before changing lane?

- ☐ **A** Sound the horn and flash your lights
- ☐ **B** Look for motorcyclists filtering through the traffic
- ☐ **C** Give a 'slowing down' arm signal
- ☐ **D** Change down to first gear

In queuing traffic, motorcyclists could be passing you on either side. Use your mirrors and check your blind area before changing lanes or changing direction.

318 Mark *one* answer
You're driving in town. Why should you be careful if there's a bus at a bus stop on the other side of the road?

☐ **A** The bus might have broken down
☐ **B** Pedestrians might come from behind the bus
☐ **C** The bus might move off suddenly
☐ **D** The bus might remain stationary

If you see a bus ahead, watch out for pedestrians. They might not be able to see you if they're behind the bus.

319 Mark *one* answer
How should you overtake horse riders?

☐ **A** Drive up close and overtake as soon as possible
☐ **B** Speed isn't important but allow plenty of room
☐ **C** Use your horn just once to warn them
☐ **D** Drive slowly and leave plenty of room

When you decide to overtake a horse rider, make sure you can do so safely before you move out. Leave them plenty of room and pass slowly. Passing too close could startle the horse and unseat the rider.

320 Mark *one* answer
Why should you allow extra room while overtaking a motorcyclist on a windy day?

☐ **A** The rider may turn off suddenly to get out of the wind
☐ **B** The rider may be blown in front of you
☐ **C** The rider may stop suddenly
☐ **D** The rider may be travelling faster than normal

If you're driving in high winds, be aware that the conditions might make a motorcyclist (or cyclist) swerve or wobble. Take this into consideration if you're following or wish to overtake a two-wheeled vehicle.

321 Mark *one* answer
Where should you take particular care to look for motorcyclists and cyclists?

☐ **A** On dual carriageways
☐ **B** At junctions
☐ **C** At zebra crossings
☐ **D** On one-way streets

Motorcyclists and cyclists are often more difficult to see at junctions. They're easily hidden from view and you may not be able to see them approaching a junction if your view is partially blocked; for example, by other traffic.

322 Mark *one* answer
The road outside this school is marked with yellow zigzag lines. What do these lines mean?

- ☐ **A** You may park on the lines when dropping off schoolchildren
- ☐ **B** You may park on the lines when picking up schoolchildren
- ☐ **C** You shouldn't wait or park your vehicle here
- ☐ **D** You must stay with your vehicle if you park here

Parking here would block other road users' view of the school entrance and would endanger the lives of children on their way to and from school.

323 Mark *one* answer
You're driving past parked cars. What should you do if you see a bicycle wheel sticking out between the cars?

- ☐ **A** Accelerate past quickly and sound your horn
- ☐ **B** Slow down and wave the cyclist across
- ☐ **C** Brake sharply and flash your headlights
- ☐ **D** Slow down and be prepared to stop for a cyclist

Scan the road as you drive. Try to anticipate hazards by being aware of the places where they're likely to occur. You'll then be able to react in good time.

324 Mark *one* answer
You're driving at night. What should you do if you're dazzled by a vehicle behind you?

- ☐ **A** Set your mirror to the anti-dazzle position
- ☐ **B** Set your mirror to dazzle the other driver
- ☐ **C** Brake sharply to a stop
- ☐ **D** Switch your rear lights on and off

The interior mirror of most vehicles can be set to an anti-dazzle position. You'll still be able to see the lights of the traffic behind you, but the dazzle will be greatly reduced.

325 Mark *one* answer
You're driving towards a zebra crossing. What should you do if a person in a wheelchair is waiting to cross?

- ☐ **A** Continue on your way
- ☐ **B** Wave to the person to cross
- ☐ **C** Wave to the person to wait
- ☐ **D** Be prepared to stop

You should slow down and be prepared to stop, as you would for an able-bodied person. Don't wave them across, as other traffic may not stop.

326 Mark *one* answer

You're about to overtake a slow-moving motorcyclist. Which sign would make you take special care?

☐ **A**

☐ **B**

☐ **C**

☐ **D**

In windy weather, watch out for motorcyclists and also cyclists, as they can be blown sideways into your path. When you pass them, leave plenty of room and check their position in your mirror before pulling back in.

327 Mark *one* answer

You're waiting to turn right out of a minor road. It's clear to the left but a lorry is coming from the right. Why should you wait, even if you have enough time to turn?

☐ **A** Anything overtaking the lorry will be hidden from view

☐ **B** The lorry could suddenly speed up

☐ **C** The lorry might be slowing down

☐ **D** The load on the lorry might be unstable

Large vehicles can hide other vehicles that are overtaking – especially motorcycles. You need to be aware of the possibility of hidden vehicles and not assume that it's safe to turn.

328 Mark *one* answer

You're following a long vehicle as it approaches a crossroads. What should you do if it signals left but moves out to the right?

☐ **A** Get closer in order to pass it quickly

☐ **B** Stay well back and give it room

☐ **C** Assume the signal is wrong and that it's turning right

☐ **D** Overtake it as it starts to slow down

A long vehicle may need to swing out in the opposite direction as it approaches a turn, to allow the rear wheels to clear the kerb. Don't try to filter through if you see a gap; as the lorry turns, the gap will close.

329 Mark *one* answer

You're following a long vehicle approaching a crossroads. What should you do if the driver signals right but moves close to the left-hand kerb?

☐ **A** Warn the driver about the wrong signal

☐ **B** Wait behind the long vehicle

☐ **C** Report the driver to the police

☐ **D** Overtake on the right-hand side

When a long vehicle is going to turn right, it may need to keep close to the left-hand kerb. This is to prevent the rear end of the trailer cutting the corner. You need to be aware of how long vehicles behave in such situations. Don't overtake the lorry, because it could turn as you're alongside. Stay behind and wait for it to turn.

330 Mark *one* answer
You're approaching a mini-roundabout. What should you do if a long vehicle in front signals left but positions over to the right?

☐ **A** Sound your horn
☐ **B** Overtake on the left
☐ **C** Follow the same course as the lorry
☐ **D** Keep well back

At mini-roundabouts, there isn't much room for a long vehicle to manoeuvre. It will have to swing out wide so that it can complete the turn safely. Keep well back and don't try to move up alongside it.

---

331 Mark *one* answer
You're driving on a single carriageway road. Why should you keep well back while you're following a large vehicle?

☐ **A** To give yourself acceleration space if you decide to overtake
☐ **B** To get the best view of the road ahead
☐ **C** To leave a gap in case the vehicle stops and rolls back
☐ **D** To offer other drivers a safe gap if they want to overtake you

When following a large vehicle, keep well back. If you're too close, you won't be able to see the road ahead and the driver of the long vehicle might not be able to see you in their mirrors.

332 Mark *one* answer
You're travelling behind a bus. What should you do if it pulls up at a bus stop?

☐ **A** Accelerate past the bus
☐ **B** Look for pedestrians
☐ **C** Sound your horn
☐ **D** Pull in closely behind the bus

People may be running to catch the bus or passengers leaving the bus might wish to cross the road in front of the bus. Look out for them if you intend to go past it. Consider how many people are waiting to get on the bus – check the queue if you can. The bus might move off straight away if no-one is waiting to get on. If a bus is signalling to pull out, give it priority if it's safe to do so.

333 Mark *one* answer
You're following a lorry on a wet road. What should you do when spray makes it difficult to see the road ahead?

☐ **A** Drop back until you can see better
☐ **B** Put your headlights on full beam
☐ **C** Keep close to the lorry, away from the spray
☐ **D** Speed up and overtake quickly

Large vehicles can throw up a lot of spray when it's wet. This makes it difficult for drivers behind to see the road ahead. You'll be able to see more by dropping back further, out of the spray. This will also increase your separation distance, giving you more room to stop if you have to.

334 Mark *one* answer
You're leaving a safe gap as you follow a large vehicle. What should you do if a car moves into this gap?

☐ **A** Sound your horn
☐ **B** Drop back further
☐ **C** Flash your headlights
☐ **D** Start to overtake

Sometimes your separation distance is shortened by a driver moving into the gap you've allowed. When this happens, react positively, stay calm and drop further back to re-establish a safe following distance.

335 Mark *one* answer
What should you do when you're approaching a bus that's signalling to move away from a bus stop?

☐ **A** Get past before it moves
☐ **B** Allow it to pull away, if it's safe to do so
☐ **C** Flash your headlights as you approach
☐ **D** Signal left and wave the bus on

Try to give way to buses if you can do so safely, especially when the driver signals to pull away from a bus stop. Look out for people getting off the bus or running to catch it, because they may cross the road without looking. Don't accelerate to get past the bus, and don't flash your lights, as this could mislead other road users.

336 Mark *one* answer
What should you do if you want to overtake a long, slow-moving vehicle on a busy road?

☐ **A** Follow it closely and keep moving out to see the road ahead

☐ **B** Flash your headlights for the oncoming traffic to give way

☐ **C** Stay behind until the driver waves you past

☐ **D** Keep well back so that you get a good view of the road ahead

When you're following a long vehicle, stay well back so that you can get a better view of the road ahead. The closer you get, the less you'll be able to see of the road. Be patient and don't take a gamble. Only overtake when you're certain that you can complete the manoeuvre safely.

337 Mark *one* answer
Which vehicles are least likely to be affected by side wind?

☐ **A** Cyclists

☐ **B** Motorcyclists

☐ **C** High-sided vehicles

☐ **D** Cars

Although cars are the least likely to be affected, side winds can take anyone by surprise. This is most likely to happen after overtaking a large vehicle, when passing gaps between hedges or buildings, and on exposed sections of road.

338 Mark *one* answer
What should you do as you approach this lorry?

☐ **A** Slow down and be prepared to wait

☐ **B** Make the lorry wait for you

☐ **C** Flash your lights at the lorry

☐ **D** Move to the right-hand side of the road

When turning, long vehicles need much more room on the road than other vehicles. At junctions, they may take up the whole of the road space, so be patient and allow them the room they need.

339 Mark *one* answer
You're following a large vehicle as it approaches a crossroads. What should you do if the driver signals to turn left?

☐ **A** Overtake if you can leave plenty of room

☐ **B** Overtake if there are no oncoming vehicles

☐ **C** Wait for the driver to cancel their signal

☐ **D** Wait for the vehicle to finish turning

Hold back and wait until the vehicle has turned before proceeding. Don't overtake, because the vehicle turning left could hide another vehicle emerging from the same junction.

340 Mark *one* answer
Why is it more difficult to overtake a large vehicle than a car?

☐ **A** It will take longer to overtake a large vehicle
☐ **B** A large vehicle will be fitted with a speed limiter
☐ **C** A large vehicle will have air brakes
☐ **D** It will take longer for a large vehicle to accelerate

Depending on relative speed, it will usually take you longer to pass a lorry than other vehicles. Hazards to watch for include oncoming traffic, junctions ahead, bends or dips that could restrict your view, and signs or road markings that prohibit overtaking. Make sure you can see that it's safe to complete the manoeuvre before you start to overtake.

341 Mark *one* answer
It's very windy. What should you do if you're behind a motorcyclist who's overtaking a high-sided vehicle?

☐ **A** Overtake the motorcyclist immediately
☐ **B** Keep well back
☐ **C** Stay level with the motorcyclist
☐ **D** Keep close to the motorcyclist

Windy weather affects motorcyclists more than other vehicles. In windy conditions, high-sided vehicles cause air turbulence. You should keep well back, as the motorcyclist could be blown off course.

342 Mark *one* answer
What should you do if there's a bus at a bus stop ahead of you?

☐ **A** Flash your lights to warn the driver of your presence
☐ **B** Continue at the same speed but sound your horn as a warning
☐ **C** Watch carefully for the sudden appearance of pedestrians
☐ **D** Pass the bus as quickly as you possibly can

As you approach, look out for any signal the driver might make. If you pass the vehicle, watch out for pedestrians attempting to cross the road from behind the bus. They'll be hidden from view until the last moment.

343 Mark *one* answer
What should you be prepared to do in this situation?

☐ **A** Sound your horn and continue
☐ **B** Slow down and give way
☐ **C** Report the driver to the police
☐ **D** Squeeze through the gap

Sometimes, large vehicles may need more space than other road users. If a vehicle needs more time and space to turn, be prepared to stop and wait.

344 Mark *one* answer
Why should drivers be more careful on roads where trams also operate?

☐ **A** Because trams don't have a horn
☐ **B** Because trams can't stop for cars
☐ **C** Because trams don't have lights
☐ **D** Because trams can't steer to avoid obstructions

You should take extra care when you first encounter trams. You'll have to get used to dealing with a different traffic system. Be aware that trams can accelerate and travel very quickly, and they can't change direction to avoid obstructions.

345 Mark *one* answer
You're towing a caravan. Which is the safest type of rear-view mirror to use?

☐ **A** Interior wide-angle mirror
☐ **B** Extended-arm side mirrors
☐ **C** Ordinary door mirrors
☐ **D** Ordinary interior mirror

Towing a large trailer or caravan can greatly reduce your view of the road behind. You may need to fit extended-arm side mirrors so that you can see clearly behind and down both sides of the caravan or trailer.

346 Mark *one* answer
You're driving in heavy traffic on a wet road. Which lights should you use if there's a lot of surface spray?

☐ **A** Main-beam headlights
☐ **B** Sidelights only
☐ **C** Rear fog lights if visibility is more than 100 metres (328 feet)
☐ **D** Dipped headlights

You must make sure that other road users can see you, but you don't want to dazzle them. Use your dipped headlights during the day if visibility is poor. If visibility falls below 100 metres (328 feet), you may use your rear fog lights, but don't forget to turn them off when the visibility improves.

347 Mark *one* answer
What should you do if you overtake a cyclist when it's very windy?

☐ **A** Overtake very slowly
☐ **B** Keep close as you pass
☐ **C** Sound your horn repeatedly
☐ **D** Allow extra room

Cyclists, and motorcyclists, are very vulnerable in high winds. They can easily be blown well off course and veer into your path. Always allow plenty of room when overtaking them. Passing too close could cause a draught and unbalance the rider.

348 Mark *one* answer
When may you overtake another vehicle on their left?

☐ **A** When you're in a one-way street
☐ **B** When approaching a motorway slip road where you'll be turning off
☐ **C** When the vehicle in front is signalling to turn left
☐ **D** When a slower vehicle is travelling in the right-hand lane of a dual carriageway

You may pass slower vehicles on their left while travelling along a one-way street. Be aware of drivers who may need to change lanes and may not expect faster traffic passing on their left.

349 Mark *one* answer
You're travelling in very heavy rain. How is this likely to affect your overall stopping distance?

☐ **A** It will be doubled
☐ **B** It will be halved
☐ **C** It will be ten times greater
☐ **D** It will be no different

The road will be very wet and spray from other vehicles will reduce your visibility. Tyre grip will also be reduced, increasing your stopping distance. You should at least double your separation distance to make sure you can stop safely in the space you've allowed.

350 Mark *one* answer
What should you do when you're overtaking at night?

☐ **A** Wait until a bend so that you can see oncoming headlights
☐ **B** Sound your horn twice before moving out
☐ **C** Go past slowly so that you can react to unseen hazards
☐ **D** Beware of bends in the road ahead

Don't overtake if there's a possibility of a road junction, bend or brow of a bridge or hill ahead. There are many hazards that are difficult to see in the dark. Only overtake if you're certain that the road ahead is clear. Don't take a chance.

351 Mark *one* answer
When may you wait in a box junction?

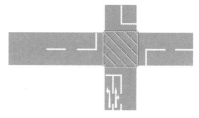

☐ **A** When you're stationary in a queue of traffic
☐ **B** When approaching a pelican crossing
☐ **C** When approaching a zebra crossing
☐ **D** When oncoming traffic prevents you turning right

The purpose of a box junction is to keep the junction clear by preventing vehicles from stopping in the path of crossing traffic. You mustn't enter a box junction unless your exit is clear. However, you may enter the box and wait if you want to turn right and are only prevented from doing so by oncoming traffic.

352 Mark *one* answer
Which plate may appear with this road sign?

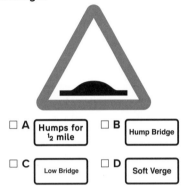

☐ **A** Humps for ½ mile

☐ **B** Hump Bridge

☐ **C** Low Bridge

☐ **D** Soft Verge

Road humps are used to slow down traffic. They're found in places where there are often pedestrians, such as

• shopping areas
• near schools
• residential areas.

Watch out for people close to the kerb or crossing the road.

353 Mark *one* answer
What's the reason for traffic-calming measures?

☐ **A** To stop road rage
☐ **B** To make overtaking easier
☐ **C** To slow traffic down
☐ **D** To make parking easier

Traffic-calming measures make the roads safer for vulnerable road users, such as cyclists, pedestrians and children. These can be designed as chicanes, road humps or other obstacles that encourage drivers and riders to slow down.

354 Mark *one* answer
What colour are the reflective studs along the left-hand edge of the motorway?

☐ **A** Green
☐ **B** Amber
☐ **C** Red
☐ **D** White

Reflective studs are used to help you in poor visibility. Different colours are used so that you'll know which lane you're in. These are

• red on the left-hand edge of the carriageway
• white between lanes
• amber on the right-hand edge of the carriageway
• green between the carriageway and slip roads.

355 Mark *one* answer
What's a rumble device designed to do?

- ☐ **A** Give directions
- ☐ **B** Prevent cattle escaping
- ☐ **C** Alert you to low tyre pressure
- ☐ **D** Alert you to a hazard

A rumble device consists of raised markings or strips, designed to give drivers an audible, visual and tactile warning. These devices are used in various locations, including in the line separating the hard shoulder and the left-hand lane on the motorway and on the approach to some hazards, to alert drivers to the need to slow down.

356 Mark *one* answer
What should you do if you have to make a journey in foggy conditions?

- ☐ **A** Follow other vehicles' tail lights closely
- ☐ **B** Avoid using dipped headlights
- ☐ **C** Leave plenty of time for your journey
- ☐ **D** Keep two seconds behind the vehicle ahead

If you're planning to make a journey when it's foggy, listen to the weather reports. If visibility is very poor, avoid making unnecessary journeys. If you do travel, leave plenty of time – and if someone is waiting for you to arrive, let them know that your journey will take longer than normal. This will also take off any pressure you may feel to rush.

357 Mark *one* answer
What must you do when you're overtaking a car at night?

- ☐ **A** Flash your headlights before overtaking
- ☐ **B** Select a higher gear
- ☐ **C** Switch your headlights to main beam before overtaking
- ☐ **D** Make sure you don't dazzle other road users

To prevent your headlights from dazzling the driver of the car in front, wait until you've passed them before switching to main beam.

358 Mark *one* answer
You're travelling on a road that has road humps. What should you do when the driver in front is travelling more slowly than you?

- ☐ **A** Sound your horn
- ☐ **B** Overtake as soon as you can
- ☐ **C** Flash your headlights
- ☐ **D** Slow down and stay behind

Be patient and stay behind the car in front. You shouldn't normally overtake other vehicles in areas subject to traffic calming. If you overtake here, you may easily exceed the speed limit, defeating the purpose of the traffic-calming measures.

359 Mark *one* answer
What's the purpose of the yellow lines painted across the road?

- ☐ **A** To show a safe distance between vehicles
- ☐ **B** To keep the area clear of traffic
- ☐ **C** To make you aware of your speed
- ☐ **D** To warn you to change direction

These lines may be painted on the road on the approach to a roundabout, a village or a particular hazard. The lines are raised and painted yellow, and their purpose is to make you aware of your speed. Reduce your speed in good time so that you avoid having to brake harshly over the last few metres before reaching the junction.

360 Mark *one* answer
What should you do when you meet an oncoming vehicle on a single-track road?

- ☐ **A** Reverse back to the main road
- ☐ **B** Carry out an emergency stop
- ☐ **C** Stop at a passing place
- ☐ **D** Switch on your hazard warning lights

Take care when using single-track roads. It can be difficult to see around bends, because of hedges or fences, so expect to meet oncoming vehicles. Drive carefully and be ready to pull into or stop opposite a passing place, where you can pass each other safely.

361 Mark *one* answer
The road is wet. Why would a motorcyclist steer around drain covers while they were cornering?

- ☐ **A** To avoid puncturing the tyres on the edge of the drain covers
- ☐ **B** To prevent the motorcycle sliding on the metal drain covers
- ☐ **C** To help judge the bend using the drain covers as marker points
- ☐ **D** To avoid splashing pedestrians on the pavement

Other drivers or riders may have to change course due to the size or characteristics of their vehicle. Understanding this will help you to anticipate their actions. Motorcyclists and cyclists will be checking the road ahead for uneven or slippery surfaces, especially in wet weather. They may need to move across their lane to avoid surface hazards such as potholes and drain covers.

362 Mark *one* answer
Why should you test your brakes after this hazard?

- ☐ **A** You'll be on a slippery road
- ☐ **B** Your brakes will be wet
- ☐ **C** You'll be going down a long hill
- ☐ **D** You'll have just crossed a long bridge

A ford is a crossing over a stream that's shallow enough to drive or ride through. After you've gone through a ford or deep puddle, your brakes will be wet and they won't work as well as usual. To dry them out, apply a light brake pressure while moving slowly. Don't travel at normal speeds until you're sure your brakes are working properly again.

363 Mark *one* answer
Why should you reduce your speed when you're driving or riding in fog?

- ☐ **A** The brakes don't work as well
- ☐ **B** You'll be dazzled by other headlights
- ☐ **C** The engine will take longer to warm up
- ☐ **D** It's more difficult to see what's ahead

You won't be able to see as far ahead in fog as you can on a clear day. You'll need to reduce your speed so that, if a hazard looms out of the fog, you have the time and space to take avoiding action. Travelling in fog is hazardous. If you can, try to delay your journey until it has cleared.

364 Mark *one* answer
What will happen to your car when you drive up a steep hill?

- ☐ **A** The high gears will pull better
- ☐ **B** The steering will feel heavier
- ☐ **C** Overtaking will be easier
- ☐ **D** The engine will work harder

The engine will need more power to pull the vehicle up the hill. When approaching a steep hill you should select a lower gear to help maintain your speed. You should do this without hesitation, so that you don't lose too much speed before engaging the lower gear.

365 Mark *one* answer
You're driving on the motorway in windy conditions. What should you do as you overtake a high-sided vehicle?

- ☐ **A** Increase your speed
- ☐ **B** Be wary of a sudden gust
- ☐ **C** Drive alongside very closely
- ☐ **D** Expect normal conditions

The draught caused by other vehicles – particularly those with high sides – could be strong enough to push you out of your lane. Be prepared for a sudden gust of wind as you overtake large vehicles. Keep both hands on the steering wheel to help you keep full control.

366 Mark *one* answer

You're driving in fog. Why should you keep well back from the vehicle in front?

- ☐ **A** In case it changes direction suddenly
- ☐ **B** In case its fog lights dazzle you
- ☐ **C** In case it stops suddenly
- ☐ **D** In case its brake lights dazzle you

If you're following another road user in fog, stay well back. The driver in front won't be able to see hazards until they're close and might need to brake suddenly. Also, the road surface is likely to be wet and could be slippery.

367 Mark *one* answer

What should you do if you park on the road when it's foggy?

- ☐ **A** Leave parking lights switched on
- ☐ **B** Leave dipped headlights and fog lights switched on
- ☐ **C** Leave dipped headlights switched on
- ☐ **D** Leave main-beam headlights switched on

If you have to park your vehicle in foggy conditions, try to find a place to park off the road. If this isn't possible, park on the road facing in the same direction as the traffic. Leave your parking lights switched on and make sure they're clean.

368 Mark *one* answer

You're driving at night. What should you do if you're dazzled by headlights coming towards you?

- ☐ **A** Pull down your sun visor
- ☐ **B** Slow down or stop
- ☐ **C** Flash your main-beam headlights
- ☐ **D** Shade your eyes with your hand

If the headlights of an oncoming vehicle dazzle you, slow down or, if necessary, stop. Don't close your eyes or swerve, as you'll increase your chances of having a collision. Don't flash your headlights either, as this could dazzle other drivers and make the situation worse.

369 Mark *one* answer

When may front fog lights be used?

- ☐ **A** When visibility is seriously reduced
- ☐ **B** When they're fitted above the bumper
- ☐ **C** When they aren't as bright as the headlights
- ☐ **D** When an audible warning device is used

Your fog lights must only be used when visibility is reduced to 100 metres (328 feet) or less. You need to be familiar with the layout of your dashboard so you're aware if your fog lights have been switched on in error, or you've forgotten to switch them off.

370 Mark *one* answer

You're driving with your front fog lights switched on. What should you do if the fog has cleared?

☐ **A** Leave them on if other drivers have their lights on

☐ **B** Switch them off as long as visibility remains good

☐ **C** Flash them to warn oncoming traffic that it's foggy

☐ **D** Drive with them on instead of your headlights

Switch off your fog lights if the weather improves, but be prepared to use them again if visibility reduces to less than 100 metres (328 feet).

371 Mark *one* answer

Why should you switch off your rear fog lights when the fog has cleared?

☐ **A** To allow your headlights to work

☐ **B** To stop draining the battery

☐ **C** To stop the engine losing power

☐ **D** To prevent dazzling drivers behind

Don't forget to switch off your fog lights when the weather improves. You could be prosecuted for driving with them on in good visibility. The high intensity of rear fog lights can dazzle drivers behind and make your brake lights difficult to notice.

372 Mark *one* answer

What will happen if you use rear fog lights in good conditions?

☐ **A** They'll make it safer when towing a trailer

☐ **B** They'll protect you from larger vehicles

☐ **C** They'll dazzle other drivers

☐ **D** They'll make drivers behind keep back

Rear fog lights shine more brightly than normal rear lights, so that they show up in reduced visibility. When the visibility improves, you must switch them off; this stops them dazzling the driver behind.

373 Mark *one* answer

Why would you fit chains to your wheels?

☐ **A** To help prevent damage to the road surface

☐ **B** To help prevent wear to the tyres

☐ **C** To help prevent skidding in deep snow

☐ **D** To help prevent the brakes locking

Chains can be fitted to your wheels in snowy conditions. They can help you to move off without wheelspin, or to keep moving in deep snow. You'll still need to adjust your driving to suit these conditions.

374 Mark *one* answer
How can you use your vehicle's engine to control your speed?

☐ **A** By changing to a lower gear
☐ **B** By selecting reverse gear
☐ **C** By changing to a higher gear
☐ **D** By selecting neutral

You should brake and slow down before selecting a lower gear. The gear can then be used to keep the speed low and help you control the vehicle. This is particularly helpful on long downhill stretches, where brake fade can occur if the brakes overheat.

375 Mark *one* answer
Why could it be dangerous to keep the clutch down, or select neutral, for long periods of time while you're driving?

☐ **A** Fuel spillage will occur
☐ **B** Engine damage may be caused
☐ **C** You'll have less steering and braking control
☐ **D** It will wear tyres out more quickly

Letting your vehicle roll or coast in neutral reduces your control over steering and braking. This can be dangerous on downhill slopes, where your vehicle could pick up speed very quickly.

376 Mark *one* answer
You're driving on an icy road. What distance from the car in front should you drive?

☐ **A** Four times the normal distance
☐ **B** Six times the normal distance
☐ **C** Eight times the normal distance
☐ **D** Ten times the normal distance

Don't travel in icy or snowy weather unless your journey is essential. Drive extremely carefully when roads are or may be icy. Stopping distances can be ten times greater than on dry roads.

377 Mark *one* answer
Which lights must you use if you're driving on a well-lit motorway at night?

☐ **A** Use only your sidelights
☐ **B** Use your headlights
☐ **C** Use rear fog lights
☐ **D** Use front fog lights

If you're driving on a motorway at night or in poor visibility, you must always use your headlights, even if the road is well lit. Other road users must be able to see you, but you should avoid causing dazzle.

378 Mark *one* answer
You're driving on a motorway at night. Which lights should you have on if there are other vehicles just ahead of you?

☐ **A** Front fog lights
☐ **B** Main-beam headlights
☐ **C** Sidelights only
☐ **D** Dipped headlights

If you're driving behind other traffic on the motorway at night, use dipped headlights. Main-beam headlights will dazzle the other drivers. Your headlights' dipped beam should fall short of the vehicle in front.

379 Mark *one* answer
What will affect your vehicle's stopping distance?

☐ **A** The speed limit
☐ **B** The street lighting
☐ **C** The time of day
☐ **D** The condition of the tyres

Having tyres correctly inflated and in good condition will ensure they have maximum grip on the road; how well your tyres grip the road has a significant effect on your car's stopping distance.

380 Mark *one* answer
When will you feel the effects of engine braking?

☐ **A** When you only use the parking brake
☐ **B** When you're in neutral
☐ **C** When you change to a lower gear
☐ **D** When you change to a higher gear

When you take your foot off the accelerator, engines have a natural resistance to turn, caused mainly by the cylinder compression. Changing to a lower gear requires the engine to turn faster and so it will have greater resistance than when it's made to turn more slowly. When going downhill, changing to a lower gear will therefore help to keep the vehicle's speed in check.

381 Mark *one* answer
Which lights should you switch on when daytime visibility is poor but not seriously reduced?

☐ **A** Headlights and fog lights
☐ **B** Front fog lights
☐ **C** Dipped headlights
☐ **D** Rear fog lights

Only use your fog lights when visibility is seriously reduced. Use dipped headlights in poor conditions because this helps other road users to see you without the risk of causing dazzle.

382 Mark *one* answer
Why are vehicles fitted with rear fog lights?

- ☐ **A** To make them more visible when driving at high speed
- ☐ **B** To show when they've broken down in a dangerous position
- ☐ **C** To make them more visible in thick fog
- ☐ **D** To warn drivers following closely to drop back

Rear fog lights make it easier to spot a vehicle ahead in foggy conditions. Avoid the temptation to use other vehicles' lights as a guide, as they may give you a false sense of security.

383 Mark *one* answer
There's been a heavy fall of snow. What should you consider before driving in these conditions?

- ☐ **A** Whether you should fit an amber flashing beacon to your car
- ☐ **B** Whether you should drive without wearing your seat belt
- ☐ **C** Whether you should wear sunglasses to reduce the glare
- ☐ **D** Whether your journey is essential

Consider whether the increased risk is worth it. If the weather conditions are bad and your journey isn't essential, then don't drive. If you have to drive, make sure you're well prepared in case you get stuck.

384 Mark *one* answer
What should you check before you start a journey in foggy weather?

- ☐ **A** The radiator has enough anti-freeze
- ☐ **B** You have a warning triangle in the vehicle
- ☐ **C** The windows and lights are clean and clear
- ☐ **D** You have a mobile phone with you

If you have to drive in fog, switch your dipped headlights on and keep all your windows clear. You should always be able to pull up within the distance you can see ahead.

385 Mark *one* answer
You've been driving in fog. What must you do when the visibility improves?

- ☐ **A** Switch off your fog lights
- ☐ **B** Keep your rear fog lights switched on
- ☐ **C** Keep your front fog lights switched on
- ☐ **D** Leave your fog lights switched on in case the fog returns

You must turn off your fog lights if visibility is more than 100 metres (328 feet). Be prepared for the fact that the fog may be patchy and you may need to turn them on again if the fog returns.

386 Mark *one* answer

Why is it dangerous to leave rear fog lights switched on after the fog has cleared?

- ☐ **A** They may be confused with brake lights
- ☐ **B** The bulbs would fail
- ☐ **C** Electrical systems could be overloaded
- ☐ **D** Direction indicators may not work properly

If your rear fog lights are left on when it isn't foggy, the glare they cause makes it difficult for road users behind to know whether you're braking or you've just forgotten to turn off your rear fog lights. This can be a particular problem on wet roads and on motorways. If you leave your rear fog lights on at night, road users behind you are likely to be dazzled and this could put them at risk.

387 Mark *one* answer

What will happen if you hold the clutch pedal down or roll in neutral for too long?

- ☐ **A** It will use more fuel
- ☐ **B** It will cause the engine to overheat
- ☐ **C** It will reduce your control
- ☐ **D** It will improve tyre wear

Holding the clutch down or staying in neutral for too long will cause your vehicle to freewheel. This is known as 'coasting' and it's dangerous because it reduces your control of the vehicle.

388 Mark *one* answer

Why is it bad technique to coast when you're driving downhill?

- ☐ **A** The fuel consumption will increase
- ☐ **B** The engine will overheat
- ☐ **C** The tyres will wear more quickly
- ☐ **D** The vehicle will gain speed more quickly

Coasting is when you allow the vehicle to freewheel in neutral or with the clutch pedal depressed. When travelling downhill, this will cause the vehicle to gain speed more quickly as you lose the benefits of engine braking; it may even lead to a loss of control. You shouldn't coast, especially when approaching hazards such as junctions or bends and when travelling downhill.

389 Mark *one* answer
What should you do when dealing with this hazard?

- ☐ **A** Switch on your hazard warning lights
- ☐ **B** Use a low gear and drive slowly
- ☐ **C** Use a high gear to prevent wheelspin
- ☐ **D** Switch on your windscreen wipers

In normal conditions, a ford can be crossed quite safely by driving through it slowly. The water may affect your brakes, so when you're clear of the ford, test them before you resume normal driving.

390 Mark *one* answer
Why is travelling in neutral for long distances (known as coasting) bad driving technique?

- ☐ **A** It will cause the car to skid
- ☐ **B** It will make the engine stall
- ☐ **C** The engine will run faster
- ☐ **D** There won't be any engine braking

Try to look and plan well ahead. Plan your approach to hazards and select the correct gear in good time. This will help give you the control you need to deal with anything unexpected that may occur.

391 Mark *one* answer
When must you use dipped headlights during the day?

- ☐ **A** All the time you're driving
- ☐ **B** When you're driving along narrow streets
- ☐ **C** When you're driving in poor visibility
- ☐ **D** When you're parking

You must use dipped headlights when daytime visibility is seriously reduced, generally to 100 metres (328 feet) or less. You may also use front or rear fog lights, but they must be switched off when visibility improves.

392 Mark *one* answer
You're joining a motorway from a slip road. How should you deal with traffic already on the motorway?

- ☐ **A** Carry on along the hard shoulder until you see a safe gap
- ☐ **B** Stop at the end of the slip road and look for a safe gap
- ☐ **C** Use the slip road to accelerate until you're moving much faster than the motorway traffic
- ☐ **D** Match your speed to traffic in the left-hand lane and filter into a safe gap

You should give way to traffic already on the motorway. Where possible, traffic may move over to let you in, but don't force your way into the traffic stream. Traffic could be travelling at high speed, so try to match your speed to filter in without affecting the traffic flow.

393 Mark *one* answer
What's the national speed limit on motorways for cars and motorcycles?

- ☐ **A** 30 mph
- ☐ **B** 50 mph
- ☐ **C** 60 mph
- ☐ **D** 70 mph

Travelling at the national speed limit doesn't allow you to hog the right-hand lane. Always use the left-hand lane whenever possible. When leaving a motorway, get into the left-hand lane well before your exit. Reduce your speed on the slip road and look out for sharp bends or curves and traffic queuing at roundabouts.

394 Mark *one* answer
Which vehicles should use the left-hand lane on a three-lane motorway?

- ☐ **A** Any vehicle that isn't overtaking
- ☐ **B** Large vehicles only
- ☐ **C** Emergency vehicles only
- ☐ **D** Slow vehicles only

On a motorway, all traffic should use the left-hand lane unless overtaking. When overtaking a number of slower vehicles, move back to the left-hand lane when you're safely past. Check your mirrors frequently and don't stay in the middle or right-hand lane if the left-hand lane is free.

395 Mark *one* answer

Which vehicles aren't allowed to use the right-hand lane of a three-lane motorway?

- ☐ **A** Small delivery vans
- ☐ **B** Motorcycles
- ☐ **C** Vehicles towing a trailer
- ☐ **D** Motorcycle and sidecar outfits

On the motorway, any vehicle towing a trailer is restricted to 60 mph. It isn't allowed in the right-hand lane, as it might hold up faster-moving traffic that wishes to overtake in that lane.

396 Mark *one* answer

Your vehicle breaks down on a motorway and you need to call for help. Why might it be better to use an emergency roadside telephone rather than a mobile phone?

- ☐ **A** It connects you to a local garage
- ☐ **B** Using a mobile phone will distract other drivers
- ☐ **C** It allows easy location by the emergency services
- ☐ **D** Mobile phones don't work on motorways

On a motorway, it's best to use a roadside emergency telephone so that the emergency services are able to find you easily. The location of the nearest telephone is shown by an arrow on marker posts at the edge of the hard shoulder. If you use a mobile, find out the number on the nearest marker post before you call. This number will let the operator know where you are and in which direction you're travelling.

397 Mark *one* answer

Your vehicle broke down on the hard shoulder of a motorway, but has now been repaired. How should you rejoin the main carriageway?

- ☐ **A** Move out onto the carriageway, then build up your speed
- ☐ **B** Move out onto the carriageway using your hazard warning lights
- ☐ **C** Gain speed on the hard shoulder before moving out onto the carriageway
- ☐ **D** Wait on the hard shoulder until someone flashes their headlights at you

Signal your intention and build up sufficient speed on the hard shoulder so that you can filter into a safe gap in the traffic. Don't push your way into a small gap or cause other traffic to alter speed or direction.

398 Mark *one* answer
You're travelling along a motorway. Where would you find a crawler or climbing lane?

- ☐ **A** On a steep gradient
- ☐ **B** Before a service area
- ☐ **C** Before a junction
- ☐ **D** Along the hard shoulder

Large, slow-moving vehicles can hinder the progress of other traffic. On a steep gradient, an extra crawler lane may be provided for slow-moving vehicles to allow faster-moving traffic to flow more easily.

399 Mark *one* answer
What do these motorway signs mean?

- ☐ **A** They're countdown markers to a bridge
- ☐ **B** They're distance markers to the next telephone
- ☐ **C** They're countdown markers to the next exit
- ☐ **D** They warn of a police control ahead

The exit from a motorway is indicated by countdown markers. These are positioned 90 metres (100 yards) apart, the first being 270 metres (300 yards) from the start of the slip road. Move into the left-hand lane well before you reach the start of the slip road.

---

400 Mark *one* answer
Where are amber reflective studs found on a motorway?

- ☐ **A** Between the hard shoulder and the carriageway
- ☐ **B** Between the acceleration lane and the carriageway
- ☐ **C** Between the central reservation and the carriageway
- ☐ **D** Between each pair of lanes

On motorways, reflective studs of various colours are fixed in the road between the lanes. These help you to identify which lane you're in when it's dark or in poor visibility. Amber-coloured studs are found on the right-hand edge of the main carriageway, next to the central reservation.

401 Mark *one* answer
What colour are the reflective studs between the lanes on a motorway?

- ☐ **A** Green
- ☐ **B** Amber
- ☐ **C** White
- ☐ **D** Red

White studs are found between the lanes on motorways. They reflect back the light from your headlights. This is especially useful in bad weather, when visibility is restricted.

402 Mark *one* answer
What colour are the reflective studs between a motorway and a slip road?

- ☐ **A** Amber
- ☐ **B** White
- ☐ **C** Green
- ☐ **D** Red

The studs between the carriageway and the hard shoulder are normally red. These change to green where there's a slip road, helping you to identify slip roads when visibility is poor or when it's dark.

403 Mark *one* answer
Your vehicle has broken down on a motorway. In which direction should you walk to find the nearest emergency telephone?

- ☐ **A** With the traffic flow
- ☐ **B** Facing oncoming traffic
- ☐ **C** In the direction shown on the marker posts
- ☐ **D** In the direction of the nearest exit

Along the hard shoulder there are marker posts at 100-metre intervals. These will direct you to the nearest emergency telephone.

404 Mark *one* answer
Why is it important to make full use of the slip road as you join a motorway?

- ☐ **A** Because there's space available to turn round if you need to
- ☐ **B** To allow you direct access to the overtaking lanes
- ☐ **C** To allow you to fit safely into the traffic flow in the left-hand lane
- ☐ **D** Because you can continue on the hard shoulder

Try to join the motorway without affecting the progress of the traffic in the left-hand lane and always give way to traffic already on the motorway. At busy times, you may have to slow down to merge into slow-moving traffic.

405 Mark *one* answer
How should you position yourself when you use the emergency telephone on a motorway?

☐ **A** Stay close to the carriageway
☐ **B** Face the oncoming traffic
☐ **C** Keep your back to the traffic
☐ **D** Stand on the hard shoulder

Traffic is passing you at speed. If the draught from a large lorry catches you by surprise, it could blow you off balance and even onto the carriageway. By facing the oncoming traffic, you can see approaching lorries and so be prepared for their draught. You'll also be in a position to see any other hazards approaching.

406 Mark *one* answer
What colour are the reflective studs between the hard shoulder and the left-hand lane of a motorway?

☐ **A** Green
☐ **B** Red
☐ **C** White
☐ **D** Amber

Red studs are placed between the edge of the carriageway and the hard shoulder. Where slip roads leave or join the motorway, the studs are green.

407 Mark *one* answer
On a three-lane motorway, which lane should you use if there's no traffic ahead?

☐ **A** Left
☐ **B** Right
☐ **C** Centre
☐ **D** Either the right or centre

On a three-lane motorway, you should travel in the left-hand lane unless you're overtaking. This applies regardless of the speed at which you're travelling.

408 Mark *one* answer
What should you do when going through a contraflow system on a motorway?

☐ **A** Use dipped headlights
☐ **B** Keep a good distance from the vehicle ahead
☐ **C** Switch lanes to keep the traffic flowing
☐ **D** Stay close to the vehicle ahead to reduce queues

At roadworks, and especially where a contraflow system is operating, a speed restriction is likely to be in place. Keep to the lower speed limit and don't

• switch lanes
• get too close to the vehicle in front of you.

Be aware that there will be no permanent barrier between you and the oncoming traffic.

409 Mark *one* answer
You're on a three-lane motorway. Which lane are you in if there are red reflective studs on your left and white ones to your right?

- ☐ **A** In the right-hand lane
- ☐ **B** In the middle lane
- ☐ **C** On the hard shoulder
- ☐ **D** In the left-hand lane

The colours of the reflective studs on the motorway and their locations are
- red – between the hard shoulder and the carriageway
- white – between lanes
- amber – between the carriageway and the central reservation
- green – along slip-road exits and entrances
- bright green/yellow – at roadworks and contraflow systems.

410 Mark *one* answer
What should you do when you're approaching roadworks on a motorway?

- ☐ **A** Speed up to clear the area quickly
- ☐ **B** Always use the hard shoulder
- ☐ **C** Obey the speed limit
- ☐ **D** Stay very close to the vehicle in front

Be aware of reduced speed limits at roadworks. Speed limits shown inside a red circle are mandatory and cameras are often used to enforce the reduced limit. Slow down in good time and keep your distance from the vehicle in front.

411 Mark *one* answer
Which vehicles are prohibited from using the motorway?

- ☐ **A** Powered mobility scooters
- ☐ **B** Motorcycles over 50 cc
- ☐ **C** Double-deck buses
- ☐ **D** Cars with automatic transmission

Motorways mustn't be used by pedestrians, cyclists, motorcycles under 50 cc, certain slow-moving vehicles without permission, and powered wheelchairs/mobility scooters.

412 Mark *one* answer
What should you do while you're driving or riding along a motorway?

- ☐ **A** Look much further ahead than you would on other roads
- ☐ **B** Travel much faster than you would on other roads
- ☐ **C** Maintain a shorter separation distance than you would on other roads
- ☐ **D** Concentrate more than you would on other roads

Traffic on motorways usually travels faster than on other roads. You need to be looking further ahead to give yourself more time to react to any hazard that may develop.

413 Mark *one* answer

What should you do immediately after joining a motorway?

☐ **A** Try to overtake
☐ **B** Re-adjust your mirrors
☐ **C** Position your vehicle in the centre lane
☐ **D** Stay in the left-hand lane

When you've just joined a motorway, stay in the left-hand lane long enough to get used to the higher speeds of motorway traffic before considering overtaking.

---

414 Mark *one* answer

When would you use the right-hand lane on a three-lane motorway?

☐ **A** When you're turning right
☐ **B** When you're overtaking
☐ **C** When you're travelling above the speed limit
☐ **D** When you're trying to save fuel

The right-hand lane of the motorway is for overtaking. Sometimes you may be directed into a right-hand lane as a result of roadworks or a traffic incident. This will be indicated by signs or officers directing the traffic.

415 Mark *one* answer

You're on a motorway that isn't subject to smart motorway regulations. When should you use the hard shoulder?

☐ **A** When you're stopping in an emergency
☐ **B** When you're leaving the motorway
☐ **C** When you're stopping for a rest
☐ **D** When you're joining the motorway

Don't use the hard shoulder for stopping unless it's an emergency. If you want to stop for any other reason, go to the next exit or service area.

---

416 Mark *one* answer

You're in the right-hand lane of a three-lane motorway. What do these overhead signs mean?

☐ **A** Move to the left and reduce your speed to 50 mph
☐ **B** There are roadworks 50 metres (55 yards) ahead
☐ **C** Use the hard shoulder until you've passed the hazard
☐ **D** Leave the motorway at the next exit

You must obey these signs even if there appear to be no problems ahead. There could be queuing traffic or another hazard that you can't see yet.

417 Mark *one* answer
When are you allowed to stop on a motorway?

☐ **A** When you need to walk and get fresh air
☐ **B** When you wish to pick up hitchhikers
☐ **C** When you're signalled to do so by traffic signals
☐ **D** When you need to use a mobile telephone

You must stop if overhead gantry signs show a red cross above every lane on the motorway. If any of the other lanes doesn't show a red cross, you may move into that lane and continue if it's safe to do so.

418 Mark *one* answer
You're travelling in the left-hand lane of a three-lane motorway. How should you react to traffic joining from a slip road?

☐ **A** Increase your speed to ensure they join behind you
☐ **B** Adjust your speed or change lane if you can do so safely
☐ **C** Maintain a steady speed
☐ **D** Switch on your hazard warning lights

Plan well ahead when approaching a slip road. If you see traffic joining the motorway, be prepared to adjust your speed or move to another lane if it's safe to do so. This can help the flow of traffic joining the motorway, especially at peak times.

419 Mark *one* answer
How should you use the lanes on a motorway?

☐ **A** Use the lane that has the least traffic
☐ **B** Keep to the left-hand lane unless you're overtaking
☐ **C** Overtake using the lane that's clearest
☐ **D** Stay in one lane until you reach your exit

You should normally travel in the left-hand lane unless you're overtaking a slower-moving vehicle. When you've finished overtaking, move back into the left-hand lane, but don't cut across in front of the vehicle that you've overtaken.

420 Mark *one* answer
You're travelling along a motorway. When are you allowed to overtake on the left?

☐ **A** When you can see well ahead that the hard shoulder is clear
☐ **B** When the traffic in the right-hand lane is signalling right
☐ **C** When you warn drivers behind by signalling left
☐ **D** When in queues and traffic to your right is moving more slowly than you are

Never overtake on the left, unless the traffic is moving in queues and the queue on your right is moving more slowly than the one you're in.

421 Mark *one* answer
When would you use an emergency refuge area on a smart motorway?

☐ **A** In cases of emergency or breakdown
☐ **B** If you think you'll be involved in a road rage incident
☐ **C** To stop and check where you are
☐ **D** To make a private phone call

On smart motorways, emergency refuge areas are built at the side of the hard shoulder. If you break down, try to get your vehicle into the refuge, where there's an emergency telephone. The phone connects directly to a control centre. Remember to take care when rejoining the motorway, especially if the hard shoulder is being used as a running lane.

422 Mark *one* answer
Traffic officers operate on motorways and some primary routes in England and Wales. What are they authorised to do?

☐ **A** Stop and arrest drivers who break the law
☐ **B** Repair broken-down vehicles on the motorway
☐ **C** Issue fixed penalty notices
☐ **D** Stop and direct anyone on a motorway

Traffic officers don't have enforcement powers but are able to stop and direct people on motorways and some 'A' class roads. They operate in England and Wales and work in partnership with the police at incidents, providing a highly trained and visible service. They're recognised by an orange-and-yellow jacket and their vehicle has yellow-and-black markings.

423 Mark *one* answer

You're on a smart motorway. What does it mean when a red cross is displayed above the hard shoulder?

☐ **A** Pull up in this lane to answer your mobile phone
☐ **B** Use this lane as a running lane
☐ **C** This lane can be used if you need a rest
☐ **D** You must not travel in this lane

Some motorways have been redesigned as smart motorways. At certain times, the hard shoulder will be open as a running lane. However, a red cross above the hard shoulder shows that it isn't open as a running lane and should only be used for emergencies and breakdowns.

424 Mark *one* answer

You're on a smart motorway. What does it mean when a mandatory speed limit is displayed above the hard shoulder?

☐ **A** You shouldn't travel in this lane
☐ **B** The hard shoulder can be used as a running lane
☐ **C** You can park on the hard shoulder if you feel tired
☐ **D** You can pull up in this lane to answer a mobile phone

A mandatory speed-limit sign above the hard shoulder shows that this part of the road can be used as a running lane between junctions. You must stay within the speed limit. Look out for vehicles that may have broken down and could be blocking the hard shoulder.

425 Mark *one* answer
How do smart motorways prevent traffic bunching?

☐ **A** By using higher speed limits
☐ **B** By using advisory speed limits
☐ **C** By using minimum speed limits
☐ **D** By using variable speed limits

When a smart motorway is operating, you must follow the mandatory signs on the gantries above each lane, including the hard shoulder. Variable speed limits help keep the traffic moving and also help to prevent bunching.

426 Mark *one* answer
What helps to reduce traffic bunching on a motorway?

☐ **A** Variable speed limits
☐ **B** Contraflow systems
☐ **C** National speed limits
☐ **D** Lane closures

Congestion can be reduced by keeping traffic at a constant speed. At busy times, maximum speed limits are displayed on overhead gantries. These can be varied quickly, depending on the amount of traffic. By keeping to a constant speed on busy sections of motorway, overall journey times are normally improved.

427 Mark *one* answer
When may you stop on a motorway?

☐ **A** If you have to read a map
☐ **B** When you're tired and need a rest
☐ **C** If your mobile phone rings
☐ **D** In an emergency or breakdown

You shouldn't normally stop on a motorway, but there may be occasions when you need to do so. If your vehicle breaks down or there's an emergency, stop on the hard shoulder and use the emergency telephones to call for assistance.

428 Mark *one* answer
What's the national speed limit for a car or motorcycle on a motorway?

☐ **A** 50 mph
☐ **B** 60 mph
☐ **C** 70 mph
☐ **D** 80 mph

The national speed limit for a car or motorcycle on a motorway is 70 mph. Lower speed limits may be in force; for example, at roadworks. Variable speed limits also operate in some areas when the motorway is very busy. Cars or motorcycles towing trailers are subject to a lower speed limit.

429 Mark *one* answer
You stop on the hard shoulder of a motorway and use the emergency telephone. Where's the best place to wait for help to arrive?

☐ **A** Next to the phone
☐ **B** Well away from the carriageway
☐ **C** With your vehicle
☐ **D** On the hard shoulder

When you're on the hard shoulder, you're at risk of being injured by motorway traffic. The safest place to wait is away from the carriageway, but near enough to see the emergency services arriving.

430 Mark *one* answer
You're on a motorway. What must you do if there's a red cross showing above every lane?

☐ **A** Pull onto the hard shoulder
☐ **B** Slow down and watch for further signals
☐ **C** Leave at the next exit
☐ **D** Stop and wait

A red cross signal above all lanes means you must stop and wait. Don't change lanes and don't try to continue any further along the motorway.

431 Mark *one* answer
You're on a smart motorway. What does it mean if a red cross is showing above the hard shoulder and mandatory speed limits above all other lanes?

☐ **A** The hard shoulder can be used as a rest area if you feel tired
☐ **B** The hard shoulder is for emergency or breakdown use only
☐ **C** The hard shoulder can be used as a normal running lane
☐ **D** The hard shoulder has a speed limit of 50 mph

A red cross above the hard shoulder shows that it's closed as a running lane and should only be used for emergencies or breakdowns. On a smart motorway, the hard shoulder may be used as a running lane at busy times. This will be shown by a mandatory speed limit on the gantry above the hard shoulder.

432 Mark *one* answer

On a smart motorway, what does this sign mean?

☐ **A** Use any lane except the hard shoulder
☐ **B** Use the hard shoulder only
☐ **C** Use the three right-hand lanes only
☐ **D** Use all the lanes, including the
hard shoulder

You must obey mandatory speed-limit signs above motorway lanes, including the hard shoulder. In this case, you can use the hard shoulder as a running lane but you should look for any vehicles that may have broken down and may be blocking the hard shoulder.

433 Mark *one* answer

Where should you stop to rest if you feel tired while you're travelling along a motorway?

☐ **A** On the hard shoulder
☐ **B** At the nearest service area
☐ **C** On a slip road
☐ **D** On the central reservation

If you feel tired, stop at the nearest service area. If that's too far away, leave the motorway at the next exit and find a safe place to stop. You mustn't stop on the carriageway or hard shoulder of a motorway except in an emergency, when in a traffic queue, or when signalled to do so by a police officer, a traffic officer or traffic signals. Plan your journey so that you have regular rest stops.

434 Mark *one* answer

You have stopped in an emergency refuge area. What must you do before you rejoin the carriageway?

☐ **A** Use the emergency telephone
☐ **B** Give an arm signal as you are
moving off
☐ **C** Switch on your vehicle's headlights
☐ **D** Switch on your vehicle's headlights

To rejoin the carriageway from an emergency refuge area, you must use the emergency telephone and follow the operator's advice. A lane may have to be closed so that you can rejoin the carriageway safely.

435 Mark *one* answer
How should you rejoin the motorway after a breakdown on the hard shoulder?

☐ **A** Build up speed on the hard shoulder before looking for a safe gap in the traffic

☐ **B** Move straight out into the left-hand lane as you are not allowed to drive on the hard shoulder

☐ **C** Wait until a vehicle in the left-hand lane signals to you that it's safe to rejoin

☐ **D** Keep your hazard lights flashing until you have safely rejoined the carriageway.

To rejoin a motorway from the hard shoulder, you first need to build up speed on the hard shoulder. You can then look for a safe gap in the traffic in the left-hand lane. Watch for traffic that may be returning from a lane on the right into the left-hand lane.

436 Mark *one* answer
What's the speed limit for a car towing a trailer on a motorway?

☐ **A** 40 mph

☐ **B** 50 mph

☐ **C** 60 mph

☐ **D** 70 mph

If you're towing a small, light trailer, it won't reduce your vehicle's performance by very much and it may not be visible in your mirrors. However, strong winds or buffeting from large vehicles might cause the trailer to snake from side to side. Be aware of your speed and don't exceed the reduced speed limit imposed on vehicles towing trailers.

437 Mark *one* answer
When should you use the left-hand lane of a motorway?

☐ **A** When your vehicle breaks down

☐ **B** When you're overtaking slower traffic in the other lanes

☐ **C** When you're making a phone call

☐ **D** When the road ahead is clear

You should drive in the left-hand lane whenever possible. Only use the other lanes for overtaking or when directed to do so by signals. Using other lanes when the left-hand lane is empty can frustrate drivers behind you.

438 Mark *one* answer
You're driving on a motorway and have to slow down suddenly due to a hazard ahead. How can you warn drivers behind of the hazard?

☐ **A** Switch on your hazard warning lights

☐ **B** Switch on your headlights

☐ **C** Sound your horn

☐ **D** Flash your headlights

Using your hazard warning lights, as well as your brake lights, will give the traffic behind an extra warning of the problem ahead. Only use them for long enough for your warning to be seen.

439 Mark *one* answer

Your car gets a puncture while you're driving on the motorway. What should you do when you've stopped on the hard shoulder?

- ☐ **A** Carefully change the wheel yourself
- ☐ **B** Use an emergency telephone and call for help
- ☐ **C** Try to wave down another vehicle for help
- ☐ **D** Only change the wheel if you have a passenger to help you

Park as far to the left as you can and leave the vehicle by the nearside door. Don't attempt even simple repairs. Instead, walk to an emergency telephone on your side of the road and phone for help. While waiting for help to arrive, stay by your car, keeping well away from the carriageway and hard shoulder.

440 Mark *one* answer

What should you do if you're driving on a motorway and you miss the exit that you wanted to take?

- ☐ **A** Carefully reverse along the hard shoulder
- ☐ **B** Carry on to the next exit
- ☐ **C** Carefully reverse in the left-hand lane
- ☐ **D** Make a U-turn at the next gap in the central reservation

It's illegal to reverse, cross the central reservation or drive against the traffic flow on a motorway. If you miss your exit, carry on until you reach the next one. Ask yourself why you missed your exit – if you think that your concentration is fading, take a break before continuing your journey.

441 Mark *one* answer

Your vehicle has broken down on a motorway. What should you do if you aren't able to get onto the hard shoulder?

- ☐ **A** Switch on your hazard warning lights
- ☐ **B** Stop the traffic behind and ask for help
- ☐ **C** Attempt to repair your vehicle quickly
- ☐ **D** Stand behind your vehicle to warn others

If you can't get your vehicle onto the hard shoulder, use your hazard warning lights to warn others. Leave your vehicle only when you can safely get clear of the carriageway. Don't try to repair the vehicle or attempt to place any warning device on the carriageway.

442 Mark *one* answer
Why is it particularly important to check your vehicle before making a long motorway journey?

☐ **A** You'll have to do more harsh braking on motorways
☐ **B** Motorway services areas don't deal with breakdowns
☐ **C** The road surface will wear down the tyres faster
☐ **D** Continuous high speeds increase the risk of your vehicle breaking down

Before you start your journey, make sure that your vehicle can cope with the demands of high-speed driving. You should check a number of things; the main ones being fuel, oil, water and tyres. You also need to plan rest stops if you're making a long journey.

443 Mark *one* answer
You're driving on a motorway. What does it mean if the car in front shows its hazard warning lights for a short time?

☐ **A** The driver wants you to overtake
☐ **B** The other car is going to change lanes
☐ **C** Traffic ahead is slowing or stopping suddenly
☐ **D** There's a police speed check ahead

If the vehicle in front shows its hazard warning lights, there may be an incident, stopped traffic or queuing traffic ahead. By keeping a safe distance from the vehicle in front, you're able to look beyond it and see any hazards well ahead.

444 Mark *one* answer
You're driving on the motorway. Which lane should you get into well before you reach your exit?

☐ **A** The middle lane
☐ **B** The left-hand lane
☐ **C** The hard shoulder
☐ **D** The right-hand lane

You'll see the first advance direction sign one mile from a motorway exit. If you're travelling at 60 mph in the right-hand lane, you'll only have about 50 seconds before you reach the countdown markers. There'll be another sign at the half-mile point. Don't cut across lanes of traffic at the last moment – move to the left-hand lane in good time.

445 Mark *one* answer
What restrictions apply to people who have a provisional driving licence?

☐ **A** They can't drive over 30 mph
☐ **B** They can't drive at night
☐ **C** They can't drive unaccompanied
☐ **D** They can't drive with more than one passenger

You won't be able to drive unaccompanied until you've passed your practical driving test. If you haven't driven on the motorway while you were learning, ask your instructor to take you for a lesson on the motorway when you've passed your test. Alternatively, you could take part in the Pass Plus scheme. This has been created for new drivers and includes motorway driving. Ask your instructor for details.

446 Mark *one* answer

Your vehicle breaks down on a motorway and you manage to stop on the hard shoulder. What should you do if you use your mobile phone to call for help?

- ☐ **A** Stand at the rear of the vehicle while making the call
- ☐ **B** Phone a friend and ask them to come and collect you
- ☐ **C** Wait in the car for the emergency services to arrive
- ☐ **D** Check your location from the nearest marker posts beside the hard shoulder

You should use an emergency telephone when you break down on the motorway; only use your mobile if this isn't possible. The emergency services need to know your exact location so they can reach you as quickly as possible. Look for a number on the nearest marker post beside the hard shoulder. Give this number when you call the emergency services.

447 Mark *one* answer   NI

You're towing a trailer along a three-lane motorway. When may you use the right-hand lane?

- ☐ **A** When there are lane closures
- ☐ **B** When there's slow-moving traffic
- ☐ **C** When you can maintain a high speed
- ☐ **D** When large vehicles are in the left and centre lanes

If you're towing a caravan or trailer, you mustn't use the right-hand lane of a motorway with three or more lanes except in certain specified circumstances, such as when lanes are closed.

448 Mark *one* answer

What would you expect to find at a contraflow system on a motorway?

- ☐ **A** Temporary traffic lights
- ☐ **B** Lower speed limits
- ☐ **C** Wider lanes than normal
- ☐ **D** Road humps

When approaching a contraflow system, reduce speed in good time and obey all speed limits. You may be travelling in a narrower lane than normal, with no permanent barrier between you and the oncoming traffic. Be aware that the hard shoulder may be used for traffic and the road ahead could be obstructed by slow-moving or broken-down vehicles.

449 Mark *one* answer
What's the meaning of this sign?

- ☐ **A** Local speed limit applies
- ☐ **B** No waiting on the carriageway
- ☐ **C** National speed limit applies
- ☐ **D** No entry for vehicles

This sign doesn't tell you the speed limit in figures. You should know the speed limit for the type of road that you're on and the type of vehicle that you're driving. Study your copy of *The Highway Code*.

450 Mark *one* answer
What's the national speed limit for cars and motorcycles on a dual carriageway?

- ☐ **A** 30 mph
- ☐ **B** 50 mph
- ☐ **C** 60 mph
- ☐ **D** 70 mph

Make sure that you know the speed limit for the road that you're on. The speed limit on a dual carriageway or motorway is 70 mph for cars and motorcycles, unless signs indicate otherwise. The speed limits for different types of vehicle are listed in *The Highway Code*.

451 Mark *one* answer
There are no speed-limit signs on the road. How is a 30 mph limit generally indicated?

- ☐ **A** By hazard warning lines
- ☐ **B** By street lighting
- ☐ **C** By pedestrian islands
- ☐ **D** By double or single yellow lines

There's a 30 mph speed limit where there are street lights unless signs show another limit.

452 Mark *one* answer
What will the speed limit usually be where you can see street lights but no speed-limit signs?

- ☐ **A** 30 mph
- ☐ **B** 40 mph
- ☐ **C** 50 mph
- ☐ **D** 60 mph

The presence of street lights generally indicates that there's a 30 mph speed limit, unless signs tell you otherwise.

453 Mark *one* answer
What does this sign mean?

- ☐ **A** Minimum speed 30 mph
- ☐ **B** End of maximum speed
- ☐ **C** End of minimum speed
- ☐ **D** Maximum speed 30 mph

The red slash through the sign indicates that the restriction has ended. In this case, the restriction was a minimum speed limit of 30 mph.

454 Mark *one* answer
What should you do if you want to overtake a tractor but aren't sure that it's safe?

- ☐ **A** Follow another vehicle as it overtakes the tractor
- ☐ **B** Sound your horn to make the tractor driver pull over
- ☐ **C** Speed past, flashing your lights at oncoming traffic
- ☐ **D** Stay behind it if you're in any doubt

Following a tractor can be frustrating, but never overtake if you're unsure whether it's safe. Ask yourself: 'Can I see far enough down the road to ensure that I can complete the manoeuvre safely?' It's better to be delayed for a minute or two than to take a chance that may cause a collision.

455 Mark *one* answer
Which vehicle is most likely to take an unusual course at a roundabout?

- ☐ **A** Estate car
- ☐ **B** Milk float
- ☐ **C** Delivery van
- ☐ **D** Long vehicle

Long vehicles might have to take a slightly different position when approaching the roundabout or going around it. This is to stop the rear of the vehicle cutting in and mounting the kerb.

456 Mark *one* answer
When may you stop on a clearway?

- ☐ **A** Never
- ☐ **B** When it's busy
- ☐ **C** In the rush hour
- ☐ **D** During daylight hours

Clearways are in place so that traffic can flow without the obstruction of parked vehicles. Just one parked vehicle can cause an obstruction for all other traffic. You mustn't stop where a clearway is in force, not even to pick up or set down passengers.

457 Mark *one* answer
What's the meaning of this sign?

- ☐ **A** No entry
- ☐ **B** Waiting restrictions
- ☐ **C** National speed limit
- ☐ **D** School crossing patrol

This sign indicates that there are waiting restrictions. It's normally accompanied by details of when the restrictions are in force. Details of most signs in common use are shown in *The Highway Code*. For more comprehensive coverage, see *Know Your Traffic Signs*.

458 Mark *one* answer
You're looking for somewhere to park at night. When may you park on the right-hand side of the road?

- ☐ **A** When you're in a one-way street
- ☐ **B** When you have your sidelights on
- ☐ **C** When you're more than 10 metres (32 feet) from a junction
- ☐ **D** When you're under a lamppost

Red rear reflectors show up when headlights shine on them. These are useful when you're parked at night, but they'll only reflect if you park in the same direction as the traffic flow. Normally you should park on the left, but in a one-way street you may also park on the right-hand side of the road.

459 Mark *one* answer
When should you use the right-hand lane of a three-lane dual carriageway?

- ☐ **A** When you're overtaking only
- ☐ **B** When you're overtaking or turning right
- ☐ **C** When you're using cruise control
- ☐ **D** When you're turning right only

You should normally use the left-hand lane on any dual carriageway unless you're overtaking or turning right. When overtaking on a dual carriageway, look for vehicles ahead that are turning right. They may be slowing or stopped. You need to see them in good time so that you can take appropriate action.

460 Mark *one* answer
You're approaching a busy junction. What should you do when, at the last moment, you realise you're in the wrong lane?

- ☐ **A** Continue in that lane
- ☐ **B** Force your way into the lane you need
- ☐ **C** Stop until the area has cleared
- ☐ **D** Use arm signals to help you change lane

There are times when road markings are obscured by queuing traffic, or you're unsure which lane to use. If, at the last moment, you find you're in the wrong lane, don't cut across or bully other drivers to let you in. Follow the lane you're in and find somewhere safe to turn around and rejoin your route.

461 Mark *one* answer
Where may you overtake on a one-way street?

☐ **A** Only on the left-hand side
☐ **B** Overtaking isn't allowed
☐ **C** Only on the right-hand side
☐ **D** On either the right or the left

You can overtake other traffic on either side when travelling in a one-way street. Make full use of your mirrors and ensure it's clear all around before you attempt to overtake. Look for signs and road markings, and use the most suitable lane for your destination.

462 Mark *one* answer
What signal should you give when you're going straight ahead at a roundabout?

☐ **A** Signal left before leaving the roundabout
☐ **B** Don't signal at any time
☐ **C** Signal right when you're approaching the roundabout
☐ **D** Signal left when you're approaching the roundabout

When going straight ahead at a roundabout, don't signal as you approach it. Signal left just after passing the exit before the one you wish to take.

463 Mark *one* answer
Which vehicle might have to take a different course from normal at a roundabout?

☐ **A** Sports car
☐ **B** Van
☐ **C** Estate car
☐ **D** Long vehicle

A long vehicle may have to straddle lanes either on or approaching a roundabout so that the rear wheels don't mount the kerb. If you're following a long vehicle, stay well back and give it plenty of room.

464 Mark *one* answer
When may you enter a box junction?

☐ **A** When there are fewer than two vehicles ahead
☐ **B** When signalled by another road user
☐ **C** When your exit road is clear
☐ **D** When traffic signs direct you

Yellow box junctions are marked on the road to prevent the road becoming blocked. Don't enter the box unless your exit road is clear. You may wait in the box if you want to turn right and your exit road is clear but oncoming traffic or other vehicles waiting to turn right are preventing you from making the turn.

465 Mark *one* answer
When may you stop and wait in a box junction?

- ☐ **A** When oncoming traffic prevents you from turning right
- ☐ **B** When you're in a queue of traffic turning left
- ☐ **C** When you're in a queue of traffic going ahead
- ☐ **D** When you're on a roundabout

The purpose of yellow box markings is to keep junctions clear of queuing traffic. You may only wait in the marked area when you're turning right and your exit lane is clear but you can't complete the turn because of oncoming traffic or other traffic waiting to turn right.

466 Mark *one* answer
Who is authorised to signal you to stop?

- ☐ **A** A motorcyclist
- ☐ **B** A pedestrian
- ☐ **C** A police officer
- ☐ **D** A bus driver

You must obey signals to stop given by police and traffic officers, traffic wardens and school crossing patrols. Failure to do so is an offence and could lead to prosecution.

467 Mark *one* answer
What should you do if you see a pedestrian waiting at a zebra crossing?

- ☐ **A** Go on quickly before they step onto the crossing
- ☐ **B** Stop before you reach the zigzag lines and let them cross
- ☐ **C** Be ready to slow down or stop to let them cross
- ☐ **D** Ignore them as they're still on the pavement

By standing on the pavement, the pedestrian is showing an intention to cross. By looking well ahead, you'll give yourself time to see the pedestrian, check your mirrors and respond safely.

468 Mark *one* answer
Which road users benefit from toucan crossings?

- ☐ **A** Car drivers and motorcyclists
- ☐ **B** Cyclists and pedestrians
- ☐ **C** Bus and lorry drivers
- ☐ **D** Tram and train drivers

Toucan crossings are similar to pelican crossings but there's no flashing amber phase. Cyclists share the crossing with pedestrians and are allowed to cycle across when the green cycle symbol is shown.

469 Mark *one* answer
You're waiting at a pelican crossing. What does it mean when the red light changes to flashing amber?

☐ **A** Give way to pedestrians on the crossing
☐ **B** Move off immediately without any hesitation
☐ **C** Wait for the green light before moving off
☐ **D** Get ready and go when the continuous amber light shows

This light allows pedestrians already on the crossing to get to the other side in their own time, without being rushed. Don't rev your engine or start to move off while they're still crossing.

470 Mark *one* answer
You see these double white lines along the centre of the road. When may you park on the left?

☐ **A** If the line nearest to you is broken
☐ **B** When there are no yellow lines
☐ **C** To pick up or set down passengers
☐ **D** During daylight hours only

You mustn't park or stop on a road marked with double white lines (even where one of the lines is broken) except to pick up or set down passengers.

471 Mark *one* answer
You're turning right at a crossroads. An oncoming driver is also turning right. What's the advantage of turning behind the oncoming vehicle?

☐ **A** You'll have a clearer view of any approaching traffic
☐ **B** You'll use less fuel because you can stay in a higher gear
☐ **C** You'll have more time to turn
☐ **D** You'll be able to turn without stopping

When turning right at a crossroads where oncoming traffic is also turning right, it's generally safer to turn behind the approaching vehicle. This allows you a clear view of approaching traffic and is called 'turning offside to offside'. However, some junctions, usually controlled by traffic-light filters - are marked for vehicles to turn nearside to nearside.

472 Mark *one* answer
You're travelling along a residential street. There are parked vehicles on the left-hand side. Why should you keep your speed down?

☐ **A** So that oncoming traffic can see you more clearly
☐ **B** You may set off car alarms
☐ **C** There may be delivery lorries on the street
☐ **D** Children may run out from between the vehicles

Travel slowly and carefully near parked vehicles. Beware of
- vehicles pulling out, especially bicycles and motorcycles
- pedestrians, especially children, who may run out from between cars
- drivers opening their doors.

473 Mark *one* answer
What should you do when there's an obstruction on your side of the road?

- ☐ **A** Carry on, as you have priority
- ☐ **B** Give way to oncoming traffic
- ☐ **C** Wave oncoming vehicles through
- ☐ **D** Accelerate to get past first

Take care if you have to pass an obstruction, such as a parked vehicle, on your side of the road. Give way to oncoming traffic if there isn't enough room for you both to continue safely.

474 Mark *one* answer
When would you use the right-hand lane of a two-lane dual carriageway?

- ☐ **A** When you're turning right or overtaking
- ☐ **B** When you're passing a side road on the left
- ☐ **C** When you're staying at the minimum allowed speed
- ☐ **D** When you're travelling at a constant high speed

Normally you should travel in the left-hand lane and only use the right-hand lane for overtaking or turning right. Move back into the left lane as soon as it's safe but don't cut in across the path of the vehicle you've just passed.

475 Mark *one* answer
Who has priority at an unmarked crossroads?

- ☐ **A** The larger vehicle
- ☐ **B** No-one has priority
- ☐ **C** The faster vehicle
- ☐ **D** The smaller vehicle

Practise good observation in all directions before you emerge or make a turn. Proceed only when you're sure it's safe to do so.

476 Mark *one* answer NI
What's the nearest you may park to a junction?

- ☐ **A** 10 metres (32 feet)
- ☐ **B** 12 metres (39 feet)
- ☐ **C** 15 metres (49 feet)
- ☐ **D** 20 metres (66 feet)

Don't park within 10 metres (32 feet) of a junction (unless in an authorised parking place). This is to allow drivers emerging from, or turning into, the junction a clear view of the road they're joining. It also allows them to see hazards such as pedestrians or cyclists at the junction.

477 Mark *one* answer
You're looking for somewhere to safely park your vehicle. Where would you choose to park?

- ☐ **A** At or near a bus stop
- ☐ **B** In a designated parking space
- ☐ **C** Near the brow of a hill
- ☐ **D** On the approach to a level crossing

It may be tempting to park where you shouldn't while you run a quick errand. Careless parking is a selfish act and could endanger other road users.

478 Mark *one* answer
You're waiting at a level crossing. What must you do if a train passes but the lights keep flashing?

- ☐ **A** Carry on waiting
- ☐ **B** Phone the signal operator
- ☐ **C** Edge over the stop line and look for trains
- ☐ **D** Park and investigate

If the lights at a level crossing keep flashing after a train has passed, you should continue to wait, because another train might be coming. Time seems to pass slowly when you're held up in a queue. Be patient and wait until the lights stop flashing.

479 Mark *one* answer
What does this sign mean?

- ☐ **A** No through road
- ☐ **B** End of traffic-calming zone
- ☐ **C** Free-parking zone ends
- ☐ **D** End of controlled parking zone

This sign shows that you're leaving a controlled parking zone and those restrictions no longer apply.

480 Mark *one* answer
What must you do if you come across roadworks that have a temporary speed limit displayed?

- ☐ **A** Obey the speed limit
- ☐ **B** Obey the limit, but only during rush hour
- ☐ **C** Ignore the displayed limit
- ☐ **D** Use your own judgment; the limit is only advisory

Where there are extra hazards, such as at roadworks, it's often necessary to slow traffic by imposing a lower speed limit. These speed limits aren't advisory; they must be obeyed.

481 Mark *one* answer
You're in a built-up area at night and the road is well lit. Why should you use dipped headlights?

- ☐ **A** So that you can see further along the road
- ☐ **B** So that you can go at a much faster speed
- ☐ **C** So that you can switch to main beam quickly
- ☐ **D** So that you can be easily seen by others

You may be difficult to see when you're travelling at night, even on a well-lit road. If you use dipped headlights rather than sidelights, other road users should be able to see you more easily.

482 Mark *one* answer
You're turning right onto a dual carriageway. What should you do if the central reservation is too narrow to contain your vehicle?

- ☐ **A** Proceed to the central reservation and wait
- ☐ **B** Wait until the road is clear in both directions
- ☐ **C** Stop in the first lane so that other vehicles give way
- ☐ **D** Emerge slightly to show your intentions

When the central reservation is narrow, it may not be able to contain your vehicle. In this case, you should treat a dual carriageway as one road. Wait until the road is clear in both directions before emerging to turn right. If you try to treat it as two separate roads and wait in the middle, your vehicle will stick out and cause an obstruction that may lead to a collision.

483 Mark *one* answer
What's the national speed limit on a single carriageway road for cars and motorcycles?

- ☐ **A** 30 mph
- ☐ **B** 50 mph
- ☐ **C** 60 mph
- ☐ **D** 70 mph

Exceeding the speed limit is dangerous and can result in you receiving penalty points on your licence. It isn't worth it. You should know the speed limit for the road that you're on by observing the road signs. Different speed limits apply if you're towing a trailer.

484 Mark *one* answer
What should you do when you park at night on a road that has a 40 mph speed limit?

- ☐ **A** Park facing the traffic
- ☐ **B** Leave parking lights switched on
- ☐ **C** Leave dipped headlights switched on
- ☐ **D** Park near a street light

You must use parking lights when parking at night on a road or in a lay-by on a road with a speed limit greater than 30 mph. You must also park in the direction of the traffic flow and not close to a junction.

485 Mark *one* answer
Where will you see these red and white markers?

- ☐ **A** Approaching the end of a motorway
- ☐ **B** Approaching a concealed level crossing
- ☐ **C** Approaching a concealed speed-limit sign
- ☐ **D** Approaching the end of a dual carriageway

If there's a bend just before a level crossing, you may not be able to see the level-crossing barriers or waiting traffic. These signs give you an early warning that you may find these hazards just around the bend.

486 Mark *one* answer
You're travelling on a motorway in England. When must you stop your vehicle?

- ☐ **A** When signalled to stop by a roadworks supervisor
- ☐ **B** When signalled to stop by a traffic officer
- ☐ **C** When signalled to stop by a pedestrian on the hard shoulder
- ☐ **D** When signalled to stop by a driver who has broken down

You'll find traffic officers on motorways and some primary routes in England and Wales. They work in partnership with the police, helping to keep traffic moving and helping to make your journey as safe as possible. It's an offence not to comply with the directions given by a traffic officer.

487 Mark *one* answer
How should you signal if you're going straight ahead at a roundabout?

- ☐ **A** Signal right on the approach and then left to leave the roundabout
- ☐ **B** Signal left after you leave the roundabout and enter the new road
- ☐ **C** Signal right on the approach to the roundabout and keep the signal on
- ☐ **D** Signal left just after you pass the exit before the one you're going to take

To go straight ahead at a roundabout, you should normally approach in the left-hand lane, but check the road markings. At some roundabouts, the left lane on approach is marked 'left turn only', so make sure you use the correct lane to go ahead. You won't normally need to signal as you approach, but signal before you leave the roundabout, as other road users need to know your

488 Mark *one* answer
When may you drive over a pavement?

☐ **A** To overtake slow-moving traffic
☐ **B** When the pavement is very wide
☐ **C** If there are no pedestrians nearby
☐ **D** To gain access to a property

It's illegal to drive on or over a pavement, except to gain access to a property. If you need to cross a pavement, give priority to pedestrians.

489 Mark *one* answer
A single carriageway road has this sign. What's the maximum permitted speed for a car towing a trailer?

☐ **A** 30 mph
☐ **B** 40 mph
☐ **C** 50 mph
☐ **D** 60 mph

When you're towing a trailer, a reduced speed limit also applies on dual carriageways and motorways. These lower speed limits apply to vehicles pulling all sorts of trailers, including caravans and horse boxes.

490 Mark *one* answer
What's the speed limit for a car towing a caravan on a dual carriageway?

☐ **A** 50 mph
☐ **B** 40 mph
☐ **C** 70 mph
☐ **D** 60 mph

The speed limit for cars towing caravans or trailers on dual carriageways or motorways is 60 mph. Due to the increased weight and size of the combination, you should plan further ahead. Take care in windy weather, as a strong side wind can make a caravan or large trailer unstable.

491 Mark *one* answer
You want to park and you see this sign. What should you do on the days and times shown?

Meter
ZONE

Mon - Fri
8.30 am - 6.30 pm
Saturday
8.30 am - 1.30 pm

☐ **A** Park in a bay and not pay
☐ **B** Park on yellow lines and pay
☐ **C** Park on yellow lines and not pay
☐ **D** Park in a bay and pay

Parking restrictions apply in a variety of places and situations. Make sure you know the rules and understand where and when restrictions apply. Controlled parking areas will be indicated by signs and road markings. Parking in the wrong place could cause an obstruction and danger to other traffic. It can also result in a fine.

492 Mark *one* answer

A cycle lane, marked by a solid white line, is in operation. What does this mean for car drivers?

- ☐ **A** They may park in the lane
- ☐ **B** They may drive in the lane at any time
- ☐ **C** They may use the lane when necessary
- ☐ **D** They mustn't drive along the lane

While it's in operation, other vehicles must not use this part of the carriageway except to pick up or set down passengers. At other times, when the lane isn't in operation, you should still be aware that there may be cyclists using the lane. Give them plenty of room as you pass and allow for their movement from side to side, especially in windy weather or on a bumpy road.

493 Mark *one* answer

You're going to turn left from a main road into a minor road. What should you do as you approach the junction?

- ☐ **A** Keep just left of the middle of the road
- ☐ **B** Keep in the middle of the road
- ☐ **C** Swing out to the right just before turning
- ☐ **D** Keep well to the left of the road

Your road position can help other road users to anticipate your actions. Keep to the left as you approach a left turn and don't swing out into the centre of the road in order to make the turn easier. This could endanger oncoming traffic and may cause other road users to misunderstand your intentions.

494 Mark *one* answer

You're waiting at a level crossing. What should you do if the red warning lights continue to flash after a train has passed by?

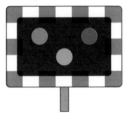

- ☐ **A** Get out and investigate
- ☐ **B** Telephone the signal operator
- ☐ **C** Continue to wait
- ☐ **D** Drive across carefully

At a level crossing, flashing red lights mean you must stop. If the train passes but the lights keep flashing, wait. Another train may be coming.

495 Mark *one* answer
What should you do if the amber lights come on and a warning sounds while you're driving over a level crossing?

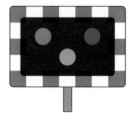

- [ ] **A** Get everyone out of the vehicle immediately
- [ ] **B** Stop and reverse back to clear the crossing
- [ ] **C** Keep going and clear the crossing
- [ ] **D** Stop immediately and use your hazard warning lights

Keep going; don't stop on the crossing. If the warning sounds and the amber lights come on as you're approaching the crossing, you must stop unless it's unsafe to do so. Red flashing lights together with the audible warning mean you must stop.

496 Mark *one* answer
You're driving on a busy main road. What should you do if you find that you're driving in the wrong direction?

- [ ] **A** Turn into a side road on the right and reverse into the main road
- [ ] **B** Make a U-turn in the main road
- [ ] **C** Make a 'three-point' turn in the main road
- [ ] **D** Turn around in a side road

Don't turn around in a busy street or reverse from a side road into a main road. Find a quiet side road and choose a place to turn around where you won't obstruct an entrance or exit. Look out for pedestrians and cyclists as well as other traffic.

497 Mark *one* answer
When may you drive without wearing your seat belt?

- [ ] **A** When you're carrying out a manoeuvre that includes reversing
- [ ] **B** When you're moving off on a hill
- [ ] **C** When you're testing your brakes
- [ ] **D** When you're driving slowly in queuing traffic

You may remove your seat belt while you're carrying out a manoeuvre that includes reversing. However, you must remember to put it back on again before you resume driving.

498 Mark *one* answer
How far are you allowed to reverse?

☐ **A** No further than is necessary
☐ **B** No more than a car's length
☐ **C** As far as it takes to reverse around a corner
☐ **D** The length of a residential street

You mustn't reverse further than is necessary. You may decide to turn your vehicle around by reversing into an opening or side road. When you reverse, always look all around you and watch for pedestrians. Don't reverse from a side road into a main road.

499 Mark *one* answer
What should you do when you're unsure whether it's safe to reverse your vehicle?

☐ **A** Sound your horn
☐ **B** Rev your engine
☐ **C** Get out and check
☐ **D** Reverse slowly

A small child could be hidden directly behind you, so, if you can't see all around your vehicle, get out and have a look. You could also ask someone reliable outside the vehicle to guide you.

500 Mark *one* answer
Why could it be dangerous to reverse from a side road into a main road?

☐ **A** Your reverse sensors will beep
☐ **B** Your view will be restricted
☐ **C** Your reversing lights will be hidden
☐ **D** Your mirrors will need adjusting

Don't reverse into a main road from a side road because your view will be restricted. The main road is likely to be busy and the traffic on it moving quickly.

501 Mark *one* answer
You want to turn right at a box junction. What should you do if there's oncoming traffic?

☐ **A** Wait in the box junction if your exit is clear
☐ **B** Wait before the junction until it's clear of all traffic
☐ **C** Drive on; you can't turn right at a box junction
☐ **D** Drive slowly into the box junction when signalled by oncoming traffic

You can wait in the box junction as long as your exit is clear. At some point there'll be a gap in the oncoming traffic, or the traffic lights will change, allowing you to proceed.

502 Mark *one* answer
You're reversing into a side road. When would your vehicle be the greatest hazard to passing traffic?

☐ **A** After you've completed the manoeuvre
☐ **B** Just before you begin to manoeuvre
☐ **C** After you've entered the side road
☐ **D** When the front of your vehicle swings out

Always check in all directions before reversing. Keep a good lookout throughout the manoeuvre and remember that the front will swing out as you reverse into the side road. Act on what you see and wait if necessary.

503 Mark *one* answer
Where's the safest place to park your vehicle at night?

☐ **A** In a garage
☐ **B** On a busy road
☐ **C** In a quiet car park
☐ **D** Near a red route

If you have a garage, use it. Your vehicle is less likely to be a victim of car crime if it's in a garage. Also, in winter, the windows will be kept free from ice and snow.

504 Mark *one* answer
When may you stop on an urban clearway?

☐ **A** To set down and pick up passengers
☐ **B** To use a mobile telephone
☐ **C** To ask for directions
☐ **D** To load or unload goods

Urban clearways have their times of operation clearly signed. You may only stop to pick up or set down passengers.

505 Mark *one* answer
You're looking for somewhere to park your vehicle. Neither you nor your passenger are disabled. What should you do if the only free spaces are marked for disabled drivers?

☐ **A** Use one of these spaces
☐ **B** Park in one of these spaces but stay with your vehicle
☐ **C** Use one of the spaces as long as one is kept free
☐ **D** Wait for a regular parking space to become free

It's illegal to park in a space reserved for disabled drivers unless you're permitted to do so. These spaces are provided for people with limited mobility, who may need extra space to get in and out of their vehicle.

506 Mark *one* answer
You're on a road that's only wide enough for one vehicle. What should you do if a car is coming towards you?

☐ **A** Pull into a passing place on your right
☐ **B** Force the other driver to reverse
☐ **C** Pull into a passing place if your vehicle is wider
☐ **D** Pull into a passing place on your left

Pull into the nearest passing place on the left if you meet another vehicle on a narrow road. If the nearest passing place is on the right, wait opposite it.

507 Mark *one* answer
You're driving at night with your headlights on main beam. A vehicle is overtaking you. When should you dip your headlights?

☐ **A** Some time after the vehicle has passed you
☐ **B** Before the vehicle starts to pass you
☐ **C** Only if the other driver dips their headlights
☐ **D** As soon as the vehicle passes you

On main beam, your lights could dazzle the driver in front. Dip your headlights as soon as the driver passes you and drop back so that the dipped beam falls short of the vehicle in front.

508 Mark *one* answer
When may you drive a car in this bus lane?

☐ **A** Outside its hours of operation
☐ **B** To get to the front of a traffic queue
☐ **C** You may not use it at any time
☐ **D** To overtake slow-moving traffic

Some bus lanes operate only during peak hours and other vehicles may use them outside these hours. Make sure you check the sign for the hours of operation before driving in a bus lane.

509 Mark *one* answer
Other than direction indicators, how can you give signals to other road users?

☐ **A** By using brake lights
☐ **B** By using sidelights
☐ **C** By using fog lights
☐ **D** By using interior lights

Your brake lights will give an indication to traffic behind that you're slowing down. Good anticipation will allow you time to check your mirrors before slowing.

510 Mark *one* answer
You're parked in a busy high street. What's the safest way to turn your vehicle around so you can drive in the opposite direction?

☐ **A** Turn around in a quiet side road
☐ **B** Drive into a side road and reverse out into the main road
☐ **C** Ask someone to stop the traffic
☐ **D** Carry out a U-turn

Make sure you carry out the manoeuvre without causing a hazard to other vehicles. Choose a place to turn that's safe and considers other road users.

511 Mark *one* answer
Where should you park your vehicle at night?

☐ **A** Near a police station
☐ **B** In a quiet road
☐ **C** On a red route
☐ **D** In a well-lit area

When you're parking at night, park in a well-lit area. This can help deter criminals from targeting your vehicle.

512 Mark *one* answer
You're driving in the right-hand lane of a dual carriageway. What should you do if you see a sign showing that the right-hand lane is closed 800 yards ahead?

☐ **A** Keep in that lane until you reach the queue
☐ **B** Move to the left immediately
☐ **C** Wait and see which lane is moving faster
☐ **D** Move to the left in good time

Keep a lookout for traffic signs. If you're directed to change lanes, do so in good time. Don't
- push your way into traffic in another lane
- try to gain advantage by delaying changing lanes.

513 Mark *one* answer

You're driving on a road that has a cycle lane. What does it mean if the lane is marked by a broken white line?

- ☐ **A** You shouldn't drive in the lane unless it's unavoidable
- ☐ **B** There's a reduced speed limit for motor vehicles using the lane
- ☐ **C** Cyclists can travel in both directions in that lane
- ☐ **D** The lane must be used by motorcyclists in heavy traffic

Cycle lanes are marked with either a solid or a broken white line. If the line is solid, you should check the times of operation shown on the signs, and not drive or park in the lane during those times. If the line is broken, you shouldn't drive or park in the lane unless it's unavoidable.

514 Mark *one* answer

When are you allowed to park in a parking bay for disabled drivers?

- ☐ **A** When you have a Blue Badge
- ☐ **B** When you have a wheelchair
- ☐ **C** When you have an advanced driver certificate
- ☐ **D** When you have an adapted vehicle

Don't park in a space reserved for disabled people unless you or your passenger are a Blue Badge holder. The badge must be displayed on the dashboard or facia panel, where it can be clearly read through the front windscreen.

515 Mark *one* answer

When must you stop your vehicle?

- ☐ **A** If you're involved in an incident that causes damage or injury
- ☐ **B** At a junction where there are 'give way' lines
- ☐ **C** At the end of a one-way street
- ☐ **D** Before merging onto a motorway

You must stop your vehicle when signalled to do so by a

- police, DVSA or traffic officer
- traffic warden
- school crossing patrol
- red traffic light.

You must also stop if you're involved in an incident that causes damage or injury to any other person, vehicle, animal or property.

516 Mark *one* answer
How can you identify traffic signs that give orders?

- ☐ **A** They're rectangular with a yellow border
- ☐ **B** They're triangular with a blue border
- ☐ **C** They're square with a brown border
- ☐ **D** They're circular with a red border

There are three basic types of traffic sign: those that warn, those that inform and those that give orders. Generally, triangular signs warn, rectangular signs give information or directions and circular signs give orders. An exception is the eight-sided 'stop' sign.

517 Mark *one* answer
What shape are traffic signs giving orders?

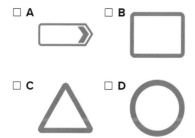

Road signs in the shape of a circle give orders. Those with a red circle are mostly prohibitive. The 'stop' sign is octagonal to give it greater prominence. Signs giving orders must always be obeyed.

518 Mark *one* answer
Which type of sign tells you what you must not do?

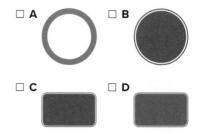

Signs in the shape of a circle give orders. A sign with a red circle means that you aren't allowed to do something. Study *Know Your Traffic Signs* to ensure that you understand what the different traffic signs mean.

519 Mark *one* answer
What does this sign mean?

☐ **A** Maximum speed limit with traffic calming
☐ **B** Minimum speed limit with traffic calming
☐ **C** '20 cars only' parking zone
☐ **D** Only 20 cars allowed at any one time

If you're in a place where there are likely to be pedestrians (for example, outside a school, near a park, in a residential area or in a shopping area), you should be cautious and keep your speed down. Many local authorities have taken steps to slow traffic down by creating traffic-calming measures such as road humps. They're there for a reason; slow down.

520 Mark *one* answer
What does this sign mean?

☐ **A** New speed limit 20 mph
☐ **B** No vehicles over 30 tonnes
☐ **C** Minimum speed limit 30 mph
☐ **D** End of 20 mph zone

Where you see this sign, the 20 mph restriction ends and a 30 mph restriction starts. Check all around for possible hazards and only increase your speed if it's safe to do so.

521 Mark *one* answer
What does this sign mean?

☐ **A** No overtaking
☐ **B** No motor vehicles
☐ **C** Clearway (no stopping)
☐ **D** Cars and motorcycles only

A sign will indicate which types of vehicles are prohibited from certain roads. Make sure that you know which signs apply to the vehicle you're using.

522 Mark *one* answer
What does this sign mean?

- ☐ **A** No parking
- ☐ **B** No road markings
- ☐ **C** No through road
- ☐ **D** No entry

'No entry' signs are used in places such as one-way streets to prevent vehicles driving against the traffic. To ignore one would be dangerous, both for yourself and for other road users, as well as being against the law.

523 Mark *one* answer
What does this sign mean?

- ☐ **A** Bend to the right
- ☐ **B** Road on the right closed
- ☐ **C** No traffic from the right
- ☐ **D** No right turn

The 'no right turn' sign may be used to warn road users that there's a 'no entry' prohibition on a road to the right ahead.

524 Mark *one* answer
Which sign means 'no entry'?

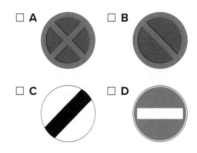

- ☐ **A**
- ☐ **B**
- ☐ **C**
- ☐ **D**

Look for and obey traffic signs. Disobeying or not seeing a sign could be dangerous. It may also be an offence for which you could be prosecuted.

525 Mark *one* answer
What does this sign mean?

Only

- ☐ **A** Route for trams only
- ☐ **B** Route for buses only
- ☐ **C** Parking for buses only
- ☐ **D** Parking for trams only

Avoid blocking tram routes. Trams are fixed on their route and can't manoeuvre around other vehicles or pedestrians. Modern trams travel quickly and are quiet, so you might not hear them approaching.

526 Mark *one* answer
Which type of vehicle does this sign apply to?

- ☐ **A** Wide vehicles
- ☐ **B** Long vehicles
- ☐ **C** High vehicles
- ☐ **D** Heavy vehicles

The triangular shapes above and below the dimensions indicate a height restriction that applies to the road ahead.

527 Mark *one* answer
Which sign means no motor vehicles allowed?

☐ **A**   ☐ **B**

☐ **C**   ☐ **D**

This sign is used to enable pedestrians to walk free from traffic. It's often found in shopping areas.

528 Mark *one* answer
What does this sign mean?

- ☐ **A** You have priority
- ☐ **B** No motor vehicles
- ☐ **C** Two-way traffic
- ☐ **D** No overtaking

Road signs that prohibit overtaking are placed in locations where passing the vehicle in front is dangerous. If you see this sign, don't attempt to overtake. The sign is there for a reason; you must obey it.

529 Mark *one* answer
What does this sign mean?

- ☐ **A** Waiting restrictions apply
- ☐ **B** Waiting permitted
- ☐ **C** National speed limit applies
- ☐ **D** Clearway (no stopping)

There'll be a plate or additional sign to tell you when the restrictions apply.

530 Mark *one* answer
What does this sign mean?

- ☐ **A** End of restricted speed area
- ☐ **B** End of restricted parking area
- ☐ **C** End of clearway
- ☐ **D** End of cycle route

Even though you've left the restricted area, make sure that you park where you won't endanger other road users or cause an obstruction.

531 Mark *one* answer
Which sign means 'no stopping'?

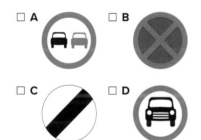

Stopping where this clearway restriction applies is likely to cause congestion. Allow the traffic to flow by obeying the signs.

532 Mark *one* answer
What does this sign mean?

- ☐ **A** National speed limit applies
- ☐ **B** Waiting restrictions apply
- ☐ **C** No stopping
- ☐ **D** No entry

This is the sign for a clearway. Clearways are stretches of road where you aren't allowed to stop unless it's an emergency. Stopping where these restrictions apply may be dangerous and is likely to cause an obstruction. Restrictions might apply for several miles and this may be indicated on the sign.

533 Mark *one* answer
What does this sign mean?

- ☐ **A** Distance to parking place ahead
- ☐ **B** Distance to public telephone ahead
- ☐ **C** Distance to public house ahead
- ☐ **D** Distance to passing place ahead

If you intend to stop and rest, this sign allows you time to reduce speed and pull over safely.

534 Mark *one* answer
What does this sign mean?

☐ **A** Vehicles may not park on the verge or footway
☐ **B** Vehicles may park on the left-hand } side of the road only
☐ **C** Vehicles may park fully on the verge or footway
☐ **D** Vehicles may park on the right-hand side of the road only

In order to keep roads free from parked cars, there are some areas where you're allowed to park on the verge. Only do this where you see the sign. Parking on verges or footways anywhere else could lead to a fine.

535 Mark *one* answer
What does this traffic sign mean?

☐ **A** No overtaking allowed
☐ **B** Give priority to oncoming traffic
☐ **C** Two-way traffic
☐ **D** One-way traffic only

Priority signs are normally shown where the road is narrow and there isn't enough room for two vehicles to pass. Examples are narrow bridges, roadworks and where there's a width restriction. Make sure you know who has priority; don't force your way through. Show courtesy and consideration to other road users.

536 Mark *one* answer
What's the meaning of this traffic sign?

- ☐ **A** End of two-way road
- ☐ **B** Give priority to vehicles coming towards you
- ☐ **C** You have priority over vehicles coming towards you
- ☐ **D** Bus lane ahead

Don't force your way through. Show courtesy and consideration to other road users. Although you have priority, make sure oncoming traffic is going to give way before you continue.

537 Mark *one* answer
What shape is a 'stop' sign?

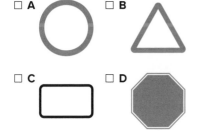

- ☐ **A**
- ☐ **B**
- ☐ **C**
- ☐ **D**

To make it easy to recognise, the 'stop' sign is the only sign of this shape. You must stop and take effective observation before proceeding.

538 Mark *one* answer
In winter, road signs can become covered by snow. What does this sign mean?

- ☐ **A** Crossroads
- ☐ **B** Give way
- ☐ **C** Stop
- ☐ **D** Turn right

The 'stop' sign is the only road sign that's octagonal. This is so that it can be recognised and obeyed even if it's obscured (for example, by snow).

539 Mark *one* answer
What does this sign mean?

- ☐ **A** Service area 30 miles ahead
- ☐ **B** Maximum speed 30 mph
- ☐ **C** Minimum speed 30 mph
- ☐ **D** Lay-by 30 miles ahead

This sign is shown where slow-moving vehicles would impede the flow of traffic; for example, in tunnels. However, if you need to slow down or even stop to avoid an incident or potential collision, you should do so.

540 Mark *one* answer
What does this sign mean?

- ☐ **A** Give way to oncoming vehicles
- ☐ **B** Approaching traffic passes you on both sides
- ☐ **C** Turn off at the next available junction
- ☐ **D** Pass either side to get to the same destination

These signs are often seen in one-way streets that have more than one lane. When you see this sign, use the route that's the most convenient and doesn't require a late change of direction.

541 Mark *one* answer
What does this sign mean?

- ☐ **A** Route for trams
- ☐ **B** Give way to trams
- ☐ **C** Route for buses
- ☐ **D** Give way to buses

Take extra care when you encounter trams. Look out for road markings and signs that alert you to them. Modern trams are very quiet and you may not hear them approaching.

542 Mark *one* answer
What messages are given by circular traffic signs that have a blue background?

- ☐ **A** They give temporary directions during a diversion
- ☐ **B** They give directions to car parks
- ☐ **C** They give motorway information
- ☐ **D** They give mandatory instructions

Signs with blue circles generally give mandatory instruction. These are often found in urban areas and include signs for mini-roundabouts and directional arrows.

543 Mark *one* answer
Where would you see a contraflow bus lane?

- ☐ **A** On a dual carriageway
- ☐ **B** On a roundabout
- ☐ **C** On an urban motorway
- ☐ **D** On a one-way street

The traffic permitted to use a contraflow lane travels in the opposite direction to traffic in the other lanes on the road.

544 Mark *one* answer
What does this sign mean?

- ☐ **A** Bus station on the right
- ☐ **B** Contraflow bus lane
- ☐ **C** With-flow bus lane
- ☐ **D** Give way to buses

There will also be markings on the road surface to indicate the bus lane. You mustn't use this lane for parking or overtaking.

545 Mark *one* answer
What does a sign with a brown background show?

- ☐ **A** Tourist directions
- ☐ **B** Primary roads
- ☐ **C** Motorway routes
- ☐ **D** Minor roads

Signs with a brown background give directions to places of interest. They're often seen on a motorway, directing you along the easiest route to the attraction.

546 Mark *one* answer
What does this sign mean?

- ☐ **A** Tourist attraction
- ☐ **B** Beware of trains
- ☐ **C** Level crossing
- ☐ **D** Beware of trams

These signs indicate places of interest and are designed to guide you by the easiest route. They're particularly useful when you're unfamiliar with the area.

547 Mark *one* answer
What's the purpose of triangular shaped signs?

- ☐ **A** To give warnings
- ☐ **B** To give information
- ☐ **C** To give orders
- ☐ **D** To give directions

Triangular signs warn you of hazards ahead. Make sure you look at each sign that you pass on the road, so that you don't miss any vital instructions or information.

548 Mark *one* answer
What does this sign mean?

- ☐ **A** Turn left ahead
- ☐ **B** T-junction
- ☐ **C** No through road
- ☐ **D** Give way

This type of sign warns you of hazards ahead. Make sure you look at each sign and road marking that you pass, so that you don't miss any vital instructions or information. This sign shows there's a T-junction with priority over vehicles from the right.

549 Mark *one* answer
What does this sign mean?

- ☐ **A** Multi-exit roundabout
- ☐ **B** Risk of ice
- ☐ **C** Six roads converge
- ☐ **D** Place of historical interest

It will take up to 10 times longer to stop when it's icy. Where there's a risk of icy conditions, you need to be aware of this and take extra care. If you think the road may be icy, don't brake or steer harshly, as your tyres could lose their grip on the road.

550 Mark *one* answer
What does this sign mean?

- ☐ **A** Crossroads
- ☐ **B** Level crossing with gate
- ☐ **C** Level crossing without gate
- ☐ **D** Ahead only

The priority through the junction is shown by the broader line. You need to be aware of the hazard posed by traffic crossing or pulling out onto a major road.

551 Mark *one* answer
What does this sign mean?

- ☐ **A** Ring road
- ☐ **B** Mini-roundabout
- ☐ **C** No vehicles
- ☐ **D** Roundabout

As you approach a roundabout, look well ahead and check all signs. Decide which exit you wish to take and move into the correct position as you approach the roundabout, signalling as required.

552 Mark *one* answer
What information would be shown in a triangular road sign?

- ☐ **A** Road narrows
- ☐ **B** Ahead only
- ☐ **C** Keep left
- ☐ **D** Minimum speed

Warning signs are there to make you aware of potential hazards on the road ahead. Take note of the signs so you're prepared and can take whatever action is necessary.

553 Mark *one* answer
What does this sign mean?

- ☐ **A** Cyclists must dismount
- ☐ **B** Cycles aren't allowed
- ☐ **C** Cycle route ahead
- ☐ **D** Cycle in single file

Where there's a cycle route ahead, a sign will show a bicycle in a red warning triangle. Watch out for children on bicycles and cyclists rejoining the main road.

554 Mark *one* answer
Which sign means that pedestrians may be walking along the road?

☐ **A**   ☐ **B**

☐ **C**   ☐ **D**

When you pass pedestrians in the road, leave plenty of room. You might have to use the right-hand side of the road, so look well ahead, as well as in your mirrors, before pulling out. Take great care if a bend in the road obscures your view ahead.

555 Mark *one* answer
Which sign means there's a double bend ahead?

☐ **A**    ☐ **B**

☐ **C**   ☐ **D**

Triangular signs give you a warning of hazards ahead. They're there to give you time to prepare for the hazard; for example, by adjusting your speed.

556 Mark *one* answer
What does this sign mean?

- ☐ **A** Wait at the barriers
- ☐ **B** Wait at the crossroads
- ☐ **C** Give way to trams
- ☐ **D** Give way to farm vehicles

Obey the 'give way' signs. Trams are unable to steer around you if you misjudge when it's safe to enter the junction.

557 Mark *one* answer
What does this sign mean?

- ☐ **A** Hump bridge
- ☐ **B** Humps in the road
- ☐ **C** Entrance to tunnel
- ☐ **D** Soft verges

These humps have been put in place to slow the traffic down. They're usually found in residential areas. Slow down to an appropriate speed.

558 Mark *one* answer
Which sign means the end of a dual carriageway?

☐ **A**   ☐ **B**

☐ **C**   ☐ **D**

If you're overtaking, make sure you move back safely into the left-hand lane before you reach the end of the dual carriageway.

559 Mark *one* answer
What does this sign mean?

- ☐ **A** End of dual carriageway
- ☐ **B** Tall bridge
- ☐ **C** Road narrows
- ☐ **D** End of narrow bridge

Don't wait until the last moment before moving into the left-hand lane. Plan ahead and don't rely on other traffic letting you in.

560 Mark *one* answer
What does this sign mean?

- ☐ **A** Side winds
- ☐ **B** Road noise
- ☐ **C** Airport
- ☐ **D** Adverse camber

A warning sign with a picture of a windsock indicates that there may be strong side winds. This sign is often found on exposed roads.

---

561 Mark *one* answer
What does this traffic sign mean?

- ☐ **A** Slippery road ahead
- ☐ **B** Tyres liable to punctures ahead
- ☐ **C** Danger ahead
- ☐ **D** Service area ahead

This sign is there to alert you to the likelihood of danger ahead. It may be accompanied by a plate indicating the type of hazard. Be ready to reduce your speed and take avoiding action.

562 Mark *one* answer
You're about to overtake. What should you do when you see this sign?

Hidden dip

- ☐ **A** Overtake the other driver as quickly as possible
- ☐ **B** Move to the right to get a better view
- ☐ **C** Switch your headlights on before overtaking
- ☐ **D** Hold back until you can see clearly ahead

You won't be able to see any hazards that might be hidden in the dip. As well as oncoming traffic, the dip may conceal
- cyclists
- horse riders
- parked vehicles
- pedestrians in the road.

563 Mark *one* answer
What does this sign mean?

- ☐ **A** Level crossing with gate or barrier
- ☐ **B** Gated road ahead
- ☐ **C** Level crossing without gate or barrier
- ☐ **D** Cattle grid ahead

Some crossings have gates but no attendant or signals. You should stop, look both ways, listen and make sure that no train is approaching. If there's a telephone, contact the signal operator to make sure it's safe to cross.

564 Mark *one* answer
What does this sign mean?

- ☐ **A** No trams ahead
- ☐ **B** Oncoming trams
- ☐ **C** Trams crossing ahead
- ☐ **D** Trams only

This sign tells you to beware of trams. If you don't usually drive in a town where there are trams, remember to look out for them at junctions and look for tram rails, signs and signals.

565 Mark *one* answer
What does this sign mean?

- ☐ **A** Adverse camber
- ☐ **B** Steep hill downwards
- ☐ **C** Uneven road
- ☐ **D** Steep hill upwards

This sign gives you an early warning that the road ahead will slope downhill. Prepare to alter your speed and gear. Looking at the sign from left to right will show you whether the road slopes uphill or downhill.

566 Mark *one* answer
What does this sign mean?

- ☐ **A** Uneven road surface
- ☐ **B** Bridge over the road
- ☐ **C** Road ahead ends
- ☐ **D** Water across the road

This sign is found where a shallow stream crosses the road. Heavy rainfall could increase the flow of water. If the water looks too deep or the stream has spread over a large distance, stop and find another route.

567 Mark *one* answer
What does this sign mean?

- ☐ **A** Turn left for parking area
- ☐ **B** No through road on the left
- ☐ **C** No entry for traffic turning left
- ☐ **D** Turn left for ferry terminal

This sign shows you that you can't get through to another route by turning left at the junction ahead.

568 Mark *one* answer
What does this sign mean?

- ☐ **A** T-junction
- ☐ **B** No through road
- ☐ **C** Telephone box ahead
- ☐ **D** Toilet ahead

You won't be able to find a through route to another road. Use this road only for access.

569 Mark *one* answer
Which is the sign for a ring road?

☐ **A**   ☐ **B**

☐ **C**   ☐ **D**

Ring roads are designed to relieve congestion in towns and city centres.

570 Mark *one* answer
What does this sign mean?

- ☐ **A** The right-hand lane ahead is narrow
- ☐ **B** Right-hand lane for buses only
- ☐ **C** Right-hand lane for turning right
- ☐ **D** The right-hand lane is closed

Yellow-and-black temporary signs may be used to inform you about roadworks or lane restrictions. Look well ahead. If you have to change lanes, do so in good time.

571 Mark *one* answer
What does this sign mean?

- ☐ **A** Change to the left-hand lane
- ☐ **B** Leave at the next exit
- ☐ **C** Contraflow system
- ☐ **D** One-way street

If you use the right-hand lane in a contraflow system, you'll be travelling with no permanent barrier between you and the oncoming traffic. Observe speed limits and keep a good distance from the vehicle ahead.

572 Mark *one* answer
What does this sign mean?

- ☐ **A** Leave motorway at next exit
- ☐ **B** Lane for heavy and slow vehicles
- ☐ **C** All lorries use the hard shoulder
- ☐ **D** Rest area for lorries

Where there's a long, steep, uphill gradient on a motorway, a crawler lane may be provided. This helps the traffic to flow by diverting the slower heavy vehicles into a dedicated lane on the left.

573 Mark *one* answer
What does a red traffic light mean?

- ☐ **A** You should stop unless turning left
- ☐ **B** Stop, if you're able to brake safely
- ☐ **C** You must stop and wait behind the stop line
- ☐ **D** Proceed with care

Whatever light is showing, you should know which light is going to appear next and be able to take appropriate action. For example, when amber is showing on its own, you'll know that red will appear next. This should give you ample time to anticipate and respond safely.

574 Mark *one* answer
At traffic lights, what does it mean when the amber light shows on its own?

- ☐ **A** Prepare to go
- ☐ **B** Go if the way is clear
- ☐ **C** Go if no pedestrians are crossing
- ☐ **D** Stop at the stop line

When the amber light is showing on its own, the red light will follow next. The amber light means stop, unless you've already crossed the stop line or you're so close to it that stopping may cause a collision.

575 Mark *one* answer
You're at a junction controlled by traffic lights. When should you wait at a green light?

- ☐ **A** When pedestrians are waiting to cross
- ☐ **B** When your exit from the junction is blocked
- ☐ **C** When you think the lights may be about to change
- ☐ **D** When you intend to turn right

As you approach the traffic lights, look into the road you wish to take. Only proceed if your exit road is clear. If the road is blocked, hold back, even if you have to wait for the next green signal.

576 Mark *one* answer
You're in the left-hand lane at traffic lights, waiting to turn left. Which signal means you must wait?

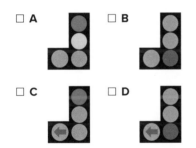

☐ A   ☐ B

☐ C   ☐ D

At some junctions, there may be separate signals for different lanes. These are called 'filter' lights. They're designed to help traffic flow at major junctions. Make sure that you're in the correct lane and proceed if the way is clear and the green light shows for your lane.

577 Mark *one* answer
What does this sign mean?

- ☐ **A** Traffic lights out of order
- ☐ **B** Amber signal out of order
- ☐ **C** Temporary traffic lights ahead
- ☐ **D** New traffic lights ahead

You might see this sign where traffic lights are out of order. Proceed with caution, as nobody has priority at the junction.

578 Mark *one* answer
Who has priority when traffic lights are out of order?

- ☐ **A** Traffic going straight on
- ☐ **B** Traffic turning right
- ☐ **C** Nobody
- ☐ **D** Traffic turning left

When traffic lights are out of order, you should treat the junction as an unmarked crossroads. Be cautious, as you may need to give way or stop. Look for traffic attempting to cross the junction, unaware that it doesn't have priority.

579 Mark *one* answer
Where would you find these flashing red light signals?

☐ **A** Pelican crossings
☐ **B** Motorway exits
☐ **C** Zebra crossings
☐ **D** Level crossings

These signals are found at level crossings, swing or lifting bridges, some airfields and emergency access sites. The flashing red lights mean stop whether or not the way seems to be clear.

580 Mark *one* answer
What do these zigzag white lines mean?

☐ **A** No parking at any time
☐ **B** Parking allowed only for a short time
☐ **C** Slow down to 20 mph
☐ **D** Sounding horns isn't allowed

The approach to, and exit from, a pedestrian crossing is marked with zigzag lines. You mustn't park on them or overtake the leading vehicle when approaching the crossing. Parking here would block the view for pedestrians and approaching traffic.

581 Mark *one* answer
When may you cross a double solid white line in the middle of the road?

☐ **A** To pass traffic that's queuing back at a junction
☐ **B** To pass a car signalling to turn left ahead
☐ **C** To pass a road maintenance vehicle travelling at 10 mph or less
☐ **D** To pass a vehicle that's towing a trailer

You may cross the solid white line to pass a stationary vehicle or to pass a pedal cycle, horse or road maintenance vehicle if it's travelling at 10 mph or less. You may also cross the solid white line to enter a side road or access a property.

582 Mark *one* answer
What does this road marking mean?

- ☐ **A** Don't cross the line
- ☐ **B** No stopping allowed
- ☐ **C** You're approaching a hazard
- ☐ **D** No overtaking allowed

A single broken line along the centre of the road, with long markings and short gaps, is a hazard warning line. Don't cross it unless you can see that the road is clear well ahead.

583 Mark *one* answer
Where would you see this road marking?

- ☐ **A** At traffic lights
- ☐ **B** On road humps
- ☐ **C** Near a level crossing
- ☐ **D** At a box junction

Because the road has a dark colour, changes in level aren't easily seen. White triangles painted on the road surface give you an indication of where there are road humps.

584 Mark *one* answer
Which diagram shows a hazard warning line?

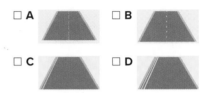

- ☐ **A**
- ☐ **B**
- ☐ **C**
- ☐ **D**

You need to know the difference between the normal centre line and a hazard warning line. If there's a hazard ahead, the markings are longer and the gaps shorter. This gives you advance warning of an unspecified hazard.

585 Mark *one* answer
Why does this junction have a 'stop' sign and a stop line on the road?

- ☐ **A** Speed on the major road is derestricted
- ☐ **B** It's a busy junction
- ☐ **C** Visibility along the major road is restricted
- ☐ **D** The junction is on a downhill gradient

Where emerging traffic has a very restricted view of the main road, you may find a 'stop' sign and a solid white stop line. You must stop at the line and then check carefully before you emerge.

586 Mark *one* answer

What does this line across the road at the entrance to a roundabout mean?

- ☐ **A** Give way to traffic from the right
- ☐ **B** Traffic from the left has right of way
- ☐ **C** You have right of way
- ☐ **D** Stop at the line

Slow down as you approach the roundabout and check for traffic from the right. If you need to stop and give way, stay behind the broken line until it's safe to emerge onto the roundabout.

587 Mark *one* answer

How will a police officer in a patrol vehicle signal for you to stop?

- ☐ **A** Flash the headlights, indicate left and point to the left
- ☐ **B** Overtake and give a slowing down arm signal
- ☐ **C** Use the siren, overtake, cut in front and stop
- ☐ **D** Pull alongside you, use the siren and wave you to stop

You must obey signals given by the police. If a police officer in a patrol vehicle wants you to pull over, they'll indicate this without causing danger to you or other traffic.

588 Mark *one* answer

You're approaching a junction where the traffic lights aren't working. What should you do when a police officer gives this signal?

- ☐ **A** Turn left only
- ☐ **B** Turn right only
- ☐ **C** Continue ahead only
- ☐ **D** Stop at the stop line

When a police officer or traffic warden is directing traffic, you must obey them. They'll use the arm signals shown in *The Highway Code*. Learn what these signals mean and obey them.

589 Mark *one* answer
What does this arm signal mean?

- ☐ **A** The driver is slowing down
- ☐ **B** The driver intends to turn right
- ☐ **C** The driver wishes to overtake
- ☐ **D** The driver intends to turn left

There might be an occasion where another driver uses an arm signal. This may be because the vehicle's indicators are obscured by other traffic. In order for such signals to be effective, all drivers should know their meaning. Be aware that the 'left turn' signal might look similar to the 'slowing down' signal.

590 Mark *one* answer
What does this motorway sign mean?

- ☐ **A** Change to the lane on your left
- ☐ **B** Leave the motorway at the next exit
- ☐ **C** Change to the opposite carriageway
- ☐ **D** Pull up on the hard shoulder

On the motorway, signs sometimes show temporary warnings due to traffic or weather conditions. They may be used to indicate
- lane closures
- temporary speed limits
- weather warnings.

591 Mark *one* answer
What does this motorway sign mean?

- ☐ **A** Temporary minimum speed 50 mph
- ☐ **B** No services for 50 miles
- ☐ **C** Obstruction 50 metres (164 feet) ahead
- ☐ **D** Temporary maximum speed 50 mph

Look out for signs above your lane or on the central reservation. These will give you important information or warnings about the road ahead. To allow for the high speed of motorway traffic, these signs may light up some distance from any hazard. Don't ignore the signs just because the road looks clear to you.

592 Mark *one* answer
What does this sign mean?

- ☐ **A** Through traffic to use left lane
- ☐ **B** Right-hand lane T-junction only
- ☐ **C** Right-hand lane closed ahead
- ☐ **D** 11 tonne weight limit

You should change lanes as directed by the sign. Here, the right-hand lane is closed but the left-hand and centre lanes are available. Merging in turn is recommended when it's safe and traffic is going slowly; for example, at roadworks or a road traffic incident. When vehicles are travelling at speed, this isn't advisable and you should move into the appropriate lane in good time.

593 Mark *one* answer
What does '25' mean on this motorway sign?

- ☐ **A** The distance to the nearest town
- ☐ **B** The route number of the road
- ☐ **C** The number of the next junction
- ☐ **D** The speed limit on the slip road

Before you set out on your journey, use a road map to plan your route. When you see an advance warning of your junction, make sure you get into the correct lane in plenty of time. Last-minute harsh braking and cutting across lanes at speed is extremely hazardous.

594 Mark *one* answer
How should the right-hand lane of a three-lane motorway be used?

- ☐ **A** As a high-speed lane
- ☐ **B** As an overtaking lane
- ☐ **C** As a right-turn lane
- ☐ **D** As an acceleration lane

You should stay in the left-hand lane of a motorway unless you're overtaking another vehicle. The right-hand lane of a motorway is an overtaking lane; it isn't the 'fast lane'. After overtaking, move back to the left when it's safe to do so.

595 Mark *one* answer
Where can you find reflective amber studs on a motorway?

- ☐ **A** Separating the slip road from the motorway
- ☐ **B** On the left-hand edge of the road
- ☐ **C** On the right-hand edge of the road
- ☐ **D** Separating the lanes

At night or in poor visibility, reflective studs on the road help you to judge your position on the carriageway.

596 Mark *one* answer
Where would you find green reflective studs on a motorway?

- ☐ **A** Separating driving lanes
- ☐ **B** Between the hard shoulder and the carriageway
- ☐ **C** At slip-road entrances and exits
- ☐ **D** Between the carriageway and the central reservation

Knowing the colours of the reflective studs on the road will help you judge your position, especially at night, in foggy conditions or when visibility is poor.

597 Mark *one* answer
What should you do when you see this sign as you travel along a motorway?

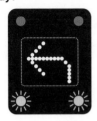

- ☐ **A** Leave the motorway at the next exit
- ☐ **B** Turn left immediately
- ☐ **C** Change lane
- ☐ **D** Move onto the hard shoulder

You'll see this sign if the motorway is closed ahead. Pull into the left-hand lane as soon as it's safe to do so. Don't wait until the last moment before you move across, because the lane may be busy and you'll have to rely on another driver making room for you.

598 Mark *one* answer
What does this sign mean?

- ☐ **A** No motor vehicles
- ☐ **B** End of motorway
- ☐ **C** No through road
- ☐ **D** End of bus lane

When you leave the motorway, make sure that you check your speedometer. You may be going faster than you realise. Slow down and look for speed-limit signs.

599 Mark *one* answer
Which sign means that the national speed limit applies?

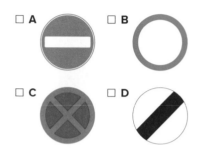

☐ A

☐ B

☐ C

☐ D

You should know the speed limit for the road on which you're travelling and for your vehicle. The different speed limits are shown in *The Highway Code*.

600 Mark *one* answer
What's the national speed limit on a single carriageway road?

☐ **A** 50 mph
☐ **B** 60 mph
☐ **C** 40 mph
☐ **D** 70 mph

If you're travelling on a dual carriageway that becomes a single carriageway road, reduce your speed gradually so that you aren't exceeding the limit as you enter. There might not be a sign to remind you of the limit, so make sure you know the speed limits for different types of road and vehicle.

601 Mark *one* answer
What does this sign mean?

☐ **A** End of motorway
☐ **B** End of restriction
☐ **C** Lane ends ahead
☐ **D** Free recovery ends

Temporary restrictions on motorways are shown on signs that have flashing amber lights. At the end of the restriction, you'll see this sign without any flashing lights.

602 Mark *one* answer
What does this sign indicate?

☐ **A** A diversion route
☐ **B** A picnic area
☐ **C** A pedestrian zone
☐ **D** A cycle route

When a diversion route has been put in place, drivers are advised to follow a symbol, which may be a black triangle, square, circle or diamond shape on a yellow background.

603 Mark *one* answer
What does this traffic sign mean?

- [ ] **A** Compulsory maximum speed limit
- [ ] **B** Advisory maximum speed limit
- [ ] **C** Compulsory minimum speed limit
- [ ] **D** Advised separation distance

The sign gives you an early warning of a speed restriction. If you're travelling at a higher speed, slow down in good time. You could come across queuing traffic due to roadworks or a temporary obstruction.

604 Mark *one* answer
What should you do when you see this sign at a crossroads?

- [ ] **A** Maintain the same speed
- [ ] **B** Carry on with great care
- [ ] **C** Find another route
- [ ] **D** Telephone the police

When traffic lights are out of order, treat the junction as an unmarked crossroads. Be very careful and be prepared to stop; no-one has priority.

605 Mark *one* answer
What does this sign mean?

- [ ] **A** Motorcycles only
- [ ] **B** No cars
- [ ] **C** Cars only
- [ ] **D** No motorcycles

You must comply with all traffic signs and be especially aware of those signs that apply specifically to the type of vehicle you're using.

606 Mark *one* answer
You're on a motorway. A lorry has stopped in the right-hand lane. What should you do when you see this sign on the lorry?

- [ ] **A** Move into the right-hand lane
- [ ] **B** Stop behind the flashing lights
- [ ] **C** Pass the lorry on the left
- [ ] **D** Leave the motorway at the next exit

Sometimes work is carried out on the motorway without closing the lanes. When this happens, signs are mounted on the back of lorries to warn other road users of the roadworks ahead.

607 Mark *one* answer

You're on a motorway. What should you do if there's a red cross showing on the signs above your lane only?

- [ ] **A** Continue in that lane and look for further information
- [ ] **B** Don't continue in that lane
- [ ] **C** Pull onto the hard shoulder
- [ ] **D** Stop and wait for an instruction to proceed

A red cross above your lane shows that your lane is closed. You should move into another lane as soon as you can do so safely.

608 Mark *one* answer

When may you sound your vehicle's horn?

- [ ] **A** To give you right of way
- [ ] **B** To attract a friend's attention
- [ ] **C** To warn others of your presence
- [ ] **D** To make slower drivers move over

Never sound your vehicle's horn aggressively. You mustn't sound it in a built-up area between 11.30 pm and 7.00 am, or when you're stationary, unless another road user poses a danger. Don't scare animals by sounding your horn.

609 Mark *one* answer

Your vehicle is stationary. When may you use its horn?

- [ ] **A** When another road user poses a danger
- [ ] **B** When the road is blocked by queuing traffic
- [ ] **C** When it's used only briefly
- [ ] **D** When signalling that you've just arrived

When your vehicle is stationary, only sound the horn if you think there's a risk of danger from another road user. Don't use it just to attract someone's attention. This causes unnecessary noise and could be misleading.

610 Mark *one* answer

What does this sign mean?

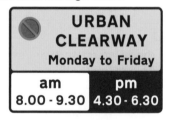

- [ ] **A** You can park on the days and times shown
- [ ] **B** No parking on the days and times shown
- [ ] **C** No parking at all from Monday to Friday
- [ ] **D** End of the urban clearway restrictions

Urban clearways are provided to keep traffic flowing at busy times. You may stop only briefly to set down or pick up passengers. Times of operation will vary from place to place, so always check the signs.

611 Mark *one* answer
What does this sign mean?

- ☐ **A** Quayside or river bank
- ☐ **B** Steep hill downwards
- ☐ **C** Uneven road surface
- ☐ **D** Road liable to flooding

You should be careful in these locations, as the road surface is likely to be wet and slippery. There may be a steep drop to the water, and there may not be a barrier along the edge of the road.

612 Mark *one* answer
Which sign means you have priority over oncoming vehicles?

☐ **A**   ☐ **B**

☐ **C**   ☐ **D**

Even though you have priority, be prepared to give way if other drivers don't. This will help to avoid congestion, confrontation or even a collision.

613 Mark *one* answer
What do the long white lines along the centre of the road mean?

- ☐ **A** Bus lane
- ☐ **B** Hazard warning
- ☐ **C** Give way
- ☐ **D** Lane marking

The centre of the road is usually marked by a broken white line, with lines that are shorter than the gaps. When the lines become longer than the gaps, this is a hazard warning line. Look well ahead for these, especially when you're planning to overtake or turn off.

614 Mark *one* answer
What's the reason for the hatched area along the centre of this road?

- ☐ **A** It separates traffic flowing in opposite directions
- ☐ **B** It marks an area to be used by overtaking motorcyclists
- ☐ **C** It's a temporary marking to warn of the roadworks
- ☐ **D** It separates the two sides of the dual carriageway

Areas of 'hatched markings' such as these separate traffic streams that could be a danger to each other. They're often seen on bends or where the road becomes narrow. If the area is bordered by a solid white line, you mustn't enter it except in an emergency.

615 Mark *one* answer
Other drivers may sometimes flash their headlights at you. What's the official meaning of this signal?

- ☐ **A** There's a radar speed trap ahead
- ☐ **B** They're giving way to you
- ☐ **C** They're warning you of their presence
- ☐ **D** There's a fault with your vehicle

If other drivers flash their headlights, this isn't a signal to show priority. The flashing of headlights has the same meaning as sounding the horn: it's a warning of their presence.

616 Mark *one* answer
What does this signal mean?

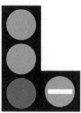

- ☐ **A** Cars must stop
- ☐ **B** Trams must stop
- ☐ **C** Both trams and cars must stop
- ☐ **D** Both trams and cars can continue

The white light shows that trams must stop. The green light shows that other vehicles can go if the way is clear. Trams are being introduced into more cities, so you're likely to come across them and you should learn which signs apply to them.

617 Mark *one* answer
Where would you find these road markings?

- ☐ **A** At a railway crossing
- ☐ **B** At a mini-roundabout
- ☐ **C** On a motorway
- ☐ **D** On a pedestrian crossing

These markings show the direction in which the traffic should go at a mini-roundabout.

618 Mark *one* answer
A police car is following you. What should you do if the police officer flashes the headlights and points to the left?

- ☐ **A** Turn left at the next junction
- ☐ **B** Pull up on the left
- ☐ **C** Stop immediately
- ☐ **D** Move over to the left

You must pull up on the left as soon as it's safe to do so and switch off your engine.

619 Mark *one* answer
You see this amber traffic light ahead. Which light, or lights, will come on next?

- ☐ **A** Red alone
- ☐ **B** Red and amber together
- ☐ **C** Green and amber together
- ☐ **D** Green alone

At junctions controlled by traffic lights, you must stop behind the white line until the lights change to green. A red light, an amber light, and red and amber lights showing together all mean stop. You may proceed when the light is green unless your exit road is blocked or pedestrians are crossing in front of you. If you're approaching traffic lights that are visible from a distance and the light has been green for some time, be ready to slow down and stop, because the lights are likely to change.

620 Mark *one* answer
What does it mean if you see this signal on the motorway?

- ☐ **A** Leave the motorway at the next exit
- ☐ **B** All vehicles use the hard shoulder
- ☐ **C** Sharp bend to the left ahead
- ☐ **D** Stop: all lanes ahead closed

You'll see this sign if there has been an incident ahead and the motorway is closed. You must obey the sign. Make sure that you prepare to leave in good time. Don't cause drivers to take avoiding action by cutting in at the last moment.

621 Mark *one* answer
What must you do when you see this sign?

- ☐ **A** Stop only if traffic is approaching
- ☐ **B** Stop even if the road is clear
- ☐ **C** Stop only if children are waiting to cross
- ☐ **D** Stop only if a red light is showing

'Stop' signs are situated at junctions where visibility is restricted or where there's heavy traffic. They must be obeyed: you must stop. Look carefully before moving off.

622 Mark *one* answer
Which shape is used for a 'give way' sign?

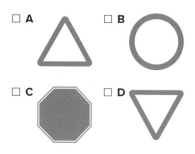

☐ **A**

☐ **B**

☐ **C**

☐ **D**

Other warning signs are the same shape and colour, but the 'give way' triangle points downwards. When you see this sign, you must give way to traffic on the road that you're about to enter.

623 Mark *one* answer
What does this sign mean?

☐ **A** Buses turning
☐ **B** Ring road
☐ **C** Mini-roundabout
☐ **D** Keep right

When you see this sign, look out for any direction signs and judge whether you need to signal your intentions. Do this in good time so that other road users approaching the roundabout know what you're planning to do.

624 Mark *one* answer
What does this sign mean?

☐ **A** Two-way traffic straight ahead
☐ **B** Two-way traffic crosses a one-way road
☐ **C** Two-way traffic over a bridge
☐ **D** Two-way traffic crosses a two-way road

Be prepared for traffic approaching from junctions on either side of you. Try to avoid unnecessary changing of lanes just before the junction.

625 Mark *one* answer
What does this sign mean?

☐ **A** Two-way traffic crosses a one-way road
☐ **B** Traffic approaching you has priority
☐ **C** Two-way traffic straight ahead
☐ **D** Motorway contraflow system ahead

This sign may be at the end of a dual carriageway or a one-way street. It's there to warn you of oncoming traffic.

626 Mark *one* answer
What does this sign mean?

- ☐ **A** Hump bridge
- ☐ **B** Traffic-calming hump
- ☐ **C** Low bridge
- ☐ **D** Uneven road

You'll need to slow down. At hump bridges, your view ahead will be restricted and the road will often be narrow. If the bridge is very steep, sound your horn to warn others of your approach. Going over the bridge too fast is highly dangerous to other road users and could even cause your wheels to leave the road, with a resulting loss of control.

627 Mark *one* answer
Which sign informs you that you're coming to a 'no through road'?

☐ **A**  ☐ **B**

☐ **C** ☐ **D**

This sign is found at the entrance to a road that can only be used for access.

628 Mark *one* answer
What does this sign mean?

- ☐ **A** Direction to park-and-ride car park
- ☐ **B** No parking for buses or coaches
- ☐ **C** Direction to bus and coach park
- ☐ **D** Parking area for cars and coaches

To ease the congestion in town centres, some cities and towns provide park-and-ride schemes. These allow you to park in a designated area and ride by bus into the centre. Park-and-ride schemes are usually cheaper and easier than car parking in the town centre.

629 Mark *one* answer
What should you do when you're approaching traffic lights that have red and amber showing together?

- ☐ **A** Pass the lights if the road is clear
- ☐ **B** Take care because there's a fault with the lights
- ☐ **C** Wait for the green light
- ☐ **D** Stop because the lights are changing to red

Be aware that other traffic might still be clearing the junction as you approach. A green light means you may go on, but only if the way is clear.

630 Mark *one* answer
You've stopped at a railway level crossing. What should you do if the red lights continue to flash after a train has gone by?

☐ **A** Phone the signal operator
☐ **B** Alert drivers behind you
☐ **C** Wait
☐ **D** Proceed with caution

You must always obey red flashing stop lights. If a train passes but the lights continue to flash, another train will be passing soon. Cross only when the lights go off and the barriers open.

---

631 Mark *one* answer
You're in a tunnel and you see this sign. What does it mean?

☐ **A** Direction to an emergency pedestrian exit
☐ **B** Beware of pedestrians: no footpath ahead
☐ **C** No access for pedestrians
☐ **D** Beware of pedestrians crossing ahead

If you have to leave your vehicle and get out of a tunnel by an emergency exit, do so as quickly as you can. Follow the signs directing you to the nearest exit point. If there are several people using the exit, don't panic but try to leave in a calm and orderly manner.

632 Mark *one* answer
Which sign shows that you're entering a one-way system?

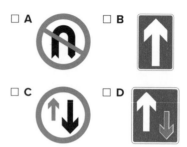

☐ **A**   ☐ **B**

☐ **C**   ☐ **D**

If the road has two lanes, you can use either lane and overtake on either side. Use the lane that's more convenient for your destination unless signs or road markings indicate otherwise.

633 Mark *one* answer
What does this sign mean?

- ☐ **A** With-flow bus and cycle lane
- ☐ **B** Contraflow bus and cycle lane
- ☐ **C** No buses and cycles allowed
- ☐ **D** No waiting for buses and cycles

Buses and cycles can travel in this lane. In this example, they'll flow in the same direction as other traffic. If it's busy, they may be passing you on the left, so watch out for them. Times on the sign will show the lane's hours of operation; if no times are shown, or there's no sign at all, this means the lane is in operation 24 hours a day. In some areas, other vehicles, such as taxis and motorcycles, are allowed to use bus lanes. The sign will show if this is the case.

634 Mark *one* answer
Which of these signs warns you of a zebra crossing?

☐ **A**   ☐ **B**

☐ **C**   ☐ **D**

Look well ahead and check the pavements and surrounding areas for pedestrians. Look for anyone walking towards the crossing. Check your mirrors for traffic behind, in case you have to slow down or stop.

635 Mark *one* answer
What does this sign mean?

- ☐ **A** School crossing patrol
- ☐ **B** No pedestrians allowed
- ☐ **C** Pedestrian zone – no vehicles
- ☐ **D** Zebra crossing ahead

Look well ahead and be ready to stop for any pedestrians crossing, or about to cross, the road. Also check the pavements for anyone who looks like they might step or run into the road.

636 Mark *one* answer
Which sign means there will be two-way traffic crossing your route ahead?

☐ A ☐ B

☐ C ☐ D

This sign is found in or at the end of a one-way system. It warns you that traffic will be crossing your path from both directions.

637 Mark *one* answer
Which arm signal tells you that the car you're following is going to pull up?

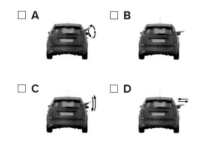

☐ A ☐ B

☐ C ☐ D

There may be occasions when drivers need to give an arm signal to confirm their intentions. This could include in bright sunshine, at a complex road layout, when stopping at a pedestrian crossing or when turning right just after passing a parked vehicle. You should understand what each arm signal means. If you give arm signals, make them clear, correct and decisive.

638 Mark *one* answer
Which sign means turn left ahead?

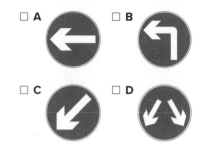

☐ A ☐ B

☐ C ☐ D

Blue circles tell you what you must do and this sign gives a clear instruction to turn left ahead. You should be looking out for signs at all times and know what they mean.

639 Mark *one* answer
What should you be aware of if you've just passed this sign?

☐ **A** This is a single-track road
☐ **B** You can't stop on this road
☐ **C** Only one lane is in use
☐ **D** All traffic is going one way

In a one-way system, traffic may pass you on either side. Always be aware of all traffic signs and understand their meaning. Look well ahead and react to them in good time.

640 Mark *one* answer
You're approaching traffic lights and the red light is showing. What signal will show next?

- ☐ **A** Red and amber
- ☐ **B** Green alone
- ☐ **C** Amber alone
- ☐ **D** Green and amber

If you know which light is going to show next, you can plan your approach accordingly. This can help prevent excessive braking or hesitation at the junction.

641 Mark *one* answer
What does this sign mean?

- ☐ **A** Low bridge ahead
- ☐ **B** Tunnel ahead
- ☐ **C** Ancient monument ahead
- ☐ **D** Traffic danger spot ahead

When approaching a tunnel, switch on your dipped headlights. Be aware that your eyes might need to adjust to the sudden darkness. You may need to reduce your speed.

642 Mark *one* answer
What does the white line along the side of the road indicate?

- ☐ **A** The edge of the carriageway
- ☐ **B** The approach to a hazard
- ☐ **C** No parking
- ☐ **D** No overtaking

A continuous white line is used on many roads to indicate the edge of the carriageway. This can be useful when visibility is restricted. The line is discontinued at junctions, lay-bys, and entrances to or exits from private drives.

643 Mark *one* answer
What does this white arrow on the road mean?

- ☐ **A** Entrance on the left
- ☐ **B** All vehicles turn left
- ☐ **C** Return to your side of the road
- ☐ **D** Road bends to the left

The arrow indicates the direction in which to pass hatch markings or double white lines. If you're overtaking, you must return to the left-hand side of the road.

644 Mark *one* answer

How should you give an arm signal to turn left?

☐ A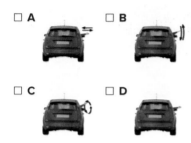

☐ B

☐ C

☐ D

There may be occasions when other road users are unable to see your indicator, such as in bright sunlight or at a busy, complicated junction. In these cases, an arm signal will help others to understand your intentions.

645 Mark *one* answer

You're waiting at a T-junction. What should you do if a vehicle is coming from the right, with its left indicator flashing?

☐ **A** Move out and accelerate hard
☐ **B** Wait until the vehicle starts to turn in
☐ **C** Pull out before the vehicle reaches the junction
☐ **D** Move out slowly

Other road users may give misleading signals. When you're waiting at a junction, don't emerge until you're sure of their intentions.

646 Mark *one* answer
When may you use hazard warning lights while you're driving?

- ☐ **A** Instead of sounding the horn in a built-up area between 11.30 pm and 7.00 am
- ☐ **B** On a motorway or unrestricted dual carriageway, to warn of a hazard ahead
- ☐ **C** On rural routes, after a sign warning of animals
- ☐ **D** On the approach to toucan crossings, where cyclists are waiting to cross

When there's queuing traffic ahead and you have to slow down or even stop, briefly showing your hazard warning lights will help alert the traffic behind to the hazard.

647 Mark *one* answer
Why should you make sure that your indicators are cancelled after turning at a junction?

- ☐ **A** To avoid flattening the battery
- ☐ **B** To avoid misleading other road users
- ☐ **C** To avoid dazzling other road users
- ☐ **D** To avoid damage to the indicator relay

Leaving your indicators on could confuse other road users and may even lead to a crash. Be aware that if you haven't turned sharply, your indicators may not self-cancel and you'll need to turn them off manually.

648 Mark *one* answer
You're driving in busy traffic. You want to pull up just after a junction on the left. When should you signal?

- ☐ **A** As you're passing or just after the junction
- ☐ **B** Just before you reach the junction
- ☐ **C** Well before you reach the junction
- ☐ **D** It would be better not to signal at all

You need to signal to let other drivers know your intentions. However, if you indicate too early, they may think you're turning left into the junction. Correct timing of the signal is very important to avoid misleading others.

649 Mark *one* answer
For how long is an MOT certificate normally valid?

- ☐ **A** Three years after the date it was issued
- ☐ **B** 10,000 miles
- ☐ **C** One year after the date it was issued
- ☐ **D** 30,000 miles

Some garages will remind you that your vehicle is due for its annual MOT test, but not all do. To ensure continuous cover, you may take your vehicle for its MOT up to one month before its existing MOT certificate expires. The expiry date on the new certificate will be 12 months after the expiry date on the old certificate.

650 Mark *one* answer
What's a cover note?

- ☐ **A** A document issued before you receive your driving licence
- ☐ **B** A document issued before you receive your insurance certificate
- ☐ **C** A document issued before you receive your registration document
- ☐ **D** A document issued before you receive your MOT certificate

Sometimes an insurance company will issue a temporary insurance certificate called a cover note. It gives you the same insurance cover as your certificate but lasts for a limited period, usually one month.

651 Mark *one* answer
You've just passed your first practical driving test. What will you have to do if you get six penalty points on your licence in the next two years?

- ☐ **A** Retake only your theory test
- ☐ **B** Retake your theory and practical tests
- ☐ **C** Retake only your practical test
- ☐ **D** Reapply for your full licence immediately

If you accumulate six or more penalty points within two years of gaining your first full licence, it will be revoked. The six or more points include any gained due to offences you committed before passing your test. If this happens, you may only drive as a learner until you pass both the theory and practical tests again.

652 Mark *one* answer
For how long is a Statutory Off-Road Notification (SORN) valid?

- ☐ **A** Until the vehicle is taxed, sold or scrapped
- ☐ **B** Until the vehicle is insured and MOT'd
- ☐ **C** Until the vehicle is repaired or modified
- ☐ **D** Until the vehicle is used on the road

A SORN allows you to keep a vehicle off-road and untaxed. SORN will end when the vehicle is taxed, sold or scrapped.

653 Mark *one* answer
What's a Statutory Off-Road Notification (SORN)?

☐ **A** A notification to tell DVSA that a vehicle doesn't have a current MOT
☐ **B** Information kept by the police about the owner of a vehicle
☐ **C** A notification to tell DVLA that a vehicle isn't being used on the road
☐ **D** Information held by insurance companies to check a vehicle is insured

If you want to keep a vehicle untaxed and off the public road, you must make a SORN. It's an offence not to do so. Your SORN is valid until your vehicle is taxed, sold or scrapped.

654 Mark *one* answer   NI
What's the maximum fine for driving or riding without insurance?

☐ **A** Unlimited
☐ **B** £500
☐ **C** £1000
☐ **D** £5000

Driving or riding without insurance is a serious offence. As well as an unlimited fine, you may be disqualified or incur penalty points.

655 Mark *one* answer
Who's legally responsible for ensuring that a vehicle registration certificate (V5C) is updated?

☐ **A** The registered vehicle keeper
☐ **B** The vehicle manufacturer
☐ **C** Your insurance company
☐ **D** The licensing authority

It's your legal responsibility to keep the details on your vehicle registration certificate (V5C) up to date. You should tell the licensing authority about any changes. These include your name, address or vehicle details. If you don't do this, you may have problems when you try to sell your vehicle.

656 Mark *one* answer
Your insurer will issue you with an insurance certificate. When must you produce this document for inspection?

☐ **A** When making a SORN
☐ **B** When buying or selling a vehicle
☐ **C** When a police officer asks you for it
☐ **D** When your vehicle is having an MOT test

You must produce a valid insurance certificate when requested by a police officer. If you can't do this immediately, you may be asked to take it to a police station. Other documents you may be asked to produce are your driving licence and the vehicle's MOT certificate.

657 Mark *one* answer
When must your vehicle have valid insurance cover?

☐ **A** Before you can make a SORN
☐ **B** Before you can sell the vehicle
☐ **C** Before you can scrap the vehicle
☐ **D** Before you can tax the vehicle

Your vehicle must have valid insurance cover before you can tax it. If required, it will also need to have a valid MOT certificate. You can tax your vehicle online, by phone or at certain post offices.

658 Mark *one* answer
What do you need before you can legally use a motor vehicle on the road?

☐ **A** An appropriate driving licence
☐ **B** Breakdown cover
☐ **C** Proof of your identity
☐ **D** A vehicle handbook

Using a motor vehicle on the road illegally carries a heavy fine and can lead to penalty points on your driving licence. You must
• hold a valid driving licence for the class of vehicle you're using
• be insured to drive the vehicle.

If required, the vehicle must have a current MOT test certificate and be taxed for use on the road.

659 Mark *one* answer
What must you have when you apply to renew your vehicle tax?

☐ **A** Valid insurance
☐ **B** The vehicle's chassis number
☐ **C** The handbook
☐ **D** A valid driving licence

You can renew your vehicle tax online, at post offices and by phone using the DVLA vehicle tax service. When applying, make sure you have all the relevant valid documents, including a valid MOT test certificate where applicable.

660 Mark *one* answer
A police officer asks to see your documents. You don't have them with you. How many days do you have to produce them at a police station?

☐ **A** 5 days
☐ **B** 7 days
☐ **C** 14 days
☐ **D** 21 days

You don't have to carry your vehicle's documents wherever you go. If a police officer asks to see them and you don't have them with you, you may be asked to produce them at a police station within 7 days.

661 Mark *one* answer
When should you update your vehicle registration certificate?

☐ **A** When you pass your driving test
☐ **B** When you move house
☐ **C** When your vehicle needs an MOT
☐ **D** When you have a collision

As the registered keeper of a vehicle, it's up to you to inform DVLA of any changes in your details; for example, your name or address. You do this by completing and sending off the relevant section of the registration certificate.

662 Mark *one* answer
What must you check before you drive someone else's vehicle?

☐ **A** That the vehicle owner has third-party insurance cover
☐ **B** That your own vehicle has insurance cover
☐ **C** That the vehicle is insured for your use
☐ **D** That the insurance documents are in the vehicle

Driving a vehicle without insurance cover is illegal, so be sure that, whoever's car you drive, you're insured – whether on their policy or on your own. If you need to take out insurance, it's worth comparing several quotes before you decide which insurance provider best meets your needs.

663 Mark *one* answer
Your car needs to pass an MOT test. What may be invalidated if you drive the car without a current MOT certificate?

☐ **A** The vehicle service record
☐ **B** The vehicle insurance
☐ **C** The vehicle tax
☐ **D** The vehicle registration document

If your vehicle requires an MOT certificate, it's illegal to drive it without one and your insurance may be invalid if you do so. The only exceptions are that you may drive to a pre-arranged MOT test appointment, or to a garage for repairs required for the test.

664 Mark *one* answer
What legal requirement must be met by a newly qualified driver?

☐ **A** They must display green L plates
☐ **B** They must have a new photograph taken for their full licence
☐ **C** They must be accompanied on their first motorway journey
☐ **D** They must have valid motor insurance

It's your responsibility to make sure you're properly insured for the vehicle you're driving. This is the case regardless of whether you're a newly qualified driver or one with more experience.

665 Mark *one* answer
What's covered by third-party insurance?

- ☐ **A** Damage to your vehicle
- ☐ **B** Fire damage to your vehicle
- ☐ **C** Flood damage to your vehicle
- ☐ **D** Damage to other vehicles

Third-party insurance doesn't cover damage to your own vehicle or injury to yourself. If you have a crash and your vehicle is damaged, you might have to carry out the repairs at your own expense.

666 Mark *one* answer
Who's responsible for paying the vehicle tax?

- ☐ **A** The driver of the vehicle
- ☐ **B** The registered keeper of the vehicle
- ☐ **C** The car dealer
- ☐ **D** The Driver and Vehicle Licensing Agency (DVLA)

The registered keeper of the vehicle is responsible for paying the vehicle tax or making a Statutory Off-Road Notification (SORN) if the vehicle is to be kept untaxed and off the road.

667 Mark *one* answer
What information is found on a vehicle registration document?

- ☐ **A** The registered keeper
- ☐ **B** The type of insurance cover
- ☐ **C** The service history details
- ☐ **D** The date of the MOT

Every vehicle used on the road has a registration document. This shows the vehicle's details, including date of first registration, registration number, registered keeper, previous keeper, make of vehicle, engine size, chassis number, year of manufacture and colour.

668 Mark *one* answer
When must you contact the Driver and Vehicle Licensing Agency (DVLA)?

- ☐ **A** When you get a parking ticket
- ☐ **B** When you change your vehicle
- ☐ **C** When you use your vehicle for work
- ☐ **D** When your vehicle's insurance is due

DVLA needs to keep its records up to date. It sends out a reminder when a vehicle's tax is due for renewal. To do this, it needs to know the name and address of the registered keeper. Every vehicle in the country is registered, so it's possible to trace its history.

669 Mark *one* answer
What circumstances require you to notify the Driver and Vehicle Licensing Agency (DVLA)?

☐ **A** When your health affects your driving
☐ **B** When you have to work abroad
☐ **C** When you lend your vehicle to someone
☐ **D** When your vehicle needs an MOT certificate

DVLA holds the records of all vehicles, drivers and riders in Great Britain and Northern Ireland. They need to know if you have a medical condition that might affect your ability to drive safely. You must tell them if your health deteriorates and you become unfit to drive.

670 Mark *one* answer NI
When could the cost of your insurance be reduced?

☐ **A** When you're under 25 years old
☐ **B** When you don't wear glasses
☐ **C** When you pass the driving test first time
☐ **D** When you complete the Pass Plus scheme

The cost of insurance varies with your age and how long you've been driving. Usually, the younger you are, the more expensive it is, especially if you're under 25. Pass Plus provides additional training to newly qualified drivers. The scheme is recognised by many insurance companies, and taking this extra training could give you reduced insurance premiums, as well as improving your skills and experience.

671 Mark *one* answer
In order to supervise a learner driver you need to have held a full driving licence for the same category of vehicle, for at least three years. What other requirement must you meet?

☐ **A** To have a car with dual controls
☐ **B** To be at least 21 years old
☐ **C** To be an approved driving instructor
☐ **D** To hold an advanced driving certificate

Learner drivers benefit by combining professional driving lessons with private practice. However, you need to be at least 21 years old and have held your driving licence for at least 3 years before you can supervise a learner driver.

672 Mark *one* answer
Your car requires an MOT certificate. When is it legal to drive it without an MOT certificate?

☐ **A** Up to seven days after the old certificate has run out

☐ **B** When driving to an MOT centre to arrange an appointment

☐ **C** When driving the car with the owner's permission

☐ **D** When driving to an appointment at an MOT centre

When a car is three years old (four years old in Northern Ireland), it must pass an MOT test and have a valid MOT certificate before it can be used on the road. Exceptionally, you may

• drive to a pre-arranged test appointment or to a garage for repairs required for the test

• drive vehicles that are more than 40 years old without an MOT test, but they must be in a roadworthy condition before being used on the road. See GOV.UK for more details.

673 Mark *one* answer [NI]
When will a new car need its first MOT test?

☐ **A** When it's one year old
☐ **B** When it's three years old
☐ **C** When it's five years old
☐ **D** When it's seven years old

The vehicle you drive must be roadworthy and in good condition. If it's over three years old, it must pass an MOT test to remain in use on the road (unless it's exempt from the MOT test – see GOV.UK).

674 Mark *one* answer
What does third-party insurance cover?

☐ **A** Damage to your vehicle
☐ **B** Damage to other vehicles
☐ **C** Injury to yourself
☐ **D** All damage and injury

Third-party insurance cover is usually cheaper than comprehensive cover. However, it doesn't cover any damage caused to your own vehicle or property. It only covers damage and injury you cause to others.

675 Mark *one* answer

What's the legal minimum insurance cover you must have to drive on public roads?

☐ **A** Third party, fire and theft
☐ **B** Comprehensive
☐ **C** Third party only
☐ **D** Personal injury cover

The minimum insurance required by law is third-party cover. This covers your liability to others involved in a collision but not damage to your vehicle. Basic third-party insurance also won't cover theft or fire damage. Ask your insurance company for advice on the best cover for you and make sure that you read the policy carefully.

676 Mark *one* answer

What does it mean if your insurance policy has an excess of £500?

☐ **A** The insurance company will pay the first £500 of any claim
☐ **B** You'll be paid £500 if you don't claim within one year
☐ **C** Your vehicle is insured for a value of £500 if it's stolen
☐ **D** You'll have to pay the first £500 of the cost of any claim

Having an excess on your policy will help to keep the premium down. However, if you make a claim, you'll have to pay the excess yourself – in this case, £500.

677 Mark *one* answer
When are you allowed to use hazard warning lights?

- ☐ **A** When stopped and temporarily obstructing traffic
- ☐ **B** When travelling during darkness without headlights
- ☐ **C** When parked on double yellow lines to visit a shop
- ☐ **D** When travelling slowly because you're lost

You mustn't use hazard warning lights while moving, except to warn traffic behind when you slow suddenly on a motorway or unrestricted dual carriageway. Never use hazard warning lights to excuse dangerous or illegal parking.

678 Mark *one* answer
What should you do if you have to stop while you're going through a congested tunnel?

- ☐ **A** Pull up very close to the vehicle in front to save space
- ☐ **B** Ignore any message signs, as they're never up to date
- ☐ **C** Keep a safe distance from the vehicle in front
- ☐ **D** Make a U-turn and find another route

It's important to keep a safe distance from the vehicle in front at all times. This still applies in congested tunnels, even if you're moving very slowly or have stopped. If the vehicle in front breaks down, you may need room to manoeuvre past it.

679 Mark *one* answer
You arrive at the scene of a crash where someone is bleeding heavily from a wound in their arm. Nothing is embedded in the wound. What could you do to help?

- ☐ **A** Walk them around and keep them talking
- ☐ **B** Dab the wound
- ☐ **C** Get them a drink
- ☐ **D** Apply pressure over the wound

If possible, lay the casualty down. Protect yourself from exposure to blood and, when you're sure there's nothing in the wound, apply firm pressure using clean material.

680 Mark *one* answer
You're at an incident. What could you do to help an unconscious casualty?

- ☐ **A** Take photographs of the scene
- ☐ **B** Check that they're breathing normally
- ☐ **C** Move them to somewhere more comfortable
- ☐ **D** Splash their face with cool water

If a casualty is unconscious, you need to check that they're breathing normally. Look for chest movements, look and listen for breathing, and feel for breath on your cheek.

681 Mark *one* answer
A casualty isn't breathing normally and needs CPR. At what rate should you press down and release on the centre of their chest?

- ☐ **A** 10 times per minute
- ☐ **B** 120 times per minute
- ☐ **C** 60 times per minute
- ☐ **D** 240 times per minute

If a casualty isn't breathing normally, cardiopulmonary resuscitation (CPR) may be needed to maintain circulation. Place two hands on the centre of the chest and press down hard and fast – around 5–6 centimetres and about twice a second.

682 Mark *one* answer
Following a collision, a person has been injured. What would be a warning sign for shock?

- ☐ **A** Flushed complexion
- ☐ **B** Warm dry skin
- ☐ **C** Slow pulse
- ☐ **D** Rapid shallow breathing

The effects of shock may not be immediately obvious. Warning signs to look for include
- a rapid pulse
- sweating
- pale grey skin
- rapid shallow breathing.

683 Mark *one* answer
An injured person has been placed in the recovery position. They're unconscious but breathing normally. What else should be done?

- ☐ **A** Press firmly between their shoulders
- ☐ **B** Place their arms by their side
- ☐ **C** Give them a hot sweet drink
- ☐ **D** Check their airway remains open

After a casualty has been placed in the recovery position, make sure their airway remains open and monitor their condition until medical help arrives. Where possible, don't move a casualty unless there's further danger.

684 Mark *one* answer
An injured motorcyclist is lying unconscious in the road. The traffic has stopped and there's no further danger. What could you do to help?

- ☐ **A** Remove their safety helmet
- ☐ **B** Seek medical assistance
- ☐ **C** Move the person off the road
- ☐ **D** Remove their leather jacket

If someone has been injured, the sooner proper medical attention is given the better. Ask someone to phone for help or do it yourself. An injured person should only be moved if they're in further danger. An injured motorcyclist's helmet shouldn't be removed unless it's essential.

685 Mark *one* answer
What should you do if you see a large box fall from a lorry onto the motorway?

- ☐ **A** Go to the next emergency telephone and report the hazard
- ☐ **B** Catch up with the lorry and try to get the driver's attention
- ☐ **C** Stop close to the box until the police arrive
- ☐ **D** Pull over to the hard shoulder, then remove the box

Lorry drivers can be unaware of objects falling from their vehicles. If you see something fall onto a motorway, look to see if the driver pulls over. If they don't stop, don't attempt to retrieve the object yourself. Pull onto the hard shoulder near an emergency telephone and report the hazard.

---

686 Mark *one* answer
You're going through a long tunnel. What will warn you of congestion or an incident ahead?

- ☐ **A** Hazard warning lines
- ☐ **B** Other drivers flashing their lights
- ☐ **C** Variable message signs
- ☐ **D** Areas with hatch markings

Follow the instructions given by the signs or by tunnel officials. In congested tunnels, a minor incident can soon turn into a major one, with serious or even fatal results.

687 Mark *one* answer
An adult casualty isn't breathing. To maintain circulation, CPR should be given. What's the correct depth to press down on their chest?

- ☐ **A** 1 to 2 centimetres
- ☐ **B** 5 to 6 centimetres
- ☐ **C** 10 to 15 centimetres
- ☐ **D** 15 to 20 centimetres

An adult casualty isn't breathing normally. To maintain circulation, place two hands on the centre of the chest. Then press down hard and fast – around 5–6 centimetres and about twice a second.

---

688 Mark *one* answer
You're the first person to arrive at an incident where people are badly injured. You've switched on your hazard warning lights and checked all engines are stopped. What else should you do?

- ☐ **A** Make sure that an ambulance has been called
- ☐ **B** Stop other cars and ask the drivers for help
- ☐ **C** Try and get people who are injured to drink something
- ☐ **D** Move the people who are injured clear of their vehicles

If you're the first to arrive at a crash scene, the first concerns are the risk of further collision and fire. Ensuring that vehicle engines are switched off will reduce the risk of fire. Use hazard warning lights so that other traffic knows there's a need for caution. Make sure the emergency services are contacted; don't assume it's already been done.

689 Mark *one* answer
You arrive at the scene of a motorcycle crash. The rider is injured. When should their helmet be removed?

☐ **A** Only when it's essential
☐ **B** Always straight away
☐ **C** Only when the motorcyclist asks
☐ **D** Always, unless they're in shock

Don't remove a motorcyclist's helmet unless it's essential. Remember they may be suffering from shock. Don't give them anything to eat or drink, but do reassure them confidently.

690 Mark *one* answer
You arrive at an incident. There's no danger from fire or further collisions and the emergency services have been called. What's your first priority when attending to an unconscious motorcyclist?

☐ **A** Check whether they're breathing normally
☐ **B** Check whether they're bleeding
☐ **C** Check whether they have any broken bones
☐ **D** Check whether they have any bruising

At the scene of an incident, always be aware of danger from further collisions or fire. The first priority when dealing with an unconscious person is to ensure they can breathe. This may involve clearing their airway if you can see an obstruction or if they're having difficulty breathing.

691 Mark *one* answer
At an incident, someone is unconscious and you want to help. What would be the first thing to check?

☐ **A** Whether their vehicle is insured
☐ **B** Whether they have any allergies
☐ **C** Whether they're comfortable
☐ **D** Whether their airway is open

Remember this procedure by saying DR ABC. This stands for Danger, Response, Airway, Breathing, Circulation. Give whatever first aid you can and stay with the injured person until a medical professional takes over.

692 Mark *one* answer
What could you do to help injured people at an incident?

☐ **A** Keep them warm and comfortable
☐ **B** Give them something to eat
☐ **C** Keep them on the move by walking them around
☐ **D** Give them a warm drink

There are a number of things you can do to help, even without expert training. Be aware of further danger from other traffic and fire; make sure the area is safe. People may be in shock. Don't give them anything to eat or drink. Keep them warm and comfortable and reassure them. Don't move injured people unless there's a risk of further danger.

693 Mark *one* answer
There's been a collision. How can you help a driver who's suffering from shock?

- ☐ **A** Give them a drink
- ☐ **B** Reassure them confidently
- ☐ **C** Ask who caused the incident
- ☐ **D** Offer them a cigarette

A casualty suffering from shock may have injuries that aren't immediately obvious. Call the emergency services, then stay with the person in shock, offering reassurance until the experts arrive.

694 Mark *one* answer
You arrive at the scene of a motorcycle crash. No other vehicle is involved. The rider is unconscious and lying in the middle of the road. What's the first thing you should do at the scene?

- ☐ **A** Move the rider out of the road
- ☐ **B** Warn other traffic
- ☐ **C** Clear the road of debris
- ☐ **D** Give the rider reassurance

The motorcyclist is in an extremely vulnerable position, exposed to further danger from traffic. Approaching vehicles need advance warning in order to slow down and safely take avoiding action or stop. Don't put yourself or anyone else at risk. Use the hazard warning lights on your vehicle to alert other road users to the danger.

695 Mark *one* answer
At an incident, how could you help a small child who isn't breathing?

- ☐ **A** Find their parents and explain what's happening
- ☐ **B** Open their airway and begin CPR
- ☐ **C** Put them in the recovery position and slap their back
- ☐ **D** Talk to them confidently until an ambulance arrives

If a young child has stopped breathing, first check that their airway is open and then begin CPR. With a young child, you may only need to use one hand and you shouldn't press down as far as you would with an adult. Continue the procedure until the child is breathing again or until a medical professional takes over.

696 Mark *one* answer
At an incident, a casualty isn't breathing. What should you do while helping them to start breathing again?

- ☐ **A** Put their arms across their chest
- ☐ **B** Shake them firmly
- ☐ **C** Roll them onto their side
- ☐ **D** Open their airway

It's important to ensure that the airway is open before you start CPR. To open the casualty's airway, place your fingers under their chin and lift it forward.

697 Mark *one* answer
At an incident, someone is suffering from severe burns. How could you help them?

☐ **A** Apply lotions to the injury
☐ **B** Burst any blisters
☐ **C** Remove anything sticking to the burns
☐ **D** Douse the burns with clean, cool water

Your priority is to cool the burns with clean, cool water. Its coolness will help take the heat out of the burns and relieve the pain. Keep the wound doused for at least 20 minutes. If blisters appear, don't attempt to burst them, as this could lead to infection.

698 Mark *one* answer
You arrive at an incident. A pedestrian is bleeding heavily from a leg wound. The leg isn't broken and there's nothing in the wound. How could you help?

☐ **A** Dab the wound to stop the bleeding
☐ **B** Keep the casualty's legs flat on the ground
☐ **C** Give them a warm drink
☐ **D** Apply firm pressure over the wound

You should protect yourself from exposure to blood, and then apply firm pressure over the wound to stem the flow of blood. As soon as practical, fasten a pad to the wound with a bandage or length of cloth. Use the cleanest material available.

699 Mark *one* answer
At an incident, a casualty is unconscious but breathing. When should you move them?

☐ **A** When an ambulance is on its way
☐ **B** When bystanders tell you to move them
☐ **C** When there's a risk of further danger
☐ **D** When bystanders offer to help you

Don't move a casualty unless there's further danger; for example, from other traffic or fire. They may have unseen or internal injuries. Moving them unnecessarily could cause further injury. Don't remove a motorcyclist's helmet unless it's essential.

700 Mark *one* answer
At an incident, it's important to look after any casualties. What should you do with them when the area is safe?

☐ **A** Move them away from the vehicles
☐ **B** Ask them how it happened
☐ **C** Give them something to eat
☐ **D** Keep them where they are

When the area is safe and there's no danger from other traffic or fire, it's better not to move casualties. Moving them may cause further injury.

701 Mark *one* answer
Which sign shows that a tanker is carrying dangerous goods?

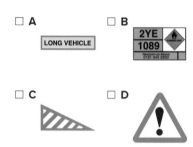

☐ **A** LONG VEHICLE

☐ **B** 2YE 1089

☐ **C**

☐ **D**

Tankers will display a hazard warning plate on the side and rear of the vehicle. Details of hazard warning symbols are given in *The Highway Code*. If a tanker is involved in a collision, you may need to report the tanker's hazard labelling to the emergency services.

702 Mark *one* answer
Which document may the police ask you to produce after you've been involved in a collision?

☐ **A** Your vehicle registration document
☐ **B** Your driving licence
☐ **C** Your theory test certificate
☐ **D** Your vehicle service record

You must stop if you've been involved in a collision that results in injury or damage. The police may ask to see your driving licence and insurance details at the time or later at a police station.

703 Mark *one* answer
After a collision, someone is unconscious in their vehicle. When should you call the emergency services?

☐ **A** Only as a last resort
☐ **B** As soon as possible
☐ **C** After you've woken them up
☐ **D** After checking for broken bones

It's important to make sure that the emergency services arrive as soon as possible. When a person is unconscious, they could have serious injuries that aren't immediately obvious.

704 Mark *one* answer
A collision has just happened. An injured person is lying in a busy road. What's the first thing you should do?

☐ **A** Treat the person for shock
☐ **B** Warn other traffic
☐ **C** Place them in the recovery position
☐ **D** Make sure the injured person is kept warm

The most immediate danger is further collisions and fire. You could warn other traffic by switching on hazard warning lights, displaying an advance warning triangle or sign (but not on a motorway), or by any other means that doesn't put you or others at risk.

705 Mark *one* answer
At an incident, how could you help a casualty who has stopped breathing?

□ **A** Keep their head tilted forwards as far as possible
□ **B** Follow the DR ABC code
□ **C** Raise their legs to help with circulation
□ **D** Try to give them something to drink

The DR ABC code has been devised by medical experts to give the best outcome until the emergency services arrive and take care of casualties.

706 Mark *one* answer
You're at the scene of an incident. How could you help someone who's suffering from shock?

□ **A** Reassure them confidently
□ **B** Offer them a cigarette
□ **C** Give them a warm drink
□ **D** Offer them some food

If someone is suffering from shock, try to keep them warm and as comfortable as you can. Don't give them anything to eat or drink but reassure them confidently and try not to leave them alone.

707 Mark *one* answer
There's been a collision. A motorcyclist is lying injured and unconscious. Why should you only remove their helmet if it's essential?

□ **A** They might not want you to remove it
□ **B** Removing it could make any injuries worse
□ **C** Removing it could let them get cold
□ **D** You could scratch the helmet as you remove it

When someone is injured, any movement that isn't absolutely necessary should be avoided, since it could make the injuries worse. Unless it's essential to remove a motorcyclist's helmet, it's generally safer to leave it in place.

708 Mark *one* answer
You're on a motorway. When can you use hazard warning lights?

□ **A** When a vehicle is following too closely
□ **B** When you slow down quickly because of danger ahead
□ **C** When you're being towed by another vehicle
□ **D** When you're riding on the hard shoulder

Briefly using your hazard warning lights will warn the traffic behind you that there's a hazard ahead. Turn them off again when following drivers have seen and responded to your signal.

709 Mark *one* answer

You've broken down on a two-way road. You have a warning triangle. At least how far from your vehicle should you place the warning triangle?

- ☐ **A** 5 metres (16 feet)
- ☐ **B** 25 metres (82 feet)
- ☐ **C** 45 metres (147 feet)
- ☐ **D** 100 metres (328 feet)

Advance warning triangles fold flat and don't take up much room. Use one to warn other road users if your vehicle has broken down or if there has been an incident. Place it at least **45 metres (147 feet)** behind your vehicle (or the incident), on the same side of the road or verge. Place it further back if the scene is hidden by, for example, a bend, hill or dip in the road. Don't use warning triangles on motorways.

710 Mark *one* answer

Your car breaks down on a level crossing. What's the first thing you should do?

- ☐ **A** Tell drivers behind what's happened
- ☐ **B** Leave your vehicle and get everyone clear
- ☐ **C** Walk down the track and signal the next train
- ☐ **D** Stay in your car until you're told to move

If your vehicle breaks down on a level crossing, your first priority is to get everyone out of the vehicle and clear of the crossing. Then use the railway telephone, if there is one, to tell the signal operator. If you have time before the train arrives, move the vehicle clear of the crossing, but only do this if the alarm signals aren't activated.

711 Mark *one* answer
What should you do if a tyre bursts while you're driving?

☐ **A** Pull on the parking brake
☐ **B** Brake as quickly as possible
☐ **C** Pull up slowly at the side of the road
☐ **D** Continue on at a normal speed

A tyre bursting can lead to a loss of control, especially if you're travelling at high speed. Using the correct procedure should help you to stop the vehicle safely.

712 Mark *one* answer
What should you do if your vehicle has a puncture on a motorway?

☐ **A** Drive slowly to the next service area to get assistance
☐ **B** Pull up on the hard shoulder or in an emergency refuge area. Change the wheel as quickly as possible
☐ **C** Pull up on the hard shoulder or in an emergency refuge area and call for assistance
☐ **D** Switch on your hazard warning lights. Stop in your lane

Pull up on the hard shoulder or in an emergency refuge area and call for assistance. Don't attempt to repair your vehicle while it's on the hard shoulder, because of the risk posed by traffic passing at high speeds.

713 Mark *one* answer
Your vehicle has stalled in the middle of a level crossing. What should you do if the warning bells start to ring while you're trying to restart the engine?

☐ **A** Get out of the car and clear of the crossing
☐ **B** Run down the track to warn the signal operator
☐ **C** Carry on trying to restart the engine
☐ **D** Push the vehicle clear of the crossing

If the warning bells ring, leave the vehicle and get any passengers well clear of the crossing immediately.

714 Mark *one* answer
What should you do before driving into a tunnel?

☐ **A** Switch off your radio
☐ **B** Take off your sunglasses
☐ **C** Close your sunroof
☐ **D** Switch on your windscreen wipers

If you're wearing sunglasses, you should remove them before driving into a tunnel. If you don't, your vision will be restricted, even in tunnels that appear to be well lit.

715 Mark *one* answer
Which lights should you use when you're driving in a tunnel?

- ☐ **A** Sidelights
- ☐ **B** Front spotlights
- ☐ **C** Dipped headlights
- ☐ **D** Rear fog lights

Before entering a tunnel, you should switch on your dipped headlights, as this will allow you to see and be seen. In many tunnels, it's a legal requirement. Don't wear sunglasses while you're driving in a tunnel.

716 Mark *one* answer
What should you do to reduce the risk of your vehicle catching fire?

- ☐ **A** Keep water levels above maximum
- ☐ **B** Check out any strong smell of fuel
- ☐ **C** Avoid driving with a full tank of fuel
- ☐ **D** Use fuel additives

The fuel in your vehicle can be a dangerous fire hazard. If you smell fuel, check out where it's coming from. Never
- use a naked flame near the vehicle if you can smell fuel
- smoke when refuelling your vehicle.

717 Mark *one* answer
You're driving on the motorway. What should you do if luggage falls from your vehicle?

- ☐ **A** Stop at the next emergency telephone and report the incident
- ☐ **B** Stop on the motorway and switch on hazard warning lights while you pick it up
- ☐ **C** Walk back up the motorway to pick it up
- ☐ **D** Pull up on the hard shoulder and wave traffic down

If any object falls onto the motorway carriageway from your vehicle, pull onto the hard shoulder near an emergency telephone and call for assistance. Don't stop on the carriageway or attempt to retrieve anything.

718 Mark *one* answer
What should you do if an instrument panel warning light comes on while you're driving?

- ☐ **A** Continue if the engine sounds all right
- ☐ **B** Hope that it's just a temporary electrical fault
- ☐ **C** Deal with the problem when there's more time
- ☐ **D** Check out the problem quickly and safely

Make sure you know what the different warning lights mean. An illuminated warning light could mean that your car is unsafe to drive. If you aren't sure about the problem, get a qualified mechanic to check it.

719 Mark *one* answer
What should you do if your vehicle breaks down in a tunnel?

- ☐ **A** Stay in your vehicle and wait for the police
- ☐ **B** Stand in the lane behind your vehicle to warn others
- ☐ **C** Stand in front of your vehicle to warn oncoming drivers
- ☐ **D** Switch on hazard warning lights, then go and call for help

A broken-down vehicle in a tunnel can cause serious congestion and danger to other road users. If your vehicle breaks down, get help without delay. Switch on your hazard warning lights, then go to an emergency telephone to call for help.

720 Mark *one* answer
What should you do if your vehicle catches fire while you're driving through a tunnel?

- ☐ **A** Leave it where it is, with the engine running
- ☐ **B** Pull up, then walk to an emergency telephone
- ☐ **C** Park it away from the carriageway
- ☐ **D** Drive it out of the tunnel if it's safe to do so

If it's possible, and you can do so without causing further danger, it may be safer to drive a vehicle that's on fire out of a tunnel. The greatest danger in a tunnel fire is smoke and suffocation.

721 Mark *one* answer
What should you do first if your vehicle has broken down on an automatic railway level crossing?

- ☐ **A** Get everyone out of the vehicle and clear of the crossing
- ☐ **B** Telephone your vehicle recovery service to move it
- ☐ **C** Walk along the track to give warning to any approaching trains
- ☐ **D** Try to push the vehicle clear of the crossing as soon as possible

First, get yourself and anyone else well away from the crossing. If there's a railway telephone, use that to get instructions from the signal operator. Then, if there's time, move the vehicle clear of the crossing.

722 Mark *one* answer
What's the first thing you must do if you have a collision while you're driving your car?

- ☐ **A** Stop only if someone waves at you
- ☐ **B** Call the emergency services
- ☐ **C** Stop at the scene of the incident
- ☐ **D** Call your insurance company

If you're in a collision that causes damage or injury to any other person, vehicle, animal or property, by law you must stop. Give your name, the vehicle owner's name and address, and the vehicle's registration number to anyone who has reasonable grounds for requesting them.

723 Mark *one* answer
What information should you share if you're involved in a collision that causes damage to another vehicle?

- ☐ **A** Your occupation and reason for your journey
- ☐ **B** Your name, address and vehicle registration number
- ☐ **C** Your national insurance number
- ☐ **D** Your internet service provider

Try to keep calm and don't rush. Make sure that you've shared all the relevant details with the other driver before you leave the scene. If possible, take pictures and note the positions of all the vehicles involved.

724 Mark *one* answer   NI
You lose control of your car and damage a garden wall. What must you do if the property owner isn't available?

- ☐ **A** Report the incident to the police within 24 hours
- ☐ **B** Go back to tell the house owner the next day
- ☐ **C** Report the incident to your insurance company when you get home
- ☐ **D** Find someone in the area to tell them about it immediately

If the property owner isn't available at the time, you must inform the police about the incident. This should be done as soon as possible, and in any case within 24 hours.

725 Mark *one* answer
What restrictions apply if you're towing a trailer on a three-lane motorway?

☐ **A** You mustn't exceed 50 mph
☐ **B** You mustn't overtake
☐ **C** You must have a stabiliser fitted
☐ **D** You mustn't use the right-hand lane

The motorway regulations for towing a trailer state that you mustn't
- use the right-hand lane of a three-lane motorway unless directed to do so (for example, at roadworks or due to a lane closure)
- exceed 60 mph.

726 Mark *one* answer
What should you do if you're towing a trailer and it starts to swing from side to side?

☐ **A** Ease off the accelerator to reduce your speed
☐ **B** Let go of the steering wheel and let it correct itself
☐ **C** Brake hard and hold the pedal down
☐ **D** Accelerate until it stabilises

Strong winds or buffeting from large vehicles can cause a trailer or caravan to swing from side to side ('snake'). If this happens, ease off the accelerator. Don't brake harshly, steer sharply or increase your speed.

727 Mark *one* answer
When would you increase the pressure in your tyres so that it's above the normal value?

☐ **A** When the roads are slippery
☐ **B** When the vehicle is fitted with anti-lock brakes
☐ **C** When the tyre tread is worn below 2 mm
☐ **D** When carrying a heavy load

Check the vehicle handbook. This should give you guidance on the correct tyre pressures for your vehicle and when you may need to adjust them. If you're carrying a heavy load, you may need to adjust the headlights as well. Most cars have a switch on the dashboard to do this.

728 Mark *one* answer

How will a heavy load on your roof rack affect your vehicle's handling?

☐ **A** It will improve the road holding
☐ **B** It will reduce the stopping distance
☐ **C** It will make the steering lighter
☐ **D** It will reduce stability

A heavy load on your roof rack will reduce the stability of the vehicle because it moves the centre of gravity away from that designed by the manufacturer. Be aware of this when you drive round bends and corners. If you change direction at speed, your vehicle and/or load could become unstable and you could lose control.

729 Mark *one* answer

What would be affected if you carry a very heavy load on your vehicle?

☐ **A** The vehicle's gearbox
☐ **B** The vehicle's ventilation
☐ **C** The vehicle's handling
☐ **D** The vehicle's battery

Any load will have an effect on the handling of your vehicle, and this becomes worse as you increase the load. You need to be aware of this when carrying passengers or heavy loads, fitting a roof rack or towing a trailer.

730 Mark *one* answer

Who's responsible for making sure that a vehicle isn't overloaded?

☐ **A** The driver of the vehicle
☐ **B** The owner of the items being carried
☐ **C** The person who loaded the vehicle
☐ **D** The licensing authority

Carrying heavy loads will affect control and the vehicle's handling characteristics. If the vehicle you're driving is overloaded, you'll be held responsible.

731 Mark *one* answer
You're planning to tow a caravan. What will help the handling of the combination?

☐ **A** A jockey wheel fitted to the tow bar
☐ **B** Power steering fitted to the towing vehicle
☐ **C** Anti-lock brakes fitted to the towing vehicle
☐ **D** A stabiliser fitted to the tow bar

Towing a caravan or trailer affects the way the towing vehicle handles. A stabiliser device isn't designed to overcome instability caused by incorrect loading but it can give added security in side winds and from buffeting caused by large vehicles.

732 Mark *one* answer
Are passengers allowed to ride in a caravan that's being towed?

☐ **A** Yes, if they're over 14
☐ **B** No, not at any time
☐ **C** Only if all the seats in the towing vehicle are full
☐ **D** Only if a stabiliser is fitted

Riding in a towed caravan is highly dangerous. The safety of the entire unit is dependent on the stability of the trailer. Moving passengers would make the caravan unstable and could cause loss of control.

733 Mark *one* answer
What safety device must be fitted to a trailer braking system?

☐ **A** Stabiliser
☐ **B** Jockey wheel
☐ **C** Corner steadies
☐ **D** Breakaway cable

In the event that the trailer becomes detached from the towing vehicle, the breakaway cable activates the trailer brakes before snapping. This allows the towing vehicle to get free of the trailer and out of danger.

734 Mark *one* answer

You wish to tow a trailer. Where would you find the maximum noseweight for your vehicle's tow hitch?

☐ **A** In the vehicle handbook
☐ **B** In *The Highway Code*
☐ **C** In your vehicle registration certificate
☐ **D** In your licence documents

You must know how to load your trailer or caravan so that the hitch exerts an appropriate downward force on the tow ball. Information about the maximum permitted noseweight can be found in your vehicle handbook or obtained from your vehicle manufacturer's agent.

735 Mark *one* answer

How should a load be carried on your roof rack?

☐ **A** Securely fastened with suitable restraints
☐ **B** Loaded towards the rear of the vehicle
☐ **C** Visible in your exterior mirror
☐ **D** Covered with plastic sheeting

Any load must be securely fastened to the vehicle. The safest way to carry items on the roof is in a specially designed roof box. This will help to keep your luggage secure and dry, and it also has less wind resistance than loads carried exposed on a roof rack.

736 Mark *one* answer

You're carrying a child under three years old in your car. Which restraint is suitable for a child of this age?

☐ **A** A child seat
☐ **B** An adult holding a child
☐ **C** An adult seat belt
☐ **D** An adult lap belt

It's your responsibility to ensure that all children in your car are secure. Suitable restraints include a child seat, baby seat, booster seat or booster cushion. It's essential that any restraint used is suitable for the child's size and weight, and fitted according to the manufacturer's instructions.

ANSWERS TO
QUESTIONS

Answers to questions

Section 1 – **Alertness**

1 C	2 B	3 D	4 C	5 C	6 C
7 C	8 B	9 C	10 B	11 A	12 A
13 D	14 B	15 A	16 B	17 B	18 B
19 C	20 D	21 D	22 D	23 D	24 C
25 C	26 D				

Section 2 – **Attitude**

27 D	28 A	29 C	30 D	31 D	32 B
33 B	34 A	35 D	36 A	37 B	38 A
39 A	40 C	41 A	42 D	43 D	44 D
45 B	46 C	47 B	48 C	49 A	50 C
51 A	52 C	53 C	54 B	55 D	56 B
57 C	58 B	59 A	60 B	61 B	62 C
63 B	64 D	65 C			

Section 3 – **Safety and your vehicle**

66 A	67 C	68 C	69 B	70 D	71 C
72 D	73 A	74 C	75 D	76 B	77 B
78 D	79 B	80 D	81 C	82 A	83 D
84 A	85 A	86 B	87 B	88 D	89 A
90 B	91 D	92 D	93 D	94 B	95 B
96 B	97 B	98 A	99 C	100 D	101 D
102 B	103 B	104 B	105 D	106 C	107 D
108 D	109 C	110 A	111 A	112 B	113 D
114 C	115 A	116 A	117 D	118 C	119 B
120 B	121 B	122 D	123 C	124 A	125 D
126 A	127 B	128 D	129 C	130 D	131 D
132 B	133 B	134 C	135 D	136 C	137 D
138 B	139 C	140 A	141 A	142 D	

Section 4 – **Safety margins**

143 D	144 D	145 A	146 B	147 D	148 B
149 C	150 A	151 D	152 A	153 A	154 B
155 D	156 B	157 B	158 D	159 A	160 C
161 A	162 C	163 B	164 D	165 D	166 B
167 D	168 A	169 A	170 A	171 C	172 B
173 C	174 C	175 C	176 A		

Section 5 – **Hazard awareness**

177 C	178 C	179 A	180 D	181 C	182 C
183 C	184 D	185 B	186 A	187 A	188 A
189 C	190 B	191 C	192 D	193 B	194 B
195 C	196 A	197 D	198 D	199 C	200 B
201 C	202 B	203 A	204 A	205 A	206 C
207 A	208 D	209 B	210 C	211 C	212 A
213 B	214 B	215 B	216 D	217 A	218 C
219 B	220 B	221 B	222 C	223 D	224 C
225 C	226 A	227 B	228 A	229 B	230 C
231 C	232 A	233 C	234 D	235 C	236 C
237 D	238 B	239 C	240 B	241 D	242 A
243 A	244 D	245 D	246 B	247 D	248 D
249 A	250 A	251 B	252 D	253 A	254 B

Section 6 – **Vulnerable road users**

255 D	256 D	257 B	258 D	259 D	260 C
261 D	262 D	263 D	264 B	265 D	266 D
267 C	268 C	269 C	270 A	271 D	272 D
273 D	274 C	275 D	276 A	277 D	278 C
279 C	280 D	281 D	282 B	283 A	284 C
285 C	286 A	287 D	288 A	289 B	290 B
291 A	292 A	293 C	294 B	295 D	296 A
297 D	298 D	299 D	300 C	301 B	302 B
303 D	304 C	305 B	306 A	307 D	308 B
309 B	310 D	311 C	312 B	313 C	314 A
315 C	316 C	317 B	318 B	319 D	320 B
321 B	322 C	323 D	324 A	325 D	

Answers to questions

Section 7 – **Other types of vehicle**

326 A	327 A	328 B	329 B	330 D	331 B
332 B	333 A	334 B	335 B	336 D	337 D
338 A	339 D	340 A	341 B	342 C	343 B
344 D	345 B	346 D	347 D		

Section 8 – **Vehicle handling**

348 A	349 A	350 D	351 D	352 A	353 C
354 C	355 D	356 C	357 D	358 D	359 C
360 C	361 B	362 B	363 D	364 D	365 B
366 C	367 A	368 B	369 A	370 B	371 D
372 C	373 C	374 A	375 C	376 D	377 B
378 D	379 D	380 C	381 C	382 C	383 D
384 C	385 A	386 A	387 C	388 D	389 B
390 D	391 C				

Section 9 – **Motorway rules**

392 D	393 D	394 A	395 C	396 C	397 C
398 A	399 C	400 C	401 C	402 C	403 C
404 C	405 B	406 B	407 A	408 B	409 D
410 C	411 A	412 A	413 D	414 B	415 A
416 A	417 C	418 B	419 B	420 D	421 A
422 D	423 D	424 B	425 D	426 A	427 D
428 C	429 B	430 D	431 B	432 D	433 B
434 A	435 A	436 C	437 D	438 A	439 B
440 B	441 A	442 D	443 C	444 B	445 C
446 D	447 A	448 B			

Section 10 – **Rules of the road**

449 C	450 D	451 B	452 A	453 C	454 D
455 D	456 A	457 B	458 A	459 B	460 A
461 D	462 A	463 D	464 C	465 A	466 C
467 C	468 B	469 A	470 C	471 A	472 D
473 B	474 A	475 B	476 A	477 B	478 A
479 D	480 A	481 D	482 B	483 C	484 B
485 B	486 B	487 D	488 D	489 C	490 D
491 D	492 D	493 D	494 C	495 C	496 D
497 A	498 A	499 C	500 B	501 A	502 D
503 A	504 A	505 D	506 D	507 D	508 A
509 A	510 A	511 D	512 D	513 A	514 A
515 A					

Section 11 – **Road and traffic signs**

516 D	517 D	518 A	519 A	520 D	521 B
522 D	523 D	524 D	525 A	526 C	527 B
528 D	529 A	530 B	531 B	532 C	533 A
534 C	535 B	536 C	537 D	538 C	539 C
540 D	541 A	542 D	543 D	544 B	545 A
546 A	547 A	548 B	549 B	550 A	551 D
552 A	553 C	554 A	555 B	556 C	557 B
558 D	559 A	560 A	561 C	562 D	563 A
564 C	565 B	566 D	567 B	568 B	569 C
570 D	571 C	572 B	573 C	574 D	575 B
576 A	577 A	578 C	579 D	580 A	581 C
582 C	583 B	584 A	585 C	586 A	587 A
588 D	589 D	590 A	591 D	592 C	593 C
594 B	595 C	596 C	597 A	598 B	599 D
600 B	601 B	602 A	603 A	604 B	605 D
606 C	607 B	608 C	609 A	610 B	611 A
612 C	613 B	614 A	615 C	616 B	617 B
618 B	619 A	620 A	621 B	622 D	623 C
624 B	625 C	626 A	627 C	628 A	629 C
630 C	631 A	632 B	633 A	634 A	635 D
636 B	637 C	638 B	639 D	640 A	641 B
642 A	643 C	644 C	645 B	646 B	647 B
648 A					

Answers to questions

Section 12 – Documents

649 C	650 B	651 B	652 A	653 C	654 A
655 A	656 C	657 D	658 A	659 A	660 B
661 B	662 C	663 B	664 D	665 D	666 B
667 A	668 B	669 A	670 D	671 B	672 D
673 B	674 B	675 C	676 D		

Section 13 – Incidents, accidents and emergencies

677 A	678 C	679 D	680 B	681 B	682 D
683 D	684 B	685 A	686 C	687 B	688 A
689 A	690 A	691 D	692 A	693 B	694 B
695 B	696 D	697 D	698 D	699 C	700 D
701 B	702 B	703 B	704 B	705 B	706 A
707 B	708 B	709 C	710 B	711 C	712 C
713 A	714 B	715 C	716 B	717 A	718 D
719 D	720 D	721 A	722 C	723 B	724 A

Section 14 – Vehicle loading

725 D	726 A	727 D	728 D	729 C	730 A
731 D	732 B	733 D	734 A	735 A	736 A

GLOSSARY

Glossary

Accelerate

To make the vehicle move faster by pressing the right-hand pedal.

Advanced stop lines

A marked area on the road at traffic lights, which permits cyclists or buses to wait in front of other traffic.

Adverse weather

Bad weather that makes driving difficult or dangerous.

Alert

Quick to notice possible hazards.

Anticipation

Looking out for hazards and taking action before a problem starts.

Anti-lock brakes

Brakes that stop the wheels locking so that you are less likely to skid on a slippery road.

Aquaplane

To slide out of control on a wet road surface.

Articulated vehicle

A long vehicle that is divided into two or more sections joined by cables.

Attitude

The way you think or feel, which affects the way you drive. Especially, whether you are patient and polite, or impatient and aggressive.

Automatic

A vehicle with gears that change by themselves as you speed up or slow down.

Awareness

Taking notice of the road and traffic conditions around you at all times.

Black ice

An invisible film of ice that forms over the road surface, creating very dangerous driving conditions.

Blind spot

The section of road behind you that you cannot see in your mirrors. You 'cover' your blind spot by looking over your shoulder before moving off or overtaking.

Brake fade

Loss of power to the brakes when you have been using them for a long time without taking your foot off the brake pedal. For example, when driving down a steep hill. The brakes will overheat and not work properly.

Braking distance

The distance you must allow to slow the vehicle in order to come to a stop.

Brow

The highest point of a hill.

Built-up area

A town, or place with lots of buildings.

Carriageway

One side of a road or motorway. A 'dual carriageway' has a central reservation.

Catalytic converter

A piece of equipment fitted in the exhaust system that changes harmful gases into less harmful ones.

Chicane

A sharp double bend that has been put into a road to make traffic slow down.

Child restraint

A child seat or special seat belt for children. It keeps them safe and stops them moving around in the car.

Clearway

A road where no stopping is allowed at any time. The sign for a clearway is a red cross in a red circle on a blue background.

Coasting
  Driving a vehicle without using any of the gears. That is, with your foot on the clutch pedal and the car in neutral.

Commentary driving
  Talking to yourself about what you see on the road ahead and what action you are going to take – an aid to concentration.

Comprehensive insurance
  A motor insurance policy that pays for all repairs even if you cause an accident.

Concentration
  Keeping all your attention on your driving.

Conditions
  How good or bad the road surface is, volume of traffic on the road, and what the weather is like.

Congestion
  Heavy traffic that makes it difficult to get to where you want to go.

Consideration
  Thinking about other road users and not just yourself. For example, letting another driver go first at a junction.

Contraflow
  When traffic on a motorway follows signs to move to the opposite carriageway for a short distance because of roadworks. (During a contraflow, there is traffic driving in both directions on the same side of the motorway.)

Coolant
  Liquid in the radiator that removes heat from the engine.

Defensive driving
  Driving safely without taking risks, looking out for hazards and thinking for others.

Disqualified
  Stopped from doing something (eg driving) by law, because you have broken the law.

Distraction
  Anything that stops you concentrating on your driving, such as talking to passengers or using your mobile phone.

Document
  An official paper or card, eg your driving licence.

Dual carriageway
  A road or motorway with a central reservation.

Engine braking – *see also* gears
  Using the low gears to keep your speed down. For example, when you are driving down a steep hill and you want to stop the vehicle running away. Using the gears instead of braking will help to prevent brake fade.

Environment
  The world around us and the air we breathe.

Equestrian crossing
  An unusual kind of crossing. It has a button high up for horse riders to push.

Exceed
  Go higher than an upper limit.

Exhaust emissions
  Gases that come out of the exhaust pipe to form part of the outside air.

Field of vision
  How far you can see in front and around you when you are driving.

Filler cap
  Provides access to the vehicle's fuel tank, for filling up with petrol or diesel.

Glossary

Fog lights

Extra bright rear (and sometimes front) lights that may be used in very poor visibility due to fog. You must remember to switch them off when visibility improves, as they can dazzle and distract other drivers.

Ford

A place in a stream or river that is shallow enough to drive across with care.

Four-wheel drive (4WD)

On a conventional vehicle, steering and engine speed affect just two 'drive' wheels. On 4WD, they affect all four wheels, ensuring optimum grip on loose ground.

Frustration

Feeling annoyed because you cannot drive as fast as you want to because of other drivers or heavy traffic.

Fuel consumption

The amount of fuel (petrol or diesel) that your vehicle uses. Different vehicles have different rates of consumption. Increased fuel consumption means using more fuel. Decreased fuel consumption means using less fuel.

Fuel gauge

A display or dial on the instrument panel that tells you how much fuel (petrol or diesel) you have left.

Gantry

An overhead platform like a high narrow bridge that displays electric signs on a motorway.

Gears

Control the speed of the engine in relation to the vehicle's speed. May be hand operated (manual) or automatically controlled. In a low gear (such as first or second), the engine runs more slowly. In a high gear (such as fourth or fifth), it runs more quickly. Putting the car into a lower gear as you drive can create the effect of engine braking – forcing the engine to run more slowly.

Handling

How well your vehicle moves or responds when you steer or brake.

Harass

To drive in a way that makes other road users afraid.

Hard shoulder

The single lane to the left of the inside lane on a motorway, which is for emergency use only. You should not drive on the hard shoulder except in an emergency, or when there are signs telling you to use the hard shoulder because of roadworks.

Harsh braking (or harsh acceleration)

Using the brake (or accelerator) too hard so as to cause wear on the engine.

Hazard warning lights

Flashing amber lights that you should use only when you have broken down. On a motorway, you can use them to warn other drivers behind you of a hazard ahead.

High-sided vehicle

A van or truck with tall sides, or a tall trailer such as a caravan or horse-box, that is at risk of being blown off-course in strong winds.

Impatient

Not wanting to wait for pedestrians and other road users.

Inflate

To blow up – to put air in your tyres until they are at the right pressures.

Instrument panel

The car's electrical controls and gauges, set behind the steering wheel. Also called the dashboard.

Intimidate

To make someone feel afraid.

Involved

Being part of something. For example, being one of the drivers in an accident.

Jump leads

A pair of thick electric cables with clips at either end. You use it to charge a flat battery by connecting it to the live battery in another vehicle.

Junction

A place where two or more roads join.

Liability

Being legally responsible.

Manoeuvre

Using the controls to make your car move in a particular direction. For example, when turning, reversing or parking.

Manual

By hand. In a car that is a 'manual' or has manual gears, you have to change the gears yourself.

Maximum

The largest possible; 'maximum speed' is the highest speed allowed.

Minimum

The smallest possible.

Mirrors

Cars have a minimum of three rear view mirrors: one in the centre of the windscreen, and one on each front door. Additional mirrors may be required on longer vehicles, or when towing a high trailer such as a caravan. Some mirrors may be curved (convex or concave) to increase the field of vision. The mirror on the windscreen can be turned to anti-dazzle position, if glare from headlights behind creates a distraction.

Mobility

The ability to move around easily.

Monotonous

Boring. For example, a long stretch of motorway with no variety and nothing interesting to see.

MOT

The test that proves your car is safe to drive. Your MOT certificate is one of the important documents for your vehicle.

Motorway

A fast road that has two or more lanes on each side and a hard shoulder. Drivers must join or leave it on the left, via a motorway junction. Many kinds of slower vehicles – such as bicycles – are not allowed on motorways.

Multiple-choice questions

Questions with several possible answers where you have to try to choose the right one.

Observation

The ability to notice important information, such as hazards developing ahead.

Obstruct

To get in the way of another road user.

Octagonal

Having eight sides.

Glossary

Oil level

The amount of oil needed for the engine to run effectively. The oil level should be checked as part of your regular maintenance routine, and the oil replaced as necessary.

Pedestrian

A person walking.

Pelican crossing

A crossing with traffic lights that pedestrians can use by pushing a button. Cars must give way to pedestrians on the crossing while the amber light is flashing. You must give pedestrians enough time to get to the other side of the road.

Perception

Seeing or noticing (as in Hazard Perception).

Peripheral vision

The area around the edges of your field of vision.

Positive attitude

Being sensible and obeying the law when you drive.

Priority

The vehicle or other road user that is allowed by law to go first is the one that has priority.

Provisional licence

A first driving licence. All learner drivers must get one before they start having lessons.

Puffin crossing

A type of pedestrian crossing that does not have a flashing amber light phase.

Reaction time

The amount of time it takes you to see a hazard and decide what to do about it.

Red route

You see these in London and some other cities. Double red lines at the edge of the road tell you that you must not stop or park there at any time. Single red lines have notices with times when you must not stop or park. Some red routes have marked bays for either parking or loading at certain times.

Red warning triangle

An item of safety equipment to carry in your car in case you break down. You can place the triangle 45m behind your car on the same side of the road. It warns traffic that your vehicle is causing an obstruction. (Do not use these on motorways.)

Residential areas

Areas of housing where people live. The speed limit is 30mph or sometimes 20mph.

Road hump

A low bump built across the road to slow vehicles down. Also called 'sleeping policemen'.

Rumble strips

Raised strips across the road near a roundabout or junction that change the sound the tyres make on the road surface, warning drivers to slow down. They are also used on motorways to separate the main carriageway from the hard shoulder.

Safety margin

The amount of space you need to leave between your vehicle and the one in front so that you are not in danger of crashing into it if the driver slows down suddenly or stops. Safety margins have to be longer in wet or icy conditions.

Separation distance

The amount of space you need to leave between your vehicle and the one in front so that you are not in danger of crashing into it if the driver slows down suddenly or stops. The separation distance must be longer in wet or icy conditions.

Security coded radio

To deter thieves, a radio or CD unit that requires a security code (or pin number) to operate it.

Single carriageway

Generally, a road with one lane in each direction.

Skid

When the tyres fail to grip the surface of the road, the subsequent loss of control of the vehicle's movement is called a skid. Usually caused by harsh or fierce braking, steering or acceleration.

Snaking

Moving from side to side. This sometimes happens with caravans or trailers when you drive too fast, or they are not properly loaded.

Staggered junction

Where you drive cross another road. Instead of going straight across, you have to go a bit to the right or left.

Steering

Control of the direction of the vehicle. May be affected by road surface conditions: when the steering wheel turns very easily, steering is 'light', and when you have to pull hard on the wheel it is described as 'heavy'.

Sterile

Clean and free from bacteria.

Stopping distance

The time it takes for you to stop your vehicle – made up of 'thinking distance' and 'braking distance'.

Supervisor

Someone who sits in the passenger seat with a learner driver. They must be over 21 and have held a full driving licence for at least three years.

Tailgating

Driving too closely behind another vehicle – usually to harass the driver in front.

Thinking distance

The time it takes you to notice something and take the right action. You need to add thinking distance to your braking distance to make up your total stopping distance.

Third party insurance

An insurance policy that insures you against any claim by passengers or other persons for damage or injury to their person or property.

Toucan crossing

A type of pedestrian crossing that does not have a flashing amber light phase, and cyclists are allowed to ride across.

Tow

To pull something behind your vehicle. It could be a caravan or trailer.

Traffic-calming measures

Speed humps, chicanes and other devices placed in roads to slow traffic down.

Tram

A public transport vehicle that moves along the streets on fixed rails, usually electrically powered by overhead lines.

Tread depth

The depth of the grooves in a car's tyres that help them grip the road surface. The grooves must all be at least 1.6mm deep.

Glossary

Turbulence
Strong movement of air. For example, when a large vehicle passes a much smaller one.

Two-second rule
In normal driving, the ideal minimum distance between you and the vehicle in front can be timed using the 'two-second' rule. As the vehicle in front passes a fixed object (such as a signpost), say to yourself 'Only a fool breaks the two second rule'. It takes two seconds to say it. If you have passed the same object before you finish, you are too close – pull back.

Tyre pressures
The amount of air that must be pumped into a tyre in order for it to be correctly blown up.

Vehicle Excise Duty
The tax you pay for your vehicle so that you may drive it on public roads, also known as road tax.

Vehicle Registration Certificate
A record of details about a vehicle and its owner, also known as a log book.

Vehicle watch scheme
A system for identifying vehicles that may have been stolen.

Vulnerable
At risk of harm or injury.

Waiting restrictions
Times when you may not park or load your vehicle in a particular area.

Wheel balancing
To ensure smooth rotation at all speeds, wheels need to be 'balanced' correctly. This is a procedure done at a garage or tyre centre, when each wheel is removed for testing. Balancing may involve minor adjustment with the addition of small weights, to avoid wheel wobble.

Wheel-spin
When the vehicle's wheels spin round out of control with no grip on the road surface.

Zebra crossing
A pedestrian crossing without traffic lights. It has an orange light, and is marked by black and white stripes on the road. Drivers must stop for pedestrians to cross.

Notes

Personal information

My driver number
_____

Driving instructor's name
and phone number
_____

_____

_____

_____

Driving instructor's number
_____

Theory test date and time
_____

Theory test pass date
_____

Theory test certificate number
_____

Driving school code
_____

Practical test date and time
_____